The Landscape We See

M<small>C</small>GRAW-HILL BOOK COMPANY   *New York, Toronto, London, Sydney*

The Landscape We See

GARRETT ECKBO

OTHER BOOKS BY THE AUTHOR

Landscape for Living
1950

The Art of Home Landscaping
1956

Urban Landscape Design
1964

PREAMBLE
The Divine Right of Technology

1702428

That the technical powers of the human species have been growing during the last quarter-millennium at an explosive speed is doubtless a commonplace.

These powers are now so great that unless they are quickly brought under controls directed toward humane purposes, they will almost certainly destroy the dominant species and all subordinate life in one gathering holocaust.

Unfortunately the prevalent technocratic philosophy works vigorously against any regeneration, reformation, salvation. That philosophy holds in essence that man's fulfillment will come automatically with the complete release of all scientific curiosity and the effective application of its finding by technology. Adherents cling to this belief with a deep emotional fervor which has little of the scientific spirit in it. The divine right of kings has given place in the prevailing mythology to the divine right of technocrats.

Conservationists are faced with the problem of protecting and restoring some semblance of the natural environment for human life on this planet. In this endeavor their most dangerous opponent is the stubborn superstition that all technological advance is good.

But a tool or a weapon is good if it is used to good purposes. Science and technology are wonderful when they are applied to beneficent ends; they can be lethal if applied to malignant ends.

The great problem and opportunity of the last half of the 20th century is to understand this truth clearly and subordinate our technological powers to lifeward, not deathward purposes.

The human species evolved with all other life and is best suited to endure in the reasonably natural environment; the forces which seek to protect and preserve this environment are beneficient; those which seek to destroy it are malignant.

A high civilization will dedicate itself to the task of providing all men with economic and cultural abundance and security within the only context wherein such abundance and security are possible, the natural setting. . . .

A great work of re-thinking, of repentance is required, a re-examination of many of our basic evaluations as a nation; only when this work has been at least commenced can we defend ourselves against the rising forces of destruction which are of our own creation.

ANTHONY WAYNE SMITH[1]

"We're nearing civilization. This foliage is plastic."
Cartoon by Harris

"Just think—once this was nothing but raw wilderness!"
Cartoon by Mauldin

Moving amidst my own people I was never impressed by any of their accomplishments; I never felt the presence of any deep religious urge, nor any great aesthetic impulse: there was no sublime architecture, no sacred dances, no ritual of any kind. We moved in a swarm, intent on accomplishing one thing—to make life easy. The great bridges, the great dams, the great skyscrapers left me cold. Only Nature could instill a sense of awe. And we were defacing Nature at every turn. . . . a wilderness of steel and iron, of stocks and bonds, of crops and produce, of factories, mills and lumber yards, a wilderness of boredom, of useless utilities, of loveless love. . . .

HENRY MILLER[2]

PROLOGUE
Beginning without End

In the beginning the land was hot and fluid. It swirled and bubbled, gave off noxious gassy clouds and poured restlessly and heavily here and there over the surface of a newborn globe that was adjusting its orbit to those of its neighbors in the universe.

As time passed, the liquid land gradually cooled and slowed, passing from thin to thick to sticky to muddy to solid, like the frosting on a cake. Clouds gathered, rain fell, water ran intricately from high parts to low parts and gradually collected in oceans. Water from these evaporated, more clouds gathered, more rain fell, more water ran over the new land, beginning to cut and shape as it ran.

Much time passed. Somewhere in the ocean there was a spark, and living microorganisms appeared. They multiplied, spread, filled the oceans with proliferating forms of many sizes and shapes. Ultimately some were cast or pushed up on shore, looked around, decided to stay, and began to develop the means for taking root or locomotion and survival on land. Further proliferation followed. Vegetable and animal kingdoms began to dominate the mineral.

Much more time passed. Blood changed from cold to warm. The young received more and more specific care. The forms of life became more and more accurately adjusted to an environment that became more complex as it became more stable.

One day an animal stood up on its hind legs to reach a higher fruit, found it could reach more and farther around itself, tried it again more and more often. Its progeny gradually learned to walk with no hands, to throw stones, to chip stones, to help each other in social groupings.

The production and control of fire was discovered, and shortly after, landscape design began. Forests, brush, and grasslands were burned to drive out game and produce more palatable vegetation. Man and landscape began a reciprocal pattern of living which has never ceased.

Came the Agricultural Revolution. Crops were sown, animals tamed, and man decided to settle down and build himself a home. Architecture began, followed soon by urbanism. Straw and mud huts clustered around central open spaces and were protected by outer walls.

The forces of nature still ruled most of the surface of the earth. Geologic stresses and strains manipulated its crust; wind, rain, ice, and running water carved and shaped its surfaces; vegetation spread rampant within the limits of moisture and temperature; wild beasts roamed everywhere in fantastic and terrifying profusion. Man's first major control by the counterterror of fire was easy to start but difficult to manage or direct. Agricultural settlements represented the first beachhead of the humanized environment.

The extraction of vegetable, animal, and mineral resources from the vast storehouse of Mother Earth expanded rapidly, as did the handicraft techniques for processing them into useful and pleasing forms. Wealth appeared in the form of surplus production and began to be unequally distributed on the basis of strength and cleverness. Conflicts between villages over meager supplies became struggles for wealth and its sources in land, raw materials, and labor. Slavery appeared, man's primary inhumanity to man. The central open space in the village was improved with an altar and a larger and more ornate hut for the chief. Palace, temple, plaza, and surrounding shelter for the citizens—these were the elements which would proliferate down through the centuries, from Egypt through Greece, Rome, medieval, Renaissance, and baroque Europe to romantic eighteenth-century England. Parallel with this urban flowering, horticultural processes expanded from simple agricultural field cropping through more intensive demonstrations of skill and productivity and the use of domesticated plants, perhaps first as favorite types and specimens, for creating pleasant spaces around the home, to nonproductive gardens designed to show skill, control, power, culture, and benevolence on the part of the rulers. All of this culminated at Versailles and Paris (as its parallel had at Peking in the East). Thereafter, the practical English (as the sensitive Japanese) began to view man's work as somewhat monstrous and to see nature as a garden rather than a wilderness.

Came the Industrial Revolution and the accelerating explosion of production and population which sweeps us along today. The techniques for the produc-

tion of humanized environment took on astonishing power and complexity with enormous speed. Wealth and the democratic idea spread with parallel force. Along with limited handicraft society went palace, temple, and plaza. Urban patterns, as they grew faster, became constantly more simple, more mechanical, more regimented and less human. The traditional, historical articulation of the community into its natural organic pattern became lost in a vast commercial anarchy. Today one finds the center of city or town only by the increasing height of buildings, the increasing clamor of lights and signs, and the increasing congestion of traffic. We still build temples and palaces and many other splendid structures, but they are lost in the modern urban jungle.

The World Set Free

That committee is now, far more than the council or any other of its delegated committees, the active government of the world. Developed from an almost invisible germ of "town-planning" that came obscurely into existence in Europe or America (the question is still in dispute) somewhere in the closing decades of the nineteenth century, its work, the continual active planning and replanning of the world as a place of human habitation, is now so to speak the collective material activity of the race. The spontaneous, disorderly spreading and recessions of populations, as aimless and mechanical as the trickling of spilt water, which was the substance of history for endless years, giving rise here to congestions, here to chronic devastating wars, and everywhere to a discomfort and disorderliness that was at its best only picturesque, is at an end. Men spread now, with the whole power of the race to aid them, into every available region of the earth. Their cities are no longer tethered to running water and the proximity of cultivation, their plans are no longer affected by strategic considerations or thoughts of social insecurity. The aeroplane and the nearly costless mobile car have abolished trade routes; a common language and a universal law have abolished a thousand restraining inconveniences, and so an astonishing dispersal of habitations has begun. One may live anywhere. And so it is that our cities are now true social gatherings, each with a character of its own and distinctive interests of its own, and most of them with a common occupation. They lie out in the former deserts, these long-wasted sun-baths of the race, they tower amidst eternal snows, they hide in remote islands, and bask on broad lagoons. For a time the whole tendency of mankind was to desert the river valleys in which the race had been cradled for half a million years, but now that the War against Flies has been waged so successfully that this pestilential branch of life is nearly extinct, they are returning thither with a renewed appetite for gardens laced by watercourses, for pleasant living amidst islands and houseboats and bridges, and for nocturnal lanterns reflected by the sea.

Man who is ceasing to be an agricultural animal becomes more and more a builder, a traveler, and a maker . . . the food now of the whole world is produced by less than one per cent of its population. . . . Far fewer people are needed upon the land than training and proclivity dispose toward it, and as a consequence of this excess of human attention, the garden side of life, the creation of groves and lawns and vast regions of beautiful flowers, has expanded enormously and continues to expand. . . .

Contentious professions cease to be an honorable employment for men. The peace between nations is also a peace between individuals. We live in a world that comes of age. Man the warrior, man the lawyer, and all the bickering aspects of life, pass into obscurity; the grave dreamers, man the curious learner, and man the creative artist, come forward to replace these barbaric aspects. . . .

Once the world was released from the hardening insecurities of a needless struggle for life that was collectively planless and individually absorbing, it became apparent that there was in the vast mass of people a long smothered passion to make things. The world broke out into making, and at first mainly into aesthetic making. . . . There is a natural order in these things, and art comes before science as the satisfaction of more elemental needs must come before art. . . .

H. G. WELLS[3]

Since the above appeared in 1914, there had been no comparably optimistic view of tomorrow's landscape until Wolf Von Eckard's Epilogue in *A Place to Live*, Delacorte Press, New York, 1967. Perhaps it marks a turning point in our journey through darkness and confusion.

FOREWORD

THE landscape is the world around us, including everything we see or sense wherever we are. It is continuous in both space and time—in space as a series of physical and social arrangements which exist at any given moment, in time as the continuity of such arrangements through the continuous changes which constitute their development.

Nature is the *status quo*, including man and all his works. It is what is (we know), resulting from what has been (we think), and leading to what will be (we hope). It resists change, wants to remain as is, even though quantitative accumulations within it move constantly toward qualitative change. Change and resistance to it are both integral elements in the *status quo* of human and nonhuman nature.

Art is, among other things, the creative portion of the processes of change. It involves human evaluation (of nonhuman changes) or direction (of human-instigated changes). It involves a value system (this change is better for people than that change). Creative change is good for people. It creates new values, new resources, new dimensions, new experiences, new relations among familiar or unfamiliar elements, new understanding of the world and our position in it. Uncreative change does none of these things, or may use one to cancel out another, or take some away entirely; therefore it is bad for people.

Creative people instigate, develop, direct, or take advantage of creative change. They do this by using the design process—observation, analysis, synthesis. Use of this process, even with creative intent, does not guarantee creative results. Historically design, in specific areas and periods, moves through a sequence of stages—innovation, consolidation, institutionalization. Consolidation results from organization, and institutionalization produces academic systems and hack reproduction. Innovators may consolidate, and consolidators may continue to innovate. Innovators may also be employed by consolidators and institutions. But institutionalization comes naturally from consolidation and tends to kill innovation. That is why new rounds of design begin with innovators attacking institutions.

Today we seem to be in the hands of the organizers. Offices are getting larger and more efficient, design is more predictable, public relations procedures are working, images are building. Design itself is organization, but only of the relationship between designer and problem —including program, solution, implementation. Subordination of the process to noncreative objectives of promotion, exploitation, or administration will tend to destroy its creative potential.

Our lives alternate between verbal and visual images. Words may clarify what we see, or they may totally distort it. Any mass-circulation picture magazine will provide examples. Visual experience may clarify verbal images and may even destroy those which are untrue. But our primary education in verbalization makes this latter alternative much slower and more difficult. We listen and read much better than we see. Literacy is no longer an unmixed blessing. It has opened the monstrous Pandora's box of dirty journalism, twisted propaganda, fragmentary advertising, comic books, pulp writing, security classification, and the big lie. It is almost impossible for us to imagine a world in which visual experience would be as important as verbal. The physical landscape is visual; the social landscape is verbal; our problem is how to integrate them in honesty and beauty.

Our verbal social world is dominated by private enterprise, which feels qualified to determine the scope and arrangement of public service and to warn us when it approaches the welfare state and socialism. Yet private enterprise seems unable to solve problems of low profitability—poverty, unemployment, low-rent housing, the good visual environment, preventive medicine, juvenile deliquency, race prejudice, land speculation, soil erosion, air and water pollution, education, recreation, comprehensive regional planning. Some solutions begin to appear through liaisons of public and private enterprise. Perhaps socialism can be forestalled by complete marriage of the two.

The key words of our time may be these: science, democracy, conspiracy. Science, because we are told that it will bring the brave new world into being, if we will only listen and learn. Democracy, because it embodies the hopes of the multitude for a better future—one in which they participate in all decisions which affect their lives. Conspiracy, because it represents those dark forces which seek to deprive us of the benefits of science and democracy. Yet science is only the pursuit of knowledge (what do we do with it?); democracy is not yet here (how long, O Lord?); and conspiracy is two people in a room with the door shut (who, me?). Art waits in the wings, toying with inadequate opportunities, ready to help complete the intuitive understanding of our potentialities which science initiates. Democracy has only to learn how to unite the best that science and art together have to offer, in order to evade the deliberate obscurantism of conspiracy theories, and set the world truly free.

I have not performed this labor alone. My wife and daughters have labored long, faithfully, and critically through many retypings of the manuscript. My partners have supported this enterprise wholeheartedly. Our associates have pitched in whenever graphic help was needed. And Dick Petrie has once again done an excellent job of design and layout.

Garrett Eckbo

CONTENTS

Total Landscape

Epilogue

Background

Through conscious planning and design the city of Fresno, California, recaptured and improved this downtown landscape for the pedestrian.

INTRODUCTION

Our concern is set firmly within the context of the humanities as defined by Ralph Barton Perry:

I define "the humanities," then, to embrace whatever influences conduce to freedom. . . . By freedom I mean enlightened choice. . . . By enlightened choice, I do not mean effective choice. For that I should prefer to reserve the term "liberty." . . . Liberty has to do with the action of circumstance upon the man, freedom with a man's action on circumstance.

The extent to which a man is free, that is, exercises enlightened choice, depends in the first place upon the extent to which he is aware of the possibilities. . . . Freedom is proportional to the range of options.

A second condition of enlightened choice is imagination. . . . [it] enables the mind to entertain more possibilities of truth. It plays wantonly with the doubtful, the improbable and the incredible. It is of the essence of fancy that it should be free. Imagination is the agency by which the human mind looks beyond every self-imposed limitation, conscious or unconscious; it is the chief antidote to habit; it recognizes no impossibility within the elastic power of invention. Learning, imagination and sympathy constitute the conditions of that freedom. . . . man owes his dignity to the possession of freedom. . . .[4]

The question explored was: What has been, and is, happening to the earth's surface as a result of man's having been on it for a long time, increasing in numbers and skills unevenly, at different places and times? (PAUL FEJOS) *It was further suggested that, whereas all articles would deal with the quantitative*

In this book we are concerned with the processes which shape the landscape, both in quantity and quality. We are particularly concerned with conscious design as the potential control of those processes, which becomes increasingly important as we become increasingly urbanized.

By *quality* I mean a relationship between an individual or a group of people and a landscape. This relationship involves human perception, comprehension, and reaction as a process which measures quality. The essence of landscape quality is neither in the landscape itself nor in people, but rather in the nature of the relationships which are established between them. Thus quality may vary with time and place, with human nature, and with the nature of the landscape in which it lives.

By *landscape* I mean everything which surrounds us wherever we are. This includes not only all physical elements—earth, water, atmosphere, buildings, trees, streets, cars—but the entire social pattern of customs, laws, traditions, permissions, prohibitions, and attitudes which anthropologists and sociologists call culture. The *physical landscape* is a product of the processes of nature and human culture, combined in varying proportions. The human expression in this physical landscape results from a series of decisions made by various people at various times and places. Insofar as these decisions produce physical results, they constitute a design process, regardless of the intent of their makers. If they are not concerned with the quality of the results, the design process is merely unconscious. Our concern is with the actual and potential results of all design processes in the physical landscape. Those who participate in unconscious design processes must begin to accept responsibility for the qualitative impact of their decisions on the landscape. Most of the history of design in the landscape is a history of special elements for special people. Our times require us to think in terms of the design of all the landscape for all the people.

Our small effort goes on within a much larger framework of attempts to synthesize thinking on the world in which we live. An outstanding example of these is the International Symposium on Man's Role in Changing the Face of the Earth which was held in Princeton, New Jersey, for one week in June, 1955.

This symposium took a very large look at our world. It covered the past (retrospect), the present (process), and the future (prospect). Its cochairmen were Carl Sauer, geographer; Marston Bates, zoologist; and Lewis Mumford, planner and urbanist.

Within this large framework we might ask: What is the relevance of the *conscious* design process to the constant changes in the landscape which go on around us? How do we relate these changes back to the individual eyes, ears, noses and other senses through which we human beings still perceive, comprehend, and react to them? Can we afford to be unconscious any more? In handicraft cultures the landscape resulting from unconscious design processes is usually charming, though insanitary. But we are no longer a handicraft society. Industrialization has released forces which will destroy the landscape unless consciously controlled.

effects of man's working and living in different parts of the world, perhaps some authors would wish to consider the qualitative effects of man on the landscape. . . . The aesthetic appreciation of the earth was important in Shaler's thinking, and it is involved, at least implicitly, too, in much contemporary thought about the future of man on the earth. . . . Man is living nearly everywhere in a cultured landscape which, during centuries, has been shaped in accordance to his needs, his taste, and his personal peculiarities. The forming of the landscape by man is an artistically unconscious process and therefore reflects the personality of a culture far more than it reflects conscious art. . . . Shall we have a wild nature or a tamed nature? . . . Within the last century man has developed the idea that change is continuous and includes himself. . . . Nature has always contained man, but all the while is being changed by man in the course of his own self-transformation. (WILLIAM L. THOMAS, JR.) *In general, individual efforts are now out of tune, in time and space, with the dynamics of social needs and aspirations. The unity between the individual scale and the totality of the environment has broken down. Something new must be put in its place. The right scale depends on the awareness of relations—of the relations between individual and group, between the functional and personal life, between the man-made landscape and the natural landscape, between all parts of the immediate environment and the wider world around us and, finally, the universe.* (E. A. GUTKIND) *In the regional city, as Stein conceived it, organization would take the place of mere agglomeration and, in doing so, would create a reciprocal relation between city and country that would not be overthrown by further population growth. . . . Neither the blotting-out of the landscape nor the disappearance of the city is the climax stage of urbanization. Rather, it is the farsighted and provident balancing of city populations and regional resources so as to maintain in a state of high development all the elements—social, economic, and agricultural—necessary for their common life.* (LEWIS MUMFORD[5])

4

Man and countryside replaced by man
and auto.

Natural and human development processes produce the landscape which surrounds us.

CHAPTER 1
Processes of Landscape Development

Dr. Richard J. Russell discusses environmental changes through forces independent of man:

It seems important to recognize and hold in mind that a variety of natural processes are operative and have not ceased to operate simply because man made his appearance on the scene. Of his general dominance there can be no question, but man's control of his own destiny is actually far from complete. He stands passive in the face of forces which he is unable to harness, subdue, or even modify. His increased technical competence brings many changes, but man's tenure on earth is still subject to many ungovernable environmental controls. The more significant affect him gradually, as a rule, but some of the less important strike him with catastrophic impact.[5]

Dr. Russell goes on to detail these primary forces of nature:

1. More stable soils and widespread vegetation have reduced the destructive effects of weather greatly since geologic times, save in a few harsh environments.

2. Though profound changes in weather and climate occur so slowly that man does not recognize them, he is *keenly aware of vagaries in local weather conditions and of short-term climatic fluctuations.*

3. . . . *on the whole, natural vegetation is distributed according to patterns determined by climates and relief features rather than by the desires of man. . . . Whether it be the most poleward trees of the taiga, the position of the cold or the dry timber line, or the boundary between tree-covered plains and adjacent steppe, the limits*

The landscape, like nature and human society which together produce it, is not static or fixed. It is constantly in development, growth, change, improving, or retrogressing. This is true even of those wild or pastoral landscapes which may appear to us to be in equilibrium. Their rate of change is merely so slow as to be imperceptible to the casual eye. But this rate can, and often does, speed up abruptly as a fruition of some combination of forces which has been developing over a considerable period of time.

The landscape is not being but becoming. It is a result of a composite of processes which are continuous from the past through the present into the future. This composite is continuous even though its content and the proportion of different elements in it are constantly shifting and adjusting, sometimes approaching balance but never quite achieving it. The rates of speed of different elements in this complex of processes are highly variable and changeable. We think of geologic change as being of infinite slowness, yet earthquakes, volcanoes, and tidal waves can create immense physical changes in the twinkling of an eye. Age-old cities, encrusted and bogged down in the residue of centuries of human social living, can be changed radically almost as quickly by the constructive inspiration or destructive energy or carelessness of people.

Natural processes are basic to, and surround, all human activity. These include those geologic forces called "constructive"—movements of the earth's crust, fires from within—and those called "destructive" or "weathering"—water (as rain, snow, and ice, as running streams and moving sheets, and as a precipitator of chemical and biologic action), wind, and temperature. Included also are biologic forces—vegetation as a soil former and stabilizer of topography and as a creator of sheltered and enriched spaces, animal and human life as sources of constructive and destructive activity. Animal life, although it has a positive impact upon the visual quality of the landscape, is in general an integrated and nondisturbing part of the near balance of natural processes. Human life emerged some fifty thousand years ago as a force capable of conscious observation, thought, and decision critical of its environment. Within the last eight thousand years, and at a constantly accelerating pace, this human force has made such an impact upon the landscape as to appear constantly more unnatural or opposed to nature.

In our basic reference[5] we find much about the natural and human processes which produce our landscape.

Human society is a product of nature, a natural force which has so expanded and developed as to be able to control, balance, or compete with many of the other forces of nature. We might say that this began when the first child of nature began to reflect upon, and be critical of, its environment. With the first tree house and skin suit the old world of nature began to feel the impact of a new force—human imagination and decision. It is a rude platitude to say that this force must now decide whether to blow up the world, including itself, or establish peaceful coexistence among its belligerent components. The optimist will expect human imagination to overcome this obstacle to progress as it has so many others.

Beginning with the first crude hut or cave painting, human changes, improvements, or additions to the landscape have always required certain basic steps: program, site selection, design, construction and installation, management and maintenance. It is always necessary to decide what is to be done, where to do it, how to do it; then to do it; and then to use what has been created so as to prolong the use as long as possible. This is as true of the latest and largest industrial development as it was of the first tree house. Consciously or unconsciously, scrambled, telescoped or ignored, these steps will assert themselves. Program and site selection are interdependent, design must know what elements are needed and where, construction and installation must follow specific plans and decisions. Failings or inadequacies in any of these steps will have to be compensated by exaggerated or distorted management and maintenance activities. Design must always proceed with clear understanding of the nature of each of the other steps on each specific project.

Programming. Action by people in the landscape always proceeds from some objective, need, or desire: cultivation of crops, extraction of resources, construction of shelter for social activity, improvement of the appearance and surroundings of this shelter, organization of community relations between shelters. Historically, these objectives have run a gamut from utility through increasing convenience, comfort, and luxury to the more and more conscious and ostentatious display of wealth and power.

People formulate programs for personal or group objectives conditioned by the overall discipline of the social fabric within which they live. These programs have increased rapidly in complexity since the long span of history from primitive communities through slave empires and feudal baronies was abruptly accelerated by the Industrial Revolution. Today, in a world split three ways between capitalist and socialist nations and those emerging from colonial or semicolonial status, development in the United States is dominated by the drives and objectives

are set by endurance to adversity, and crucial tests depend on extreme, rather than average, climatic years. Man has succeeded in breeding a few domestic crops, such as rapidly maturing wheat or cotton, that cope successfully with limited degrees of climatic adversity, and his activities may extend grasslands beyond their original limits. . . .

4. *The greatest beneficial effect of the wind . . . is the drifting of moisture from ocean toward continental interior, making possible the existence of life away from coasts. . . . Winds of less than storm velocities are of utmost consequence to man. A sharp differentiation between windward and leeward landscapes is strikingly exhibited in trade-wind islands, and rain-shadow effects exist in the lee of uplands in all latitudes. . . .*

5. *Cloudbursts seldom occasion serious damage in Louisiana or other places where rainfall is torrential, for the reason that soils, slopes, and vegetation are thoroughly conditioned for them. But in semi-arid southern California even a small rain may cause disaster. . . .*

6. *Man's contact with the processes of alluvial morphology has been intimate. . . . Changes in river courses affect man severely and at times disastrously. . . . Encroaching sand has driven him from habitable sites. . . .*

DR. RICHARD RUSSELL[5]

On *human processes* Dr. Paul B. Sears[5] gives us the classical conservation outlook:

Man is clearly the beneficiary of a very special environment which has been a great while in the making. This environment is more than an inert stockroom. It is an active system, a pattern, and a process as well. Its value can be threatened by disruption no less than by depletion. . . . Any species survives by virtue of its niche—the opportunity afforded it by environment. But in occupying its niche it also assumes a role in relation to its surroundings. . . . The habitat furnishes the niche, and, if any species breaks up the habitat, the niche goes with it. . . . Since living systems are active and dynamic, they tend to approximate what is known as a steady state rather than a condition of repose. . . .

While these principles have been shown to apply to what is generally called the world of nature, that is, the world apart from man, there is considerable resistance to the idea that they apply to him in any serious way. Much of this resistance is emotional, having its roots in that part of Judeo-Christian tradition which separates man from nature to a greater extent than perhaps was common in oriental and Mediterranean thought. Some of it certainly comes from those who resent, for whatever reasons, any warning sign along the road to a perpetually expanding economy. And surprisingly, perhaps, some resistance comes from scientists and technologists, especially those unacquainted with the general field that used to be called natural history. . . . the changes induced by man, whether by sheer destruction or indirectly by accelerating natural processes, are probably more serious to him than the so-called "natural changes" for which he is not responsible. . . . Unfortunately, the situation is clouded by a wide-spread confidence that this impact of man upon environment can continue indefinitely. . . . It is true that we are far from the end of the rope. . . . There are many interesting approaches to the problem of man and his environment, and all, save perhaps the technological . . . indicate that humanity should strive toward a condition of equilibrium with its environment. This is the verdict of ethics, aesthetics, and natural science. . . .

In spite of the recurring abuses of power throughout history, commerce and industry were until the Reformation, in principle at least, subordinate to other cultural forces and restraints, notably religion. . . . the very structure of our modern economy, based as it is on mass production, intensifies the problem that here concerns us. Everything is geared to the speedy conversion of raw materials into consumers' goods at a rate governed only—when it is governed—by the capacity of the public to buy. . . . DR. PAUL SEARS[5]

A high level of production has become the keystone of effective economic security. There remains, however, the task of justifying the resulting flow of goods. Production . . . must have a raison d'etre of its own. . . . the result has been an elaborate and ingenious defense of the importance of production

of private enterprise. We might say that we have in general three types of programs: private for profit, private nonprofit, public nonprofit. These often overlap or function jointly on specific projects. Commercial and industrial development is programmed directly and explicitly in terms of private profit expectations; private homes, social and cultural developments, public building, recreation, utility, and conservation projects, while not directly in search of profits, are conditioned by the demands of real estate, banking, and the construction industry.

The scale of programming has grown with industrialization, from the isolated piece-by-piece development of the early nineteenth century to the community, state, or nationwide programs of corporations, school and park districts, and other large planning units. Within the past decade certain large national programs concerned with defense and security have come increasingly to dominate our lives and our landscape. The new Federal highway program and the increasing ownership of enormous areas of land by the military are symptomatic. C. Wright Mills suggests that these large programs are written by a "power elite" composed of top corporation executives, military officers, and political leaders.[6] This is more commonly called the "power structure."

Within these large patterns the individual and family still pursue the age-old universal objectives of mankind: good surroundings for private home life, learning, play, relaxation, and cultural development, for work in the multiple enterprises which produce the necessities and luxuries of modern life, and for the travel between these which consumes so much of our time and energy today. The definition of "good" is specific in time and place. It is part of what we call "the American standard of living." This is becoming more and more consistent from coast to coast as the typical middle-class suburban pattern. The detached private house of 1,500 square feet or more, the lot and the garden of ¼ acre or more, two cars in every garage, the quiet secluded street; convenient shopping, school, park-playground, church; sources of employment, higher education, and metropolitan amenities within easy commuting distance by train or freeway; multiple regional recreational facilities available for weekend trips—these might be called the normal components of the American dream today. Variations toward slum or palace and toward urban apartment or country farm home are variations around this dominant central suburban norm. This is an ideological fact; quantitative proportioning of the variations to the norm will vary from region to region and community to community. (See *The Exploding Metropolis* by the Editors of *Fortune*, and *American Skyline* by Tunnard and Reed.[7])

Site Selection. This is the procurement of, or securing of control over, a piece of land adequate and suitable to the physical development of the program. Physical and social forces are both involved and must be harmonized. Either programming or site selection may come first: sites may be searched out for the development of specific programs, or programs may be developed for specific sites within a general pattern

9

of zoning or local custom. Sites may be picked and developed for their own sakes—strategic locations for war or commerce, locations with good view, climate and topography for fine homes, accessibility to raw materials and transportation for industry. Historically the acquisition of such desirable sites has been a source of much conflict, maneuvering, bargaining, and war.

Seldom do program and site fit each other as hand and glove. Sometimes the site may be larger than the program requires, as in the opulent country estate. Much more often, however, a site adequate in size or conditions for the specific program cannot be found or cannot be obtained economically. Such congestion and inflation of land values are among the well-known by-products of urbanization and community development. Discrepancies between program and site result, too, from the primitive and inadequate nature of the land subdivision process. It often occurs before programs for specific land use are even written, yet it establishes a rigid and inflexible framework within which those programs must develop. Average housing, substandard housing, and community facilities in general tend to come after superstandard housing, industry and commerce, and streets and highways in the allocation of land. Zoning and general real estate development programs are notoriously inaccurate in their prognostications of the relative land areas needed for these various land uses. These inaccuracies in housing areas are rationalized by the "trickle down" theory—surplus upper-class housing is abandoned for the lower classes.

Each specific act of site selection and programming takes place within a specific context of physical and social conditions. These include topography; soil; climate—general macroregional and specific microlocal; water features or bodies; vegetation; level of community development—urban, suburban, rural, or primeval; level of real estate activity, inflation of land values, etc.; community pattern—relations between homes of various economic levels, centers of work, production and distribution, recreation and other community facilities, schools, health centers, resources (mineral rights), etc.; and social attitudes—who should be near whom and what should be near what.

It is interesting and instructive to investigate the historical processes by which our various developed regions and communities came from raw wilderness to their present states of confused urbanity. But programming and site selection for the needs and desires of present and future generations go on within the natural and social framework which exists today. "There is no use telling our troubled society what would have been right the last time. As Emerson said: 'Him I reckon the most learned scholar, not who can unearth the buried dynasties of Sesostris and Ptolemy . . . but who can unfold the theory of this particular Wednesday.' "[10] The greatest concentration of need and desire exist precisely in the urban centers of greatest congestion, anarchy, and deterioration.

We are in passage from a pattern of many small competitive decisions

as such. It is a defense which makes the urgency of production largely independent of the volume of production. . . . However there is a flaw in the case. If the individual's wants are to be urgent they must be original with himself. They cannot be urgent if they must be contrived for him. And above all they must not be contrived by the process of production by which they are satisfied. . . . One cannot defend production as satisfying wants if that production creates the wants. . . . Production only fills a void that it has itself created. JOHN KENNETH GALBRAITH[8]

The relation between a society and its environment can be understood only when we see how the environment is organized in terms of the verbal categories of those who use it. EDMUND R. LEACH[9]

The Increasing Intensity in Land Use: . . . Agriculture requires the removal of native vegetation, while pastoral life is sustained by such vegetation. . . . With agriculture, urban life and the leisure arts and crafts became possible. Repeatedly in human history, this appears to have thrown the art of husbandry and the importance of good land use out of perspective. . . . Two aspects of the growth of cities were particularly important. One was the expansion of irrigation works; the other, the harvesting of timber for fuel and structural purposes, thus clearing land not needed for, or suitable to, agriculture. . . . the clearing of forests, no doubt followed by heavy grazing, stimulated erosion. . . .

It is in the world of today, where industrialization and death control have produced an explosive growth of population, that land-use problems have become most acute and dramatic. . . .

The effect has been confusing almost to the point of disaster, as can be seen in any metropolitan "urban fringe" area. Allocation of space by planning and zoning, while not a new idea, has been outlined on a scientific basis by Geddes and his followers. . . . In the United States it faces grave political obstacles, made worse by the fact that we do still have a margin of safety and by the prevalence of our conviction that an economy can continue to expand without limits. . . .

Soil Erosion: It would be misleading to say that man is the cause of erosion or that erosion per se is a bad thing. As frequently pointed out, it is a normal part of the natural process of base-leveling and has been the source of some of the richest alluvial terraces and plains on earth. . . . It is when we remove this natural cover without providing a substantial artificial equivalent that the rate of erosion is accelerated to a dangerous degree. . . .

The Problem of Water: If the water cycle be roughly described as (1) evaporation from the seas, (2) transport over the land, (3) rainfall or snowfall, and (4) flow back to the sea, it is chiefly during stage (4) that water is available for the sustenance of life on land. By prolonging this stage, terrestrial life gets the maximum benefit from moisture. Whatever shortens the time that water is in or on the land decreases its utility to land life, including our own. Continuous vegetative cover retards the flow of water. It also renders the ground more permeable, thus maintaining the water table. . . . A closely related phenomenon is the rapid increase of virtually waterproofed surface areas represented by cities and highways. . . . we have the phenomenon of a technological culture whose demand for water is steadily rising at the same time that its processes accelerate the return of water to the sea. . . .

The problem of water involves quality as well as quantity. . . . Our streams are utilized as sources for domestic and industrial water supply and concurrently as convenient sewers for domestic and industrial waste—beyond the capacity of their normal process to purify. To urban wastes is often added the silt from eroded surfaces. . . .

Any discussion of water involves not only shortage and quality but also the question of flood. It is difficult to say to what extent floods have been increased by man's activity. . . . there are at least local floods that can be traced to human disturbance. . . . On general principles we would expect denuded and exploited headwater regions to intensify the destructive character and frequency of floods. . . . far greater funds are expended upon efforts to control flood after water has reached the river channels than are devoted to securing proper land use of the tribu-

in the landscape, made by many small owners, builders, bankers, etc., to one of fewer, larger, and more centralized decisions. Typical of these are mass building of tract housing; mass building of multiple housing both private and public; urban renewal, a formula whereby large sections of urban land can be taken over by the community, cleared, unified, and turned over to private enterprise for controlled redevelopment; large industrial and commercial projects, some of phenomenal size; large farming, ranching, and mining operations. In general this process centralizes larger and larger decisions about the general landscape in fewer and fewer hands. How responsible are these few hands to the general public? What voice do the people have in the development and redevelopment of their environment? Are the ballot box and the law of supply and demand adequate controls?

Programming and site selection are normal planning procedures—part of a rational pattern of analyzing human needs and desires and projecting their satisfaction. Complications in the realization of these aims seem to come from speculative operations and from the demands of both short- and long-term investors. Inasmuch as profit seeking has been and still is our normal incentive for development, how and how much to control it is a central problem of American planning and design.

Design. Design, our central subject, is the process by which we determine precisely how best to develop our program on the site selected, in specific forms and materials. It is a process of making all of the specific decisions about development, from general arrangements down to the smallest detail. Design is a special process, not a special person, although we expect people with training and talent to do it better than those with little of either. The designer must base himself on a clear understanding of the problem, expressed in a program of needs and desires which he may have to help write if the owner has difficulty in analyzing or articulating. The designer must also base himself on complete familiarity with the site and its surroundings.

Often designers, through sensitive understanding of the program, can be very helpful in the site-selection process. They must also base themselves on clear understanding of the construction and installation resources available to the project and of the management and maintenance policies and facilities which can be anticipated when the project is turned over for occupancy and use. Working drawings and specifications constitute a demand for certain materials and techniques which must be available. Very often the design process should include writing a program for management and maintenance, in order to guarantee the success of the development.

The normal space scale of conscious design is established by the more or less arbitrary boundaries of real property and political subdivision of the land. Its normal time scale is established by the durability of material installations and of the human programs for their use. In times past, programs tended to outlive installations, but since the Industrial Revolution this tendency has been reversed.

11

Construction and Installation. These comprise one of the largest segments of the American economy, a complex and anarchic monster which can produce gigantic buildings, freeways, and dams with assembly-line efficiency, yet may take many months to fit together the cabinets and appliances in the custom-built house. It includes all degrees of technology, from primitive handicraft to precise automatic machine production, and all combinations of these techniques. The construction industry includes within itself all of the ways and means whereby man can improve nature, destroy it, or live in peaceful coexistence with it.

Construction must be based on, and controlled by, program, site, and design. If one or more of them are inadequate, the problem must be solved during construction or passed on to management. Such problems, plus the fact that construction and site procurement are geared to the pursuit of profit, lead to a certain amount of conflict and competition with the design stage. The ethics of the professional designer, functioning as the owner's agent, deny him the pursuit of profit from materials and labor. He is paid a predetermined fee for service, advice and ideas, design and supervision. Furthermore, serious professional designers tend to project unprecedented forms and arrangements and unprecedented techniques for achieving them, rather than follow those tried and true paths dear to the heart of the practical construction industry. Typical of its reaction is the anti-intellectual and antiprofessional attitude found among many people in the industry and in local departments of building and safety.

Management and Maintenance. These become responsible for the operation and continued good condition and development of the project once construction has been completed. Housewives and private gardeners are managers and maintainers just as much as are superintendents of the largest industrial plants, parks, schools, cemeteries, and golf courses. Inadequacies in the previous four stages will become problems for management; in the extreme the manager may find himself writing the program for the problem solution which design is supposed to have produced. Sometimes, if coordination has been inadequate, aggressive management may disagree with the program and design which have been formulated and set about redoing them. As communities grow older, changes of ownership and use lead to remodeling and to the writing of new programs for old projects designed for different uses. The tendency toward rapid obsolescence of programs is reflected architecturally today in buildings which are open shells in which all partitions are movable, and is reflected in the outdoors in the high mortality of mature trees in urban areas, the fear of planting new trees which will not mature in five years, and the search for economical, quick, automatic tree-moving techniques.

Finally, we may conclude that the human processes of landscape development go on through a team of five disciplines, which may very likely be combined among fewer people for small projects or spread out over many more for large developments. These five basic disciplines—pro-

tary uplands to retain the water where it falls. This is an interesting aspect of a technological culture whose emphasis is on engineering rather than on biological controls. . . . The impoundment of water for various reasons is rapidly increasing, owing to the substitution of powerful earth-moving machinery for hand labor. . . .

The Atmosphere: . . . Of perhaps more immediate concern is the growing volume of volatile and solid wastes which pollute the air of great urban centers across the United States. . . . the problem of protecting the quality of two basic resources, formerly regarded as free economic goods—water and air—remains urgent. . . . Modern society is not yet organized to control the powers which science already has placed at its disposal. . . . Through science, man now has the means to be aware of change and its effects and the ways in which his cultural values and behavior should be modified to insure their own preservation. Whether we consider ethics to be enlightened self-interest, greater good for the greater number, ultimate good rather than present benefit, or Schweitzer's reverence for life, man's obligation toward environment is equally clear. DR. PAUL B. SEARS[5]

12

gramming, site selection, design, construction and installation, and management and maintenance—may all be the responsibility of one owner-builder of the farmhouse or mountain cabin, or they may be spread among several dozen people in the large corporation development involving complex planning problems. However many people are involved, the successful development will carefully recognize, and give full importance to, each of the five steps.

Copenhagen (LEFT) and Philadelphia (BELOW) represent qualitative concentration in their renewal efforts.

CHAPTER 2
Quality in the Landscape

We are accustomed to quantitative measurements in the landscape as a barometer of economic progress—volume of building permits, mileage of roads and streets built, acres subdivided. The notion of qualitative measurement distinct from, or even opposed to, quantitative standards may strike a discordant note in many ears. In fact, to the prophets of progress quantity and quality are almost synonymous. (There is, of course, a different relationship in the grading of merchandise by price: the more quality [higher price], the less quantity, and vice versa.) More is better, and the double squirrel cage of production and consumption, not completely synchronized, spins merrily on. More is also newer, and the expanding concentration on new forms and styles seems to overshadow the old-fashioned threat of innovation to established investments in land and building development.

The notion of the public as an intake mechanism for continuously expanding consumption, driven by the drums of advertising, and at the same time as an unfailing reservoir of labor for production to meet these demands seems to underlie most official views of the landscape around us. More industry (but less agriculture), more extraction of raw materials, more housing, more commercial structures, more office space—these are the primary concentrations, followed with considerable lag by more community facilities—schools, hospitals, churches, parks, playgrounds.

Certain qualitative expectations exist for most of these independently. Industry, office space, schools, and hospitals must be functional; commercial structures, such as shopping centers and supermarkets, must be glamorous. Housing and churches embody peculiarly distorted relations between functionalism and romanticism or sentimentalism, typified by the seesawing competition between Cinderella, ranch-style, and "modern" tract houses. Parks and playgrounds are usually so frustrated by inadequate budgets as to have little opportunity to explore the association of functional and romantic design.

There is a constantly shifting relationship between quantity and quality. With man comes the development of qualitative judgments—this is better than that—and the resultant remodeling of nature. Each remodeling is creative if it goes beyond its precedents, hence represents a qualitative improvement. Once accepted and established, however, a new work becomes an integral part of the current natural world (man plus wild nature). As long as it remains superior to others of its type, it continues to set a qualitative standard. But imitations and equal or superior new works push it gradually or quickly from qualitative to quantitative status. Few works survive this tendency to move from qualitative identity to quantitative anonymity. The first malcontent who left cave or treetop to build himself a hut of handy sticks and mud began ten thousand years of alternations between quantity and quality in housing. This has produced some magnificent palaces and the modern American tract house, each edition of which is the ultimate answer to the housing problem. But millions in underdeveloped countries around the world are still moving every day from street sleeping to trash huts in squatter colonies essentially the same as the original model.[11] The first sewage system and indoor bathrooms were major qualitative advances. Now they are part of the normal quantitative expectations in North America and Europe, though still future qualitative objectives for the have-not two-thirds of the world. Here in the United States we compete eagerly for new bathroom concepts which will render the old obsolete— sunken tubs, noiseless fixtures, new finishes, outdoor showers. For a city without parks or open space it is a qualitative improvement to clear a block in the center of town and plant it with grass and trees of any sort. However this act immediately moves the city from the class without parks to the class with parks, and we begin to compare the new park with parks in other cities. We find that some have more advanced concepts of design and facilities. Immediately our new park becomes one of the run-of-the-mill quantity of ordinary parks, and we are faced with the problem of improving it to give it qualitative status in the world of parks.

In professional design practice, too, there is a shifting relationship between quality and quantity. We leave school filled with brave ideas about the pursuit of truth and beauty and the search for ideal form. As time goes on success creeps up, respectability sets in, and our own precedents accumulate. Perhaps the essence of professionalism is the fortitude to resist the quantitative reproduction of precedent (hackwork) and to persist in the never-ending search for meaningful form and vital relationships.

In the inextricably interrelated seesaw between quantity and quality there is a distinct social tendency, particularly in cases of great need or deterioration (housing, schools, parks), to concentrate on quantity and forget about quality. This results partly from the immensity of our urban problems; partly from an oversimplification of their nature; partly from the treatment of planning as an emergency measure—too little, too late; partly from compartmental (housing, parks, traffic) rather

In *Markets of the Sixties* the Editors of *Fortune* say:

Not so long ago American taste was the concern chiefly of the country's architects, artists, writers, and intellectual leaders. Now it is also the concern of its business leaders—of anyone, that is, who sells consumer goods and services. . . . Taste is perhaps best defined as the capacity to discern fitness, beauty, order, congruity, or whatever constitutes excellence. When patterns of taste are dictated by purely commercial considerations, one argument goes, this capacity is stunted, and nearly all taste must conform to the average. . . . In this essay, Fortune puts aside statistics to argue a speculative and controversial thesis: it is that American taste, at least by prevailing standards, is changing for the better, and will continue to do so. The change will be pervasive, encompassing nearly all social and income groups and will be evident not only in the things people buy, but in the way people use their leisure. . . .

Four major forces are working to elevate American taste: (1) rising real income; (2) more education, both formal and informal; (3) the efforts of the tastemakers to spread their own gospel; and (4) the old American striving for self-betterment.[12]

COMMUNITY LIFE. Agnes Meyer comments on the impact of World War II upon community life:

These results would never have been so catastrophic nor so widespread, if deep cracks had not already existed in our social situation before the strain of total war was imposed upon it. . . . It was as revealing as it was disheartening to walk out of orderly, efficient, beautifully managed factories into a community turmoil so shocking. . . . Here was the visible proof of the gap that exists in our society between our mechanical genius and our social ineptitude, between our ability to apply scientific methods to industry and our failure to apply similar methods to human problems. . . .

Even before the war our community organization had been shattered by a technological revolution and the invasion of large impersonal forces that have revolutionized living conditions in the western world more drastically in the

last fifty years than in the preceding fifty centuries. The environment has been transformed, but in our habits, thoughts and feelings we are still living in bygone eras. . . . During the first World War, the depression, and the Second World War, the previous disruption of society was accelerated by the constant migration, the atomization of society, and the isolation of the individual. . . . Voluntary groups have proliferated to try to bring order out of chaos; but our social endeavors, whether public or private have not kept pace with the mass problems that now confront us . . . [This expresses] the survival of an outmoded individualism that is no longer able to cope with problems so widespread, so deep, and so intricate.[10]

William Appleman Williams, in discussing the 1820s, says:

Leadership ceased to be defined by the problems and responsibilities of general development; the encompassing view, based upon a sense of interrelated wholeness and community and defined by a system of equity and balance, failed to withstand the forces it had done so much to create. Leadership became instead a task of representing a specific element of the system and attempting to secure its objectives through conflict and compromise with the other elements.[15]

And Agnes Meyer says of community life:

There is a deep hunger in our land and throughout the world for a new sense of community. The old world order with its traditional loyalties has been shattered and a new social order has not yet come into being. Today, methods of communication are rapid and numerous. Yet they have not brought men closer together. To communicate is one thing. To commune together is quite another. And what humanity longs for, consciously and unconsciously, is the close communion of simpler days, when it was possible to hold intimate discourse, to enjoy an emotional sharing of ideas, to live a life of warmth and meaningful association with family, neighbors and friends. . . .

The problem before us is clear. First, this happy union of science and voluntary action must recreate a true local community in which our people can

than comprehensive planning; partly from unconscious acceptance of the real estate segregation of standards into high, middle, and low. Democratic standards are optimum or median, with floors but no ceilings. Our minimum floors tend automatically to become maximum ceilings.

Now it is said that people have no taste. Technology has robbed them of the opportunity for creative craftsmanship and hence of their standards for judgment. It has handed them instead a post on the assembly line (or at the automatic control board), a mess of disconnected fact learning, "interpreted" news, and high-pressure advertising. The dreariness and ugliness of much of the American scene is a result of the debacle of popular taste, a taste which rules the market, is expressed in the great bulk of American building, either responds to ugliness or does not recognize it when they meet face to face. This is the standard rationalization for the failure of American enterprise to produce a landscape that is pleasant or comfortable, let alone beautiful.

But consider who makes the actual specific decisions about form and arrangement which are responsible for the appearance of tract housing, stores, restaurants, roadside stands, and all of the other horrible examples that any enterprising photographer can collect by the gross along the highways and byways of the United States.[13] These decisions are not made by the average man—he works for someone else for a living. They are made by the owners, proprietors, and managers of the specific enterprises involved, and these are a small minority of the population. (In 1964 there were 7,586,000 "managers, officials and proprietors, except farm" out of a total of 68,517,000 "employed persons."[14] While these people may feel that they are deferring to popular taste, this would seem to boil down to their personal conceptions of popular taste, based on little or no reciprocal communication. Nor do they make any effort (with some notable exceptions) to assist this popular taste to improve itself, by bringing it in contact with the best cultural and design forces our country has produced. By and large their decisions are based on their own tastes, prejudices, and objectives. They are in a strategic position in relation to the quality of the general landscape. Their responsibilities are great; it is their attitudes and the results of their work which are often described as "popular." These are only popular in the sense that they dominate the landscape.

Quality in the landscape has various aspects. There is technical quality, in which certain technical problems are solved adequately or skillfully—soil erosion is stopped or prevented, wind is broken, sun is screened out, sound is blocked, plants are well grown. There is functional quality, in which use and circulation demands are met—it is convenient to get from street to house by foot or car, to walk around the garden, and to carry on such outdoor activities as may be desired. The popular theory of modern design has been that if technical and functional problems are solved, beauty will take care of itself. But we have found that this is not true. Beauty cannot take care of itself in this hasty, heedless, machine-ridden age. It is necessary to study with great care the visual quality that will result from arrangements proposed to solve technical and functional problems. Usually it is necessary to make careful and detailed adjustments in these arrangements to achieve maximum ultimate visual quality. Often it is necessary to design additional arrangements, not based on such problems, to achieve such quality. The ultimate combination of technical, functional, and visual qualities may produce final, complete emotional-intellectual satisfaction.

We find that we have no real basis for qualitative judgment of the physical environment. What we think are qualitative standards are really quantitative. We think the good environment is an expanding collection of *things,* whereas it is really a flexible yet balanced relationship of *processes.* The house may include a certain number of rooms, square feet, doors, windows, appliances, plumbing and electrical outlets, etc. But it is the relations between all these elements, and many more, that determine the quality of the house. The way that everything in the house is put together determines whether it is special, average, or substandard. This includes the way the house, lot, and street are put together, the way the houses and lots in the block and neighborhood are put together, the way schools, parks, churches, and shopping centers are put together with the neighborhood, the way neighborhoods and work and recreation places are put together in the community or metropolitan area, and so on. Each item in this constant network of relations affects all the others, be it ever so slightly. It is as though we all lived on a giant rope net, hung so loosely that whenever one moved, everyone else had to adjust.

One of the most widespread and naïve notions is that the efficient environment will be good and beautiful to live in. We are surrounded by the anarchic and shabby results of this idea, and yet our leaders in business, technology, and engineering cling to it stubbornly. The persistent concept of our times seems to be that nature is only an enlarged complex of machinery, people are real or potential robots, all problems are basically technical in nature and solution, aesthetics is an irrelevant defense system built up by maladjusted intellectuals and artists, and the computer is the final answer to everything.

Every travel book and tourist, weekend, or vacation guide is a commentary on the landscape. Sometimes socially oriented, sometimes physically, more often both together, such publications describe and pass judgment on landscapes from the point of view of their writers and readers. While there are great differences between traveler's-eye and resident's-eye views of the same landscape, the tremendous volume of travel literature does demonstrate that the general quality of landscape can be measured and is measured, and that there is fair unanimity as to the findings. The national parks, the Alps, and the Mediterranean are considered great scenery. New York, San Francisco, and Rio de Janeiro are great segments of urban scenery. Ordinarily pleasant rural, pastoral, or wilderness scenes will draw crowds of urbanites on weekends. These are not design commentaries from the point of view of production,

find the emotional security they need as much as they need their daily bread. The methods of achieving community solidarity can be as various as life will always be in a free democracy. But its objective must be the same, to reestablish the warm relationships and attachments which are the source of the deepest human influences and the highest human satisfactions. It must be a vision of community so closely bound that it is to each of its members an extended personality, an enlargement of the self. From such roots a stronger national community would come into being. . . .[10]

These intertwined yet mortal enemies, the creative and the neurotic processes, are universal; because both arise in early childhood, not out of exceptional circumstances but out of simple and ubiquitous human experiences. Subsequently these are reinforced by later stresses, among which that which we euphemistically call education plays an important role. . . .

The goal to seek is to free preconscious processes from the distortions and obstructions interposed by unconscious processes and from the pedestrian limitations of conscious processes. The unconscious can spur it on. The conscious can criticize and correct and evaluate. But creativity is a product of preconscious activity. This is the challenge which confronts the education of the future. LAWRENCE S. KUBIE, M.D.[16]

We have art in the American school systems, but it peters out, except for the talented or lazy, after the eighth grade. We have a citizenry that, although concerned about the quality of education in this country, is itself a product of it and therefore ignorant of the true role of art in the history of mankind. We have professional educators who are in the same position of ignorance, but less willing to admit it. We have over 15,000,000 adolescents and young men and women who are being deprived of any deep understanding of man's oldest form of communication and expression. . . .

The last hope is the disinterested critic of the educational system as a whole. This may be an interested citizen, a citizen's group or a dedicated expert. But the critics are strangely silent. It is almost impossible to explain

18

the position of a man of the caliber of James B. Conant who writes an influential critique of American high schools in which he recommends no improvements whatsoever in the field of broad art education. He does not stand alone, however. No critic, to my knowledge, has yet proposed a serious program to end this ignorance.

This neglected area is the 30,000 years of Man's art. It includes works that have transcended all material values. It includes men who have risen to the stature of giants. It includes the development of mental abilities without which man cannot survive. It includes all these, but it is ignored in discussion in favor of "basic" or "fundamental" work. . . . these same taxpayers and educators . . . would hardly want to display their ignorance publicly. . . . The result is a form of intellectual guilt. They cannot buck the tradition of art in Western culture, but neither can they offer intelligent criticism of its position in the present school system. Thus, they simply ignore it. . . . This situation should be a matter of national concern; at present, it is a matter of national apathy. G. SCOTT WRIGHT, JR.[17]

George Geiger's words in Saturday Review connecting creativity and education are heartening:

The attempt is to extend Dewey's suggestions to new fields, or, at any rate, to new developments within familiar fields. . . . the careful reader will find in what the present writers are going to call Creative Education the outline of a fresh and provocative program. It is a program underscoring the kind of experience Dewey called esthetic, experience completed and fulfilled. . . . fragmentation appears to be the contemporary expression of an abiding cleavage in Western culture, a persistent dualism between polar concepts like mind and matter, ends and means, values and facts, and, in present-day controversy, the humanities and the sciences. . . . this taken-for-granted distinction loses its force once we turn to esthetic experience. Here everything intermingles; the fitting together constitutes the quality of an esthetic experience. As Dewey puts it: "All the cases in which means and ends are external to one another are non-esthetic. This externality may even be regarded as a definition of the non-esthetic."[18]

but they are from the point of view of consumption. We can usually agree on a beautiful or pleasant landscape, scene, or view when it can be found full-blown as a result of natural or human processes. But the great question is how do we produce these by design? Only a few great parks and segments of urban scenery suggest the answer.

Such fine objectives as those expressed by Agnes Meyer must be viewed in relation to the actual patterns of contemporary American community life, in which the community organization and apparatus, both official and unofficial, are run by a minority of more or less hard-working "ins," who are watched with varying mixtures of apathy, envy, and animosity by a majority of more or less alienated "outs." Topping it all is the local power structure with which every planner or reformer must acquaint himself before he can hope to accomplish anything.

The importance of the quality of the landscape lies, not in any abstract aesthetics, but in its effect on the physical and mental health of its inhabitants. While Meyer lays stress upon the importance of stable home life and creative education, we must stress the unified effect of the total environment. It is not enough for home and school to make up for the inadequacies of the community; they must help the community to improve itself and share some of the burdens. The most obvious examples of the bad environment—the slum and the blighted neighborhood with their chain of crime, delinquency, immorality, and disease—are not the only examples. Many a bright and shining new tract of houses, many an older suburb, inadequately related to work, community, or commercial facilities, contains the seeds of blight and deterioration. Many a peripheral subdivision of half-acre and acre lots, "estate type," will never become more than a visual shambles because the land development problems are beyond the owners' resources. Social and physical patterns develop hand in hand, and social planning must recognize that sensory experience is an important function in its own right. It is precisely the well-planned and sensitively designed integration of schools, parks, playgrounds, shops, stores, offices, and cultural and health facilities that brings both physical and social landscapes to life, gives them vigor and vitality.

Education. Twentieth-century man has been called untutored in matters of taste and aesthetics. This is true. We are not born with taste or aesthetic judgment, we develop them under the influence of our environment. Consider the fact that American education for almost all students at the elementary and secondary levels contains absolutely no material dealing with the quality of the physical environment. It contains a great deal of quantitative and functional analysis of the physical world and a great deal on both quantity and quality in the social environment. But never a word on the visual quality of our surroundings. How then can we expect the average citizen, the public official, the entrepreneur, or anyone else to have any standards for aesthetic judgment? How can they select a good house, a good public building, or a good commercial structure, let alone a good neighborhood or community plan? Colleges, universities, and the communication media of adult life offer little more. Art-appreciation courses, columns, and articles are too little and too late. The visitor from Mars, after examining our mass education and communication structures, would conclude that officially the United States does not care what the visual quality of its physical environment is. And many a weary laborer in the stony fields of good community design would agree with him. To the answer that this is all a reflection of popular taste we must say again that it is necessary to make a more realistic and accurate analysis of who and how many make the basic decisions as to the content of education and communication at all levels, and how responsible they really are to the general public. Experience as a student, teacher, and father participating in American education leads one to the conclusion that the great debate set off by Sputnik was long overdue, and has not yet been satisfactorily resolved.

Creative education which concerned itself with the quality of the physical environment might endeavor to provide citizens with bases for judgment, objective factors for analysis of their surroundings. Without trying to make designers out of all laymen, such education might well try to make all laymen into good clients for designers, able to participate in the creative give-and-take which is essential to all healthy design processes. Citizens schooled in understanding the standards and processes by which designers judge and criticize each others' work would not be nearly so easily taken in by the eager speculator or the apathetic public official. Such a truly enlightened citizenry (the true aim of democratic education and communication processes) could easily prevent the debauchery of landscape, destruction of scenery, and wastage of natural resources which is now the private and exhausting worry of a minority of conservationists, nature lovers, urban improvers, and aestheticians.

The factors for analysis might begin with the functional-technical-sensory triangle. The average citizen is close to specific functional problems and articulate about them. He know when housing, schools, parks, shopping, and traffic flow are unsatisfactory and inadequate, but is easily taken in by piecemeal programs for improving them separately (and therefore inadequately) because he cannot visualize the apparently complex processes required to solve all of the problems together in their interrelated patterns. This is largely because these processes are rarely described in plain language. Technical problems are accepted as being of primary importance and as being the province of expert engineering skills which are beyond the grasp of the average citizen, except in fragments. The much more complex processes of balancing and integrating the many different technical aspects and costs of environmental problems (involving disconnected competitive disciplines, for example, construction versus landscape, earthwork versus structures adjusted to topography, or "development" versus conservation) are again beyond the average understanding, although not beyond its capacity if put into simple complete statements in plain language. Sensory (aesthetic, visual,

Although the natural and institutional environments are dealt with in a number of academic disciplines, also the fine arts, the man-made physical environment—including the city itself—has been a neglected focus in general education in any broad sense, whether in historical, functional, behavioral or purely aesthetic terms.

This gap should be filled, not only for professional background but also, perhaps even more important, for non-professional students. This is a vital step in the public education which is so badly needed, to stimulate greater awareness and understanding of the physical environment and its design, from household objects to buildings, cities and regions. . . . Hopefully, this new focus in the humanities would help to develop some able critics in the field of environmental policy and design, to meet a widely felt need and rising demand. CATHERINE BAUER WURSTER[19]

Though ours is already the most costly school system in the world, in terms of its yield in genuine education, money has not been a major bar to reform. The following factors have: members of the educational establishment were slow to grasp the significance of Sputnik for education, reluctant to admit that drastic reforms are necessary, strongly opposed to changes in the status quo which would adversely affect their vested interests.

. . . Then, too, we have never agreed on precise goals for American education; it is therefore not surprising we have been unable to set clear-cut goals for educational reform. Even if we agreed on goals, where would we find the skilled manpower to attain these goals? No really significant improvement is possible unless we raise the intellectual and educational qualifications of teachers. How can we do this, in the face of the determination of educational officialdom that existing certification requirements must be enforced? These are an insult to intelligent people, a useless bore to bright students. Intelligence is at a premium today; it will not be lured into education unless it is appreciated and rewarded in our school system.

From whatever point we look at the reform problem, we come up against

organized opposition by defenders of the status quo.

. . . We are still the only advanced country where direction of the educational enterprise is in the hands of administrators rather than teachers; our teachers still are less qualified than their counterparts abroad; we prolong comprehensive schooling unduly; there is chaos in educational nomenclature and academic degrees.

ADM. HYMAN RICKOVER[20]

Different environments resist or facilitate the process of image-making. . . . This probability can be stated with greater and greater precision as the observers are grouped in more and more homogeneous classes of age, sex, culture, occupation, temperament, or familiarity. Each individual creates and bears his own image, but there seems to be substantial agreement among members of the same group. It is these group images, exhibiting consensus among significant numbers, that interest city planners who aspire to model an environment that will be used by many people.

Therefore this study will tend to pass over individual differences, interesting as they might be to a psychologist. The first order of business will be what might be called the "public images," the common mental pictures carried by large numbers of a city's inhabitants: areas of agreement which might be expected to appear in the interaction of a single physical reality, a common culture, and a basic physiological nature. KEVIN LYNCH[21]

and experience) problems are fuzziest and least understood by the average mind, perhaps because they are most ignored or deprecated by those who feel that an expanding economy should not be hampered by such trifling considerations. And yet there is an unprecedented interest in, and demand for, aesthetic considerations in the environment, and education and development both public and private are recognizing it.

Factors for physical analysis might expand into studying utility in the environment as measured by the quality of human relations which are produced or encouraged by it. Space relations as a composite qualitative image of the environment as a whole or a sequence of wholes might be studied along the lines suggested by Lynch.[21] The use of materials both structural and natural, in technical, economic, and aesthetic terms, could be analyzed in detailed studies. The development of principled relations—unity-variety, proportion-scale, rhythm-repetition, balance-emphasis—could be clarified and demonstrated. The successful and continuing series of landscape design study courses which have recently been developed by the National Council of State Garden Clubs are a very substantial indicator of the popular demand for design education.

Heterogeneity. Many subjective factors will influence attempts at qualitative analysis of the landscape. The heterogeneous racial, religious, economic, educational, geographic, and social backgrounds of our people bring a multiplicity of attitudes to bear on the problem. These variable backgrounds, conditioned by the current social-cultural relations into which they are thrown by the powerful, disconnected, and narrow-minded dynamics of our economy, add up to a national attitude which is in constant flux on such questions as what makes a good place to live? play? visit? travel to?

A basic and complete study of the total landscape would have to establish relations between individual and group images and structural continuities between each individual and the large units of community, region, and nation. Only this will make possible both the breaking down of the separation between the special private and general public environments and the creative interaction between the two which will improve the latter without losing the former.

Landscape thinking includes the objectivity of the rational planner and the subjectivity of artist, photographer, or tourist. One of the latter may find beauty in slums which the former will demolish and replace with dull but sanitary housing. Pictorial qualities, which a good photographer or painter can find almost anywhere, are part of, and included within, actual spatial quality, which can only be experienced directly. But the continuity of the landscape experience—seen on a walk or from a car, train, or plane—distinguishes it entirely from isolated samples taken out of context by photographer or artist. Space articulation and organization, the actual three-dimensional relations between all physical elements, have central importance in determining the quality of the landscape.

21

	PEOPLE	LAND, SQ MI	DENSITY, PERSONS PER SQ MI
UNITED STATES (Continental excluding Alaska)	179,114,000	2,976,381	60.0
REGIONS			
Northeast	81,080,000	408,404	218.2
Southeast	38,161,000	447,603	82.0
Central	32,453,000	939,006	34.85
West	6,927,000	856,951	8.0
Pacific	20,493,000	319,530	65.0
GROUPS OF PLACES BY POPULATION			
1,000,000 — 5	17,484,059	1,261	13,865.0
500,000 — 16	11,110,991	1,888	5,885.0
250,000 — 29	10,765,881	2,401	4,484.0
100,000 — 81	11,652,426	2,728	4,271.0
50,000 — 201	13,835,902	3,539	3,910.0
25,000 — 429	14,950,612	5,319	2,811.0
10,000 — 1,130	17,568,286	6,939	2,532.0
5,000 — 1,388	9,779,714	5,005	1,954.0
2,500 — 2,140	7,580,028	5,242	1,446.0
Other urban territories 596	10,540,851	5,917	1,781.0
Rural territory	53,914,025	2,937,671	18.0
URBANIZED AREAS (Including one city of 50,000 or more)			
213 areas	95,848,487	25,544.3	3,752.0
Central cities	57,975,132	10,837.7	5,349.0
Urban fringe	37,873,355	14,706.6	2,575.0

Less than	1,000 per sq mi	2 areas	32 sections
Less than	5,000	198	343
Less than	10,000	16	93
Less than	15,000		20
More than	15,000	1	12

URBAN AREAS	40,238 sq mi*
RURAL AREAS	1,755,481
PRIMITIVE AREAS	1,753,255

OWNERSHIP, United States land, %

Private	58.7
Indian	2.3
Public	39.0
Federal	33.7
State	4.5
County and municipal	0.8

* Author's note: This is not, however, a true picture of urban land use. Urban residents do not stay within the boundaries of "urban areas." If we assume an urban region to be a 40-mile, or one-hour, travel radius around each urban center, we have a more reasonable unit of intensive land use. If we apply this figure to our "groups of places by population" we get an area almost twice that of the continental U.S.! The density in these urban regions ranges from 4,082 persons per sq mi in the 5 largest to 4 per sq mi in the 2,140 smallest.

LAND USE[14]

FEDERAL

Forest and wildlife	515,102,000 acres
Grazing	164,392,000
Military, except airfields	16,378,000
Airfields	1,923,000
Parks and historic sites	22,405,000
Reclamation and irrigation	8,020,000
Flood control and navigation	6,225,000
Power development and distribution	1,917,000
Other	33,542,000
TOTAL FOREST LAND	772,000,000
Commercial	530,161,000
Private	358,250,000
Federal	98,874,000
State, county, municipal	27,216,000

FARMS

6,103,000 in 1940	1,065,114,000 acres
3,711,000 in 1959	1,123,508,000

RECREATION

National parks

182 in 1950 (33,253,000 visitors)	23,882,000 acres
201 in 1963 (102,711,000 visitors)	25,810,000

State parks

1,725 in 1950 (114,291,000 visitors)	4,657,000 acres
2,544 in 1962 (284,795,000 visitors)	5,766,000

Municipal parks in cities of 100,000 or more

8,671 in 1950	301,492 acres
10,209 in 1960	362,935

Municipal and county parks

24,708 in 1960	1,015,461 acres

Nonurban public outdoor recreation areas—park, forest, fish and wildlife, water development, transportation, special, and other agencies

24,048	234,000,000 acres
1,059 Federal	198,341,000
20,429 state	32,113,000
2,560 local	3,546,000

HIGHWAYS

1950	3,313,000 miles
1962	3,600,000
Municipal	455,244
Rural (nonmunicipal)	3,144,337
Surfaced	2,228,570
Nonsurfaced	915,767
Federal control	119,763
State "	673,139
Local "	2,351,435

RAILROADS

1940	234,398 miles
1962	215,090

HOUSING[14]

All units (58,318,000)	100.0%
No piped water inside	7.1
No flush toilet	10.3
No bathtub or shower	11.9
No furnace or built-in electric heat	34.7
No radio	8.5
No television	12.7
No telephone	21.5
No auto	21.5
Dilapidated or lacking one or more plumbing facilities	18.2

NEW CONSTRUCTION BY DOLLAR VALUE, 1963

Total	$62,451,000,000
Private	43,772,000,000
Residential	25,843,000,000
Industrial	2,962,000,000
Commercial	5,200,000,000
Other nonresidential	3,697,000,000
Farm	1,266,000,000
Public utilities	4,494,000,000
All other	310,000,000
Public	18,679,000,000
Residential	782,000,000
Educational	3,043,000,000
Other nonresidential	2,481,000,000
Military	1,222,000,000
Highways	6,670,000,000
Sewer and water	1,966,000,000
Conservation and development	1,553,000,000
All other	861,000,000

CHAPTER 3
Language, Man, and Nature

The wordfact makes words a precise substitute for reality. This is an enormous convenience. It means that to say that something exists is a substitute for its existence. And to say that something will happen is as good as having it happen. The saving in energy is nearly total. JOHN KENNETH GALBRAITH[23]

Language, like so many other human inventions, has enormous potentialities both for good and for evil. . . . Its principal danger for us humans lies in the fact that we tend to guide ourselves by verbal maps instead of by actual experience . . . since verbal maps can become increasingly divorced from experience without us becoming aware of the lost contact with reality. . . . ANATOLE RAPOPORT[24]

The function of words is to conceal thought. TALLEYRAND[25]

Design is a problem-solving activity. Being basically concerned with problems stemming from relations between man and nature, it must begin by understanding them. It must be aware of the varying explanations which are offered by science and religion for the world we live in. And it must understand its role as an art process.

Language is the most flexible and adaptable tool for communication among men and women. And yet when we are discussing work which has physical form, physical properties, and conscious aesthetic content, there is a danger in words, no matter how many or how convincing. They can create the foundation, the groundwork, the background, the climate of opinion for the designer and planner, and they can establish certain theoretical principles of approach, but they cannot do the work. Always, in physical design, there is an intangible, a quality and a value that cannot be conveyed with words or even with drawings or reproductions, but only by the experience of the actual work. In our age of slick facility with words and instantaneous communication of words and pictures around the world, of the camera angle and the professional photographer and model maker, this becomes a complex problem. Words or pictures or drawings can never convey the actual quality of work, only the ideas behind it and in it.

On the other hand, although the concepts of design are largely visual and graphic, language is still our primary means of communicating basic ideas. One picture may be worth ten thousand words, but the caption which is applied to the picture will make it or break it. It will ensure the uniform interpretation of the picture desired by the editor in the minds of all or most of his readers, eliminating the freedom of interpretation their varied backgrounds might produce.

Language is never static. It grows and changes from year to year with growth and change in people, society, and the world. This process has been accelerated in recent decades by the pressure of tremendous world events and the consequently increased activities of those who most influence the language—politicians, lawyers, commentators, journalists, writers, educators, publishers, editors. Words tend to change or lose their meaning. Sometimes the dictionary is no help at all.

Nature is the world in which we live—a ball of rock, minerals, and earth, surrounded by a layer of atmosphere and weather, spinning with gigantic precision through a galaxy of other worlds and suns, inhabited by vegetable and animal life in a myriad of forms from the simple protozoon to complex man. Two systems of explanation are offered for this fantastically complicated and apparently irrational collection of phenomena. One, religion, presents complete ready-made answers, including original creation, overall plan, and continuous control from outside this world. These answers substitute the authority of centuries of acceptance for the necessity of proof or evidence. From them, as Dr. Sears indicates, stems our Western habit of separating man from nature. The other system of explanation, science, takes nothing for granted, accepts neither traditions, precedents, authorities, nor ready-made answers. It says that all answers must prove themselves in practice, that no answer is final, static, or universal. We must lift ourselves by our own bootstraps, building our knowledge of the world on that which has already been proved beyond a reasonable doubt by rational controlled experiment, setting up hypotheses which may only stand until disproved, which serve merely as vehicles for experiment.

Preindustrial society was dominated by religion, with its institutional answers. Postindustrial society has been dominated by science, with its instrumental answers. But both processes have been continuous throughout history. The instrumental process moved us from cave and treetop to modern life. Institutional structures hang on today, summed up as The Establishment, in all parts of the world, in all capitalist, socialist, and new countries. Social development has been a struggle to know (about man, nature, the world) and then to make the best use of that knowledge. This has been an instrumental process alternately resisted and taken over by institutions. The institutional process is the defense of The Establishment against the discomfort of change, or it is the hasty absorption and assimilation of change when it can no longer be avoided.

The struggle to know has become science. The struggle to do has become art. These are both instrumental processes. The first statement is obvious; the second seems farfetched. Science pervades our world, all-wise, all-knowing, all-reaching, the great white father behind our standard of living. Art, on the other hand, is a special cubbyhole, something for leisure time or special people, entertaining, occasionally disturbing, but we can take it or leave it. Certainly we never let it interfere with the day-to-day business of life—unless we can make something material of it.

Science in general needs neither definition nor explanation in our world. Perhaps it even needs some deflation. It is a knowledge-finding, not a decision-making, process. Occasionally the knowledge is such as to allow no alternatives, as in the treatment of plague or malaria. Then the decision is built into the knowledge. But usually the knowledge in-

Now Facts are all very well but they have their little weaknesses. Americans often assume that Facts are solid, concrete (and discrete) objects like marbles, but they are very much not. Rather are they subtle essences, full of mystery and metaphysics, that change their color and shape, their meaning, according to the context in which they are presented. They must always be treated with skepticism, and the standard of judgement should be not how many Facts one can mobilize in support of a position but how skillfully one discriminates between them, how objectively one uses them to arrive at Truth, which is something different from, though not unrelated to, the Facts.

Another aspect of Facts is that there can be too many of them. . . .
                          DWIGHT MACDONALD[26]
Nature:
A collective abstract term for the entire universe.

The system of natural existences, forces, changes and events, regarded as distinguished from, or exclusive of, the supernatural. . . .

The sum of physical or material existences and forces, regarded as exclusive of man. . . .

. . . the constitution or inherited or habitual conditions and tendencies of man. . . .

The character, constitution or essential traits of a person, thing or class, especially if original rather than acquired. FUNK & WAGNALLS[27]

Allen Wheelis, in *The Quest for Identity*, includes religion and science in a broader concept:

It is not possible to view the life of man apart from culture; . . . in man—even the most primitive man— these (animal) activities are shaped by two superimposed modes of action which are distinctively human. These are the use of tools and the creation of myths. . . . They are the instrumental process and the institutional process. Each of them encompasses a vast range of phenomena, yet they bear a precise meaning.

The instrumental process . . . in words, would be somewhat as follows: "Let us first examine the facts, and draw only such conclusions as the facts warrant. If no conclusion is warranted but some conclusion is necessary—since life does not wait on certainty—then

volves alternatives (shall we make a bomb?). Then the decisions are not made by scientists but by society, by the people, through our elected or self-appointed leaders. J. Arthur Thomson has clearly stated the limited enterprise of science. "Science," he says, "is a particular way of looking at the world, but it is not the only way. . . . We learn by feeling and living as well as by scientifically knowing. Science is one of the pathways toward the truth, but there are other pathways. . . ."[28]

Art, among other things, is the process of deciding what to do with knowledge, new or old. "What!" you may say. "Art is painting, sculpture, music—literature, drama, dance—architecture, landscape architecture, interior decoration—ceramics, graphics, industrial design, furniture design—movies, television, radio, advertising—well, anyway, that is about all." But in the classical definition art was skill. There was an art of medicine, of law, of business, of politics, of military tactics and strategy—finally of life. The scope of art seems to depend on who is defining it. It may be as narrow as his special interest or as broad as

let us hold the conclusion tentative and revise it as new evidence is gathered." Scientific method, therefore, approximates the essence of the matter; but the instrumental process is a larger concept. The origin of scientific method falls within recorded history, but the instrumental process is as old as man. . . . It includes, also, art, both fine and applied. For art, as all artists know, is a problem-solving activity in which answers are achieved by taking pains, not by revelations from on high or seizure by a muse. . . . The authority of the instrumental process is rational, deriving from its demonstrable usefulness to the life process. The final appeal is to evidence.

The institutional process designates all those activities which are dominated by the quest for certainty. . . . Religion conveys the essence, but the institutional process is of greater scope. Religion was a relatively late development in the institutional process. . . . Far older are animism and the alleged omnipotence of thought, which is magic. . . . the authority of the institutional process is arbitrary; the final appeal is to force.

The instrumental process is bound to reality. Facts are facts, it seems to say. . . . Reality can be altered, particularly if it is closely observed. . . . The instrumental process is generally disparaged as mere problem-solving; for the security it creates, though real, is limited.

The institutional process is bound to human desire and fear. Wishing will make it so, it seems to say. . . . Honor and prestige accrue to the institutional process; for the security it creates, though illusory, is unlimited.

. . . For though the idea of society is the soul of the institutional process, it is the very essence, also, of the instrumental process. The fall of institutional patterns, therefore, does not preclude value and meaning at the social level. It is only because histories record primarily the vicissitudes of institutional conflict that the life of man on earth is a chaotic story of foolishness and destruction. Divested of all institutional patterns, the life of man would portray the organic unity of the instrumental process, the continuity of arts and of technology. This process is one of increasing knowledge and control. It has no terminus, but it has direction; and this direction is away from ignorance, superstition, cruelty and helplessness. Individual life has value and meaning by virtue of its participation in this process. The fact of death, in this view, is reconcilable with the activities of life; for a social process of which the individual was a part, to which he has contributed, and with which he can identify, survives his individual extinction. Indeed, without individual mortality the instrumental process could not exist. For if no one dies, then soon no one could be born; and growth and development would pass from the experience

of mankind. The progress of man is thus contingent upon the succession of generations.[29]

Accommodation between religion and science has gone on within each individual, as well as among people in general.

This firm belief, a belief bound up with deep feeling, in a superior mind that reveals itself in the world of experience, represents my conception of God. In common parlance this may be described as "pantheistic" (Spinoza).
EINSTEIN[30]

Now it is quite clear that the leaders of scientific and those of religious thought do not waste as much time quarreling with each other as they did a half-century ago. But this cessation of hostilities did not come about through a real reunion, with more scientists discovering grounds for faith through their science, and more theologians relying on science for evidence of their beliefs. On the contrary, during the past quarter-century the most important leaders in both fields have been inclined simply to pull their troops back from the battle, and to respect the territory of the other camp. . . .

If science and theology are less in conflict today, it is only partly because science is now less inclined to insist that its method is the only way to think about man and the universe; it is more because theology—or at any rate, leading theologians—make much less con-

life and the world. For art is human creativity in action, the process, and its results. Certain arts, called fine, best exemplify this process by direct, immediate, and repeated experience. Other arts, called applied, combine utility and beauty in forms which complicate or muffle the creative process. But the process itself is a constant human characteristic. It may appear in business, in labor, in school or church or home. It expresses itself by formulating and solving problems in ways which add something, small or large, to previous solutions. In the fine arts the artist formulates and solves his own problem with little reference to social context (although it was not ever thus). In the applied arts the problem comes from society, but must often be formulated and articulated by artist or designer before solutions can be found. In the general arts of life which go on around us day after day, screened and muffled by humdrum routine, the formulation and the solution of problems go on continuously with little thought that there may be creative forces at work. Decision making is always a potentially creative process, and life, as we know, is just one decision after another.

Life might be considered a constant reciprocal relationship between fantasy and reality. Reality is the world which exists around us in space, behind and before us in time, independent of us, and yet responsive to our actions. Fantasy is the multitude of interpretations of, or substitutions for, that world which exists in our various individual consciousnesses and in organized institutional form in religion, politics, art, and society. Reciprocity exists because fantasy must, at least occasionally and partially, recognize reality; and yet fantasies of sufficient force may change reality. Reality at any given time is the result of the entire continuity of natural and social processes since time began. Fantasy is a prime and ineradicable element in the social process.

Fantasy is a product of the human consciousness, which came late in the stream of evolution. Therefore reality was here first—unless you prefer to think that the human consciousness is one of the great fantasies of the Infinite Consciousness which produces all reality. This is a fantasy shared by millions.

If we say that religion is the great fantasy of man, in the sense of a fantastic authoritarian explanation of the world not supported by direct experience or established facts, we will raise the hackles on some 80 million American church members. And yet is not this devout adult majority divided into a multitude of denominations and sects, each one of which considers the beliefs of all of the others to be fantastic and unbelievable in whole or in part?

Science is no doubt the chief eliminator of fantastic explanations of the world, the chief destroyer of supersitition, myth, folklore, and irrational customs, through its insistence on empirical proof of all propositions. Yet hypothesis, which is calculated intuition or fantasy, is one of the chief tools of science in exploring the material world. And what could be more fantastic than the splitting of the atom, the possibility of blowing up our world or flying to the moon?

fident claims today than a century ago that their form of knowledge can be related with certainty to material and political affairs. DON K. PRICE[31]

The biggest mass production known to man came from the mind of God! Or if no god lived, then, from the indifferent energy of nature. SEAN O'CASEY[32]

Art, popularly contrasted with science as a world of fantasy opposed to a world of hardheaded reality, is truly a world of fantasy in a much more subtle and complex way. The art process, fully developed, makes possible the physical expression or communication of our most deep-seated, organic, and unconscious fantasies and intuitions about life and the world. Poetry and literature communicate these directly. Painting and music give form to feelings and experiences that cannot be put into words. Sculpture, architecture, and landscape architecture reshape the hard physical world on the basis of fantasies which may begin far removed from reality. These arts represent the widest spread in the patterns of reciprocity between fantasy and reality. Science, as the pursuit of knowledge, can only explain and clarify the world to us, as a structure in constant process. Art, as the expansion of experience and the deepening of understanding, can make possible for us the best (most life-giving) uses and directions for this knowledge. (Some sciences equal art in their wide spread from fantasy to reality.)

Politics, the art of the possible, also has its fantasies, at times grandiose. We have only to remember a man named Adolf. The fantasies of communism, once single, now multiple, seem more durable—hence more realistic? Every political campaign, every party platform, is a structure of fantasy which may or may not achieve reality when the dust of the election has settled. John Birchism and White Citizenism are structures of fantasy stubbornly and at times violently opposed to reality. The foreign and domestic policies of constituted governments seem likewise at times to be totally and fantastically disconnected from reality. And yet to their proponents these policies are real and all opposition is fantastic. The wordfact (this is so because I say it is so) is the ultimate fantasy of a world of mass literacy and instant communication.

Society is a structure of fantasy designed to make it possible for each individual to cope with reality. Laws, customs, morals, mores, culture—all begin as fantasies impelled by real situations, develop their own reality through usage and support, and may become fantastic and unrealistic again through changes in the real situation around them. Consider cannibalism, infanticide, monarchy, polygamy, nobility, war, torture, religious sacrifice. Snobbery is a fantasy of superiority, producing a hierarchy in which everyone is above or below everyone else. This produces opposing fantasies of equalitarianism, in which society is totally horizontal. Reality is somewhere between such extremes. Snobbery, whether of birth, money, property, color, size, shape, talent, skill, or intelligence, is arbitrary and fantastic as a measure of total social rating. But equalitarians may become mature enough to recognize superiority among themselves. Self-proclaimed superiority is a fantasy unless and until it is given reality by recognition from those around us. It may be natural to live a life of 20 to 30 percent fantasy and 70 to 80 percent reality—perhaps the reality needs the fantasy to push it ahead. But when these proportions are reversed, as in certain substantial areas of American life, there is danger ahead.

Life and Environment. Life is the total process of each of us from birth to death, as well as the total manifestation of all of us and all of organic biology on earth (perhaps elsewhere?) through time. Environment is the total complex of elements and forces which surrounds and impinges upon each unit of life throughout its span. Environment for each living unit thus includes other living units (men, animals, plants), the inorganic world above and below, nature as a vast structure of self-propelled and self-adjusting processes, and society as a human creation subjected to human decisions. The Western Judeo-Christian tradition, according to which man came from out of this world and has lived ever since in constant conflict with it and with most of his fellows, contrasts sharply with the Eastern tradition of Tao, the inevitable interdependence of all elements of life and environment, life and the world being a continuous seamless network of reciprocal relations in which each movement or change produces reactions of unpredictable extent in all directions. The practical fact that official histories of both East and West, as chronicles of continuous conflict, make this contrast appear to be a romanticized theory does not negate its basic relevance. Conflict both East and West overlays the fundamental bedrock of reciprocal social cooperation without which society would disappear. In instrumental life the two conflicting ideas are diffused around the world and throughout history, regardless of their institutionalization as Eastern or Western phenomena.

Control of our physical and social environment is one of the chief problems of life for all of us. We want to live in a nice home in a good neighborhood in a stable community in a reliable region in the greatest nation in the world. We want good workplaces, good schools, good centers for shopping, recreation, health care, culture, worship, and services. Yet in spite of these widespread and earnest desires and the greatest prosperity we have ever known, the American physical environment is deteriorating before our eyes, through new mass construction rather than blight and obsolescence, and the social environment is full of strange, violent, and demanding forces.

Life, then, is a struggle to improve one's environment, to adjust to it, or to preserve it if it requires neither improvement nor adjustment. This is roughly the arc of political thought and action from liberal to conservative, with radical extremes of progressive or reactionary ideology determined to expedite the movement of the clock forward or backward. All such programs require designed action to implement them, and their success or failure depends upon their creative content, i.e., how close they come to solving the problems of those to whom they appeal.

Life might be characterized as a continuous struggle for control of the environment. All the utopias that have been held out to us through centuries of struggle have presented controlled, stabilized, harmonious environments.[33] The progress of civilization might be called a progress from disorder. The fact that society began in the relative Eden of primitive communism and developed for many centuries through expanding disorderly struggles over the production and distribution of wealth is only a complication. The current confrontation between two large systems, each claiming possession of the keys to utopia, may mean that we are actually approaching an orderly answer.

Man and Nature. Man is people—men, women, old folks, young folks, adolescents, and children, as individuals, families, and larger social and political groupings. The social landscape is the product of the political, economic, cultural, and personal relations between people, from day to day and generation to generation throughout history. The site for this social landscape development has expanded from the primeval cave to the one world of today. The physical landscape is a product of the interactions between this social landscape and the world of nature.

In the largest sense we are a product and still a part of the natural world in which we live. There is no other world known to us, and whatever the proportions of human and nonhuman elements around us, our world is one world in our experience. The fact that man has emerged from the rest of nature to a position of decision and control sufficient to have major impact on large sections of the physical landscape does not take either him or those sections out of this world, nor does he come from out of this world. Man is the only known force capable of conscious choice and decision and therefore of control of future directions for development. Nonhuman nature, insofar as science has explained it, is a complex of forces and processes constantly in motion and change, never static even when they appear to be, almost but never quite in full equilibrium, easily disturbed and slow to recover, constantly producing new developments and directions, but with no central intelligence or consciousness to choose among or control them. Man is the only natural force able to become this central intelligence, and in many areas he has.

The basic principle of the "natural" designer—that man mars nature—is in fact a negation of our twentieth-century civilization. For a nation cannot be considered civilized until it lives in harmony with nature, and this is certainly not the case if there is a feeling of opposition between the two. The basic problem of landscape design is not man *versus* nature, it is man *and* nature. Man and nature are one thing, not two. Man is a natural product, and every one of his creations, even the most highly refined precision machine product, is a natural material refined through his imagination. Design may place nature before man, yet its whole purpose is the re-creation of man. How does it reconcile these variant ideas? The truth is that man is nothing without nature, and nature, so far as man is concerned, is nothing without him. They are two parts of a whole, not two opposing wholes. Of course the whole philosophic difficulty arises from the fact that, because our cities suffer from an excess of building and too little gardening, we feel that we must flee from them to a place in which gardening is maximum and building is minimum.

We search for, and can sense, a way of living in which one is always

31

conscious of being an integrated and reciprocal part of a total environment which includes both nature and society. This is not the Western way, in which the individual lives in alienation from his environment, competing with it, exploiting it, resisting it, or ignoring it in favor of a structure of abstractions. For centuries Western physical development followed formal geometric patterns, an expression of human dominance and independence of nature. The romantic revolts against rational formalism might be considered a search for reunion with nature, from which Eastern man has never, in principle, been parted.

If most people agree that most wild landscapes are more beautiful or pleasant than most humanized landscapes, that does not necessarily mean that nature knows best or that man automatically produces ugliness. It only means that man is able to select the most beautiful or pleasant landscapes but is still unable to control and direct the processes which produce them. The very qualities of beauty or ugliness do not exist in the landscape itself. They only exist in the relationship between it and people. They are human reactions to the landscape, and therefore are compounded with human subjectivity and frailty. Northeastern forest, Southwestern desert, and downtown urban center may be equally beautiful to some and ugly to others. With few exceptions there are no absolutes or unanimous agreements in such judgments. They cannot take place, nor can the problem arise, until people are brought face to face with the landscape. This is the point at which the work of architecture and landscape design begins. One functioning building, with its network of external connections, will humanize a great area of rural or wild landscape. One bit of landscape, properly related, will naturalize a considerable area of urbanization.

The house and garden, or other complex of specific development on one site, may view a wild landscape shaped by natural forces of geology, climate, and vegetation; or it may view a humanized landscape shaped by equally natural forces of human needs and desires, exploitation of resources, speculation in land and building, transportation and communication, power politics, and so on. In either case the fact that the forces are natural (they exist and have been there for some time) does not necessarily mean that they are permanent, right, or good. They all contain within themselves the seeds of their own change, and the direction of that change can only be guided by intelligence, reason, and sound emotion.

Such questions are basic to a mature discussion of the landscape as it relates to conscious design. They crop up in one form or another every time a building is designed (is it natural? appropriate? does it belong there?) or a garden planned (shall it be formal or informal?). The difference between Frank Lloyd Wright, who consciously and with great care integrated building with site and surroundings, and Le Corbusier, who thought in terms of conflict and contrast between the precise creation of man and the shaggy wildness of nature (the cube in the meadow), perhaps marks the spread in architectural conceptions of land-

The Taoist philosophy of nature . . . is primarily a way of life in which the original sense of the seamless unity of nature is restored without the loss of individual consciousness. It involves a new style of human action in relation to the environment, a new attitude to technical skills whereby man seems to interfere artificially with the natural world. It requires a fundamental revision of the very roots of our common sense. . . . The Taoist idea of naturalness goes far beyond the merely normal, or the simply ostentatious way of behaving. It is the concrete realization that all our experiences and actions are movements of the Tao, the way of nature, the endless knot, including the very experience of being an individual, a knowing subject. . . . Thus all art and artifice, all human action, is felt to be the same as natural or spontaneous action—a world-feeling marvelously expressed in Chinese poetry and landscape painting, whose technique involves the fascinating discipline of the "controlled accident," of doing exactly the right thing without force or self-conscious intention. . . .

A world of interdependent relationships, where things are intelligible only in terms of each other, is a seamless unity. In such a world it is impossible to consider man apart from nature. . . . Man is himself a loop in the endless knot, and as he pulls in one direction he finds that he is pulled from another and cannot find the origin of the impulse. For the mold of his thoughts prevents him. He has an idea of himself, the subject, and of nature, the object. . . . Man is one with nature in a seamless unity. . . . ALAN WATTS[34]

Originally the ego includes everything, later it detaches from itself the external world. The ego-feeling we are aware of now is thus only a shrunken vestige of a far more extensive feeling—a feeling which embraced the universe and expressed an inseparable connection of the ego with the external world. FREUD[35]
See KALAHARI by Jens Bjerre for an insight into natural man.[36]

K. Jaspers: . . . our freedom has been only "a real but passing moment between two immeasurably long periods of sleep," those of the life of nature and the life of technique.[33]

32

scape relations. The general schism in architectural thinking, between pride in pure creative geometry and a feeling that it is unnatural or inappropriate on the site and must be softened and harmonized with vegetation, is another expression of the same problem.

If life is a search for order, harmony, and repose, then it is instructive to examine the patterns of nature and of man in these terms. The natural scene at its best is in delightful equilibrium; but let some disturbing force—fire, flood, earthquake, pests, man—enter, and this balance is apt to go by the boards. It will be followed by distressing chaos, disorder, ugliness, destruction, and then perhaps by a more or less extended period of reconstruction ending in a return to the natural balanced ecological climax for the region.

Man begins with nature and projects new developments which either include or eliminate it. Such a project is apt to begin with some clear sense of order and purpose, with a plan, whether it be building, farm, mine, or city. But usually this order seems to dissipate and get lost as the project develops in use. The anarchy of a building and its surroundings, a mine and its tailings, or a city and its environs is comparable to that of nature thrown off balance by catastrophe. Farms are less apt to deteriorate thus, being of necessity a close harmony between man and nature. But when they become marginal economically, they do tend to deteriorate physically. Historical periods which have produced landscapes of considerable harmony and repose—the Greco-Roman world, the Renaissance, seventeenth-century Japan—have been upset by the introduction of new forces—barbarians, industrialism, the West.

Examination of the space patterns in the physical landscape leads inevitably, as it has for centuries, to comparison of the patterns produced by nature and by man. The long struggle between the formal rationalism of Rome and the Renaissance, proud to extend obvious human control over the landscape, and the informal naturalism of eighteenth-century England and the Orient left us with a warehouse full of academic rules and regulations. Only now are we beginning to see beyond these. Such books as Kepes's *The New Landscape*[37] and Feininger's *The Anatomy of Nature*[38] make us conscious of the harmonious quality of nature's irregularity, far from the savage wilderness of the romantic poets.

For nearly eight thousand years the hand of man has made its mark on the landscape through hand tools. For nearly two hundred it has been enormously extended and expanded by machine tools of fantastic scope and flexibility. Suddenly we find ourselves between three horns rather than two: the ageless landscape of nature; the charming though unsanitary landscapes produced by handicraft cultures throughout history and the world; and the gigantic, remorseless, and inhuman landscapes produced by machine cultures with sudden and appalling acceleration. We begin to see certain affinities between the wild scenes described by countless nature lovers and natural scientists and the picturesque scenes of handicraft humanization and urbanization described by countless travelers, architects, and urbanists from Baedeker to Sitté.

33

We begin to see these affinities as an incomplete or inaccurate regularity, an orderly irregularity, felt and processed rather than measured and planned, in contrast with the precise and unvarying regularity of mass production, its resistance to change once geared up for production of bottles, houses, or bombs. It begins to be clear that the soulless giantism of our machine world—typified by assembly-line production, tract housing, multiple high-rise housing, Federal and state highway systems, airports—is a primitive or adolescent stage of industrialism. It is concerned primarily with size and quantity, obsolescence through innovation, constantly expanding production for its own sake. It is possible today to envision the end product of nature-respecting cultured industrialism as variable and flexible in size of facility and quantity of products; capable of producing commodities as regular and similar as necessary yet never identical save where visual quality is irrelevant; decentralized and adjustable, able to go to the problem and meet its demands rather than vice versa; with production sensitively adjusted to human needs, rather than forcing humanity to adjust to its demands.

Dunham says, ". . . an artist has a technique but not a technology."[39] By this he seems to mean that the artist must dominate his technique, whereas technology tends to dominate the artist. Coomaraswamy says, "We cannot measure qualities of art by measuring degrees of skill."[40] Our society adjusts itself to technology, which means to those who control technology. Witness "technological unemployment." When we grow up, technology will adjust to society, that is, to general human needs and desires. Our production now depends on desires rather than needs. Needs can be measured objectively. Desires are subjective and can be manipulated by those who control education, information, and communication. Therefore society must control them. Society is the majority voice free of minority control but respectful of minority opinion. This is the two-hundred-year-old problem of democracy.

Design and Nature. The problem for planners and designers is what is wrong in the original conception of most plans of man which leads them to deteriorate from the point of conception on? Should they not improve from then on, in development and use? The designer must consider reality as physical, visual, and comprehensible, even though science tells us it is basically energy in motion. Design is concerned with the tangible, physical world as it appears to the average citizen, colored and influenced by the teachings of science and religion. Design must function to a great extent as a bridge between general or average and specialized or advanced conceptions of the physical world. In the design of physical relations between man and nature there is an expanding gap between the world of nature and the world of technology. While the slow-swirling spiral of evolution moves the former from reptiles and ferns to mammals and flowering trees, the latter leaps from fire and handicraft to nuclear physics and astronautics. Site-space design for the air-conditioned glass cube is different from, and yet the same as, that for the Renaissance palace, the Georgian manor house, or the Japanese

*Renaissance materialism was natural-
istic, and as man began to tap the more
hidden powers and resources of nature,
he de-natured nature, and so attacked
the very basis of his faith. . . . The
fast and chaotic rise of the industrial
centres of Europe . . . ravaged the
countryside and drew ever-growing
numbers of people into congested and
devitalised cities. . . . With a nature
in retreat, man found himself segre-
gated from the universe and he could
no longer enjoy the hope and idealism
of Renaissance materialism. . . . Up to
now, only the more sublime, beautiful
aspects of nature had been considered
worthy subjects of art. Now . . . artists
were no longer satisfied with the merely
beautiful; they began to seek the bi-
zarre, the out of the ordinary, the altered and even the deformed. . . . Finally, nature, and the old pursuit of
beauty, are rejected altogether. . . .
Those who see in a better planned future a restitution of nature have failed
to realise, or do not wish to realise,
that no matter how we let nature in
again, she cannot possibly provide us
with the emotional sustenance which
our irreversibly architectonic, mechanical and scientificated environment requires. Nature can be hated, ignored,
regretted, used as a means of escape
from the contemporary, but she can
never again fulfill man's primary aesthetic needs.* FRANK AVRAY WILSON[41]

*Nature does not make Art. She works
by circumstance and law. Only man
makes Art. Because man chooses. He
invents. He can make the doors smaller
than people and the skies black in the
daytime if he wants to. He assembles.
He can bring together the mountain,
the serpent, and the child.* LOUIS
KAHN[42]

*Certain people always say we should
go back to nature. I notice they never
say we should go forward to nature.
It seems to me they are more concerned
that we should go back, than about nature.* ADOLPH GOTTLIEB[43]

tea pavilion. It is different because of the reciprocal creative stimulus between modern science and modern art and the expanding gap between design concepts and the visual reality of raw nature. It is the same because ever since man acquired sufficient control over his environment to lose his fear of nature, he has yearned to surround his buildings with spatial compositions constructed of earth, rock, vegetation, and water, representing the world of nature and of man in happy coexistence. Only the protective battlements of the medieval stone castle and the self-centered introspection of the modern air-conditioned concrete cube exclude this contemplative possibility. **1702428**

The philosophic relationship between man and nature has long been a source of design theories in which geometry and biology, formality and informality, were set in conflict with each other. Today we are able to project theories in which these conflicting ideas work together to produce richness beyond the potential of either alone. For we know that the new world of automation and atomic power must still be visually related to the old world of nature everywhere, specific bit by specific bit. The cultural impact of this knowledge is expressed by the phrase "indoor-outdoor living." Is this marriage possible? Certainly not physi-cally with air conditioning—you must open and close a door between. Air conditioning has reduced the physical possibility—a primitive hut is more indoor-outdoor. But glass has expanded the visual possibility— with the glass wall we can sit in air-conditioned comfort with the greatest extremes of jungle, desert, or mountain landscape just beyond. The origi-nal implication of the glass wall was precisely to make the outdoors part of indoor living, thereby expanding its scale and richness, regardless of climate. The concentration in California and other mild climates on moving indoor living outdoors has been an extra dividend, not applicable to all climates. The problem of indoor-outdoor living in Ne-braska or Louisiana can be solved by the sentitive and intelligent use of the glass wall, rather than by the attempt to import California gar-dens. Likewise, the delightful integration of indoors and out achieved in Japan in summer can be equaled rather than imitated.

35

Claire Falkenstein, in Venice, Italy (LEFT), and George Hall, in Pasadena, California (BELOW), have integrated art with specific landscapes.

CHAPTER 4
Art and Design

The Oxford Dictionary defines art as skill:

Human skill. . . . Learning, science. . . . Technical or professional skill. . . . The application of skill to subjects of taste. . . . Perfection of workmanship or execution. . . . skill applied to . . . Painting, Architecture, etc. . . . Anything wherein skill may be attained. . . . certain brands of learning which are instruments for more advanced studies or for the work of life. . . . A body of rules for practice. . . .[44]

When we introduce the concept *art* into a world divided between *nature* and *man* we introduce further confusion and controversy. Fear and timidity enter, great conflicts of mysticism and reason occur, and those bugaboos of design crop up: "unnatural," "arbitrary," "self-conscious," "contrived." Is the world of art separate from, and in conflict with, the world of nature? Is nature the most perfect art? Does "nature know best"? Can we have art disconnected from nature?

Susanne K. Langer says, ". . . the whole function of a work of art . . . is to symbolize subjective experience—that is, to formulate and convey ideas of sentience and emotion."[45] Does this mean that art is limited to objects, or to acts of communication? that the landscape cannot become a work of art? or perhaps that only a fragment of a certain size can become such a work? Frank Avray Wilson accepts no such limitations: "Art is revelation . . . nothing more than the accentuation of an innate human propensity for symbolic expression and communication. . . . The final test of the value of any art is this: Can it help us to reach that state of sensitivity and inspired vision which will progressively enable us to convert our entire environment into one vast work of art? For that is the challenge facing us. Once nature provided us with this all-embracing milieu; now that we have ousted nature, we must set about providing ourselves with a new environment which is as inspiring, as harmonising and as mentally integrating as was once nature, and this we now know is eminently possible. . . ."[41]

In classical thought we have many arts—medical, military, legal, governmental, fine, and applied. On the other hand, one can find critics who place rigid limits on what may be called art, including music, painting, sculpture, and perhaps poetry and theater, but no more, not even architecture. Art has many definitions,[46] but these seem to center on a creative act whose effects expand among people and endure in time. The creative act establishes new relations, adds new dimensions, new qualities, and new arrangements. Art may be classical (the search for

37

rules of order) or romantic (the search for wonder and fantasy). But it ceases to be art when it finds either without some of the other. Among the functions of art is the improvement of man's relationship with his world, by (1) the communication of concepts of that world which clarify and strengthen his understanding of its qualities, and (2) direct improvement of the world itself by creative change. All artists are designers, but not all designers are artists. Likewise, some artists may be merely designers.

Art begins with fresh inspirations produced by uninhibited talents in new and growing situations, proceeds through skillful and powerful expansions by those who know how, and ends as accepted and sterilized components of The Establishment.

Culture, or civilization . . . is that complex whole which includes knowledge, belief, art, law, morals, custom, and many other capabilities of man as a member of society. TYLOR[47]

Culture comprises inherited artifacts, goods, technical processes, ideas, habits, and values. MALINOWSKI[48]

Culture is all behavior mediated by symbols. BAIN[49]

By culture I mean the symbolic expressions in the realms of ideas and art of the experience of individuals in those (social) relationships. DANIEL BELL[50]

The relation between cultural ends and actual means is not (and cannot be?) one of coincidence, and it is rarely, if ever, one of harmony. . . . The distinction between culture and civilization, according to which "culture" refers to some higher dimension of human autonomy and fulfillment, while "civilization" designates the realm of necessity, of socially necessary work and behavior, where man is not really himself and in his own element but is subject to heteronomy, to external conditions and needs [, is important]. . . . The concept of progress is applicable only to this realm (technical progress), to the advance in civilization; but such advance has not eliminated the tension between culture and civilization. It may even have aggravated the dichotomy to the degree to which the immense potentialities opened by technical progress appear in sharpening contrast with their limited and distorted realization. At the same time, however, this tension itself is being suppressed by the systematic, organized incorporation of culture into daily life and work—and suppressed so effectively that the question arises whether, in view of the tendencies prevalent in advanced industrial society, the distinction between culture and civilization can still be maintained. More exactly, has not the tension between means and ends, cultural values and social facts, been resolved in the absorption of the ends by the means—has not a "premature," repressive, and even violent coordination of culture with civilization occurred by virtue of which the latter is freed from some effective brakes on its destructive tendencies? With this integration of culture into society, the society tends to become totalitarian even where it preserves democratic forms and institutions.

Technological civilization tends to eliminate the transcendent goals of culture (transcendent with respect to the socially established goals), thereby eliminating or reducing those factors and elements of culture which were antagonistic and alien to the given forms of civilization. . . . the facile assimilation of work and relaxation, of frustration and fun, of art and the household, of psychology and corporate management alters the traditional function of these elements of culture: they become affirmative, that is to say, they serve to fortify the hold of the Establishment over the mind—that Establishment which has made the goods of culture available to the people—and they help to strengthen the sweep of what is over what can be and ought to be, ought to be if there is truth in the cultural values. This proposition is not condemnation: wide access to the traditional culture, and especially to its authentic oeuvres, is better than the retention of cultural privileges for a limited circle on the basis of wealth and birth. But in order to preserve the cognitive content of these oeuvres, intellectual faculties and an intellectual awareness are required which are not exactly congenial to the modes of thought and behavior required by the prevailing civilization in advanced industrial countries. . . .

The gap between scientific and nonscientific culture today may be a very promising circumstance. The neutrality of pure science has made it impure, incapable or unwilling to refuse collaboration with the theoreticians and practitioners of legalized destruction and exploitation. The aloofness of nonscientific culture may preserve the much needed refuge and reservation in which forgotten or suppressed truths and images are sustained. When society tends toward total coordination and administration (through scientific means), the alienation of nonscientific culture becomes a prerequisite of opposition and refusal. . . . HERBERT MARCUSE[51]

Culture is the state of being of a young society awakening to new life. . . . The result is an entirely new outlook on the world and, therefore, original creation in every field of human activity—religious, artistic, intellectual, political. Culture is essentially trailblazing.

Culture is a pulsating organism endowed with immense flexibility and vitality, in a state of constant, irrepressible growth. Civilization, on the other hand, is the rigid crystallization of a particular society; it is the unavoidable horizonal tread on history's stairway, the inevitable pause of a society whose creativity has been exhausted by its cultural growth and which seeks to digest, duplicate, spread and distribute mechanically the output of its parent culture. Culture lays the emphasis on the original and unique, Civilization on the common and general: they are respectively the Greek and the Roman ideals. AMAUSY DE RIENCOURT[51a]

Culture in a natural society will not be a separate and distinguishable thing—a body of learning that can be put into books and museums and mugged up in your spare time. Just because it will not exist as a separate entity, it would be better to stop using the word "culture." We shall not need it in the future and it will only confuse the present issue. Culture belongs to the past: the future will not be conscious of its culture. HERBERT READ[52]

Culture, as I see it, is consciousness in perpetual evolution as man derives it from himself and the world in which he lives, works and struggles. If this consciousness is just, if it is not systematically falsified, then despite our errors and ignorances we bequeath a valuable inheritance to those who follow. But if we subordinate our work to bellicose imperatives, our children will consume poisoned truths, they will be fascists or desperados. . . . two contradictory traits . . . together define all of culture: nationalist particularism, and the potential universality that is in the smallest thing. A work's profundity derives from the national history, the language, the traditions, the specific and frequently tragic problems that the epoch and place present to the artist through the living community in which he finds himself integrated. . . . Because of this particularity all works tend to the universal. . . . It is significant that the uniquely Russian aspect of a work, viewed anew by a Frenchman in the light of French customs and preoccupations, reveals to the reader aspects of itself and its country until then unknown and obscure. In a similar fashion the Americans "gave" us Faulkner and . . . besides understanding ourselves through him, we reveal aspects of his work that the Americans could not know. All of which renders clear the celebrated saying of Andre Gide: "The more individual one is, the more universal one becomes." . . . But the warrior's tactic, in time of Cold War, consists of separating these two aspects of a work in order to oppose them. In place of a dialectic step which transforms the particular into the general, culture on a wartime footing starts by affirming its particularity (it is Greco-Latin, European or Western); in spite of which it decides that this particu-

larity is universal, for the simple reason that there is only one culture and elsewhere there exists only barbarism. In this way universality is negated in the name of the universal. Thus bourgeois humanism can simultaneously afford itself the luxury of being racist. . . .
JEAN PAUL SARTRE[53]

A vital relation between theory and practice is one of mobile interactions, each exerting an effect on the other. It calls for skepticism, freedom of inquiry, and tolerance of doubt. It presupposes the freedom to revise theory in the light of experience, and the intuition to look for undiscovered aspects of reality because of the implications of theory. This is lost by him who takes refuge in dogma. Henceforth the criterion of truth is not experience, but the book. ALLEN WHEELIS[29]

[Art is] the legitimate and recognizable child of experience. . . . The true artist lets himself go. He is natural. He "swims easily in the stream of his own temperament." He listens to himself. He respects himself. . . . He comes into the light of every-day like a great leviathan of the deep, breaking the smooth surface of accepted things, gay, serious, sportive. His appetite for life is enormous. He enters eagerly into the life of man, all men. He becomes all men in himself.

The function of the artist is to disturb. His duty is to arouse the sleepers, to shake the complacent pillars of the world. He reminds the world of its dark ancestry, shows the world its present, and points the way to its new birth. He is at once the product and preceptor of his time. After his passage we are troubled and made unsure of our too-easily accepted realities. He makes uneasy the static, the set and the still. In a world terrified of change, he preaches revolution—the principle of life. He is an agitator, a disturber of the peace—quick, impatient, positive, restless and disquieting. He is the creative spirit working in the soul of man. DR. NORMAN BETHUNE[54]

Art is such by virtue of that characteristic which the Scholastics call quiddity, that whatness which makes an object its unique self, and which is in itself more interesting than anything

that we could say about it. HARRY LEVIN[55]

I felt I'd made something that existed apart from me, from my ego, something that had its own objective reality. It was the first piece in which the material and the style and the form and the meaning all seemed to come together as one, and it was the first time I'd lost all sense of myself in the process. RICHARD LIPPOLD[56]

Edgar Wind points out that *Plato viewed the divine madness of inspiration . . . with grave suspicion, that he saw Greek art and Greek poetry achieve their subtlest powers of persuasion at the very time when he saw the Greek state disintegrate,* and that *Plato did not foresee that the dangers of art, which he feared so greatly, might not affect a people who had become immune to them.* Now, Wind suggested *that the wide diffusion of art today, and with it the great expansion of our artistic horizon, is made possible by a light response to art, by a certain ease we have acquired in touching the surface of many different artistic experiences without getting seriously involved in any. And I assumed a connexion between this detached way of looking at art and the fact that art has become marginal in our lives, the centre being occupied by science. . . .*

We have, however, another fear which I believe was unknown to Plato—the fear that knowledge might hurt the imagination, that the exercise of artistic faculties, both in the artist and in the spectator, might be weakened by the use of reason. . . . the Romantic revolt against reason was so effective in art that the didactic art became a compromise.[57]

Genuine poets or artists are, as Plato said, a subversive and unpredictable element, and a nuisance, in any well-knit society, in which every class of person knows his place and function. . . . inspired art . . . can never be harmless, because it appeals to the lower side of our mind, to our senses, and not to our intellect. . . . it is concerned, not with knowledge, with true propositions, but with appearances and the imitation of appearance. . . . an inspired artist or poet is subversive of the social

In a recent lecture S. I. Hayakawa made important statements on creativity.[58] These may be paraphrased as follows:

Culture is not produced by people compensating for their deficiencies in the "normal" drive for sex, money, and power. Creativity is a necessary symptom of psychological health; the neurotic creator is not creative *because* he is neurotic. His creativity overcomes—often utilizes—his neurosis for the purpose of his art. Creativity appears in all fields in the form of unique and original solutions, bringing something new into birth. Creativity, beginning as hunch or intuition, requires total receptivity in the individual, rather than pure intellect. Emotion is a part of scientific endeavor. Receptivity involves openness to the fullness of experience. In the outside world no two things are identical. They are in constant change. The habit of categorizing leads us to say, "They all look alike." We must check such abstractions against experience. Without labels and classification we realize the fullness and uniqueness of everything in the world. There must be *flexibility,* permeable boundaries, *tolerance of ambiguity* and conflicting knowledge.

From within, our emotions and tensions must be accessible to awareness. Most people do not know how they feel because they are too busy feeling as they are supposed to. Unexpected feelings are suppressed by unhealthy people. Creative emotional health knows how it feels. The creative person has the ability to toy with elements and concepts. Absurd and impossible ideas may lead to hunches of permanent value. Fear of ridicule destroys creativity. We must have the freedom to make mistakes. Many discoveries begin with half-baked theories and with the encouragement of uncertainty and confusion.

Too often techniques govern problems, rather than vice versa. Creativity is characterized by intensity of encounter, heightened consciousness, the same energizing of the organism as for fighting or fleeing, but resulting not in fear or anger, but joy.

of visual art which is serious art could men be restored to the full play of their powers of perception. Popular illustration and inferior art . . . provide no shock of regained recognition of the variety and independence of objects.

The important difference between art and commercial entertainment lies somewhere here, in their relative resistance to fantasy and wish; and that is why we think of popular entertainment, commercially supplied, as leaving the spectator passive, with his mind and feelings operated upon by an external agency, while the enjoyment of serious works of art is an activity, and activity that enlarges understanding of reality. It is an activity because we have to interpret the object before us and to view it from different points of view and as admitting more than one interpretation. . . . STUART HAMPSHIRE[59]

You employ stone, wood and concrete [plants, rocks, and water], and with these materials you build houses and palaces [gardens and parks]. That is construction. Ingenuity is at work.

But suddenly you touch my heart, you do me good, I am happy and I say: "This is beautiful." That is Architecture. Art enters in.

My house is practical. I thank you, as I might thank Railway engineers, or the Telephone service. You have not touched my heart.

But suppose that walls rise toward heaven in such a way that I am moved. I perceive your intentions. Your mood has been gentle, brutal, charming or noble. The stones you have erected tell me so. You fix me to the place and my eyes regard it. They behold something which expresses a thought. A thought which reveals itself without word or sound, but solely by means of shapes which stand in a certain relationship to one another. These shapes are such that they are clearly revealed in light. The relationships between them have not necessarily any reference to what is practical or descriptive. They are a mathematical creation of your mind. They are the language of Architecture. By the use of inert materials and starting from conditions more or less utilitarian, you have established certain relationships which have aroused my emotions. This is Architecture. LE CORBUSIER[60]

and moral order because he is versatile. He can adopt many different roles, simulate and represent many different feelings and kinds of experience. . . . With his wayward inspiration he cannot easily be directed, and he is therefore . . . a loose and destroying element in a well-knit society. . . . The ability to imagine and to represent in sensuous form new roles, to enter into, and to convey, different modes of feeling and states of mind, gradually corrupts those who have this ability. . . . Art unavoidably forms men's habits and feelings and therefore affects the quality and stability of social life, and the whole culture. Therefore it must be responsibly controlled, as part of education. . . .

Schiller (1795) [in] Letters on Aes-

thetic Education [gives] the most plausible of all the many speculative accounts of the place of art in human life. . . . it does meet Plato's challenge. . . . art is . . . play, the uneconomic and free, because purposeless, exercise of all our faculties simultaneously. All our faculties here means both the intellectual and the sensuous, and the enjoyment, and the sense of the value of their free exercise, lies in the combining of that which is ordinarily separated in day-to-day thought and action . . . the strain of thinking in abstract terms . . . would become intolerable, . . . men would demand some release in the use of their powers of sensuous discrimination and enjoyment. Only by introducing them to the kind

40

Generally speaking, science means research on the basis of something existing, whereas art means the creation of something new. ELIEL SAARINEN[61]

The main difference between the problems of artist and those of scientist is the difference in the form of their materialization and grasp. Plastic art is expressed with means largely comprehensible by sensory experiences on a non-verbal level. Even if, as in old paintings, the creative impetus is screened by the logical presentation of a describable theme, it is not the landscape or still-life that results in art, but the creative act by which the subject matter is transmuted into visual form. On the other hand, a scientific discourse is stated in rational intellectual terms even if the impulse to it comes from subconscious regions of the intuition. LASZLO MOHOLY-NAGY[62]

The Poetry of Knowledge: One step more and we are at the threshold of the thought of Baudelaire in which the apparent antinomy between art and science is resolved in a few words: "The imagination is the most scientific of the faculties, because it alone understands the universal analogy." . . . There is in the poet as much rigorous knowledge as there is in the scientist himself, but he only formulates it tacitly, giving sudden shape to the lightning-like hypothesis that is born of its slow assimilation; he makes use of the object to prove his hypothesis. There is, in the scientist, as much synthetic intuition as there is in the poet: he starts from the hypothesis in order to define the object.
. . . Intuition has its certitudes which proof does not know. ELIE FAURE[63]

First, the problem is clearly outlined. Second, all possible information that has a bearing on it is assembled. To this end, the investigator both searches for all relevant discoveries that have been made by others and carries out carefully planned observations and experiments of his own.
Third, all the evidence at hand is evaluated to see if a theory cannot be formed that will show agreement between the various facts.
Fourth, this theory is tested in every way possible to discover flaws. So long as discrepancies are not found, it stands;

We cannot will insights or creativity, but we can will awareness and readiness and commitment.

Ideas produced by the creative process must be understood by the cultural community in order to be appreciated. They must be communicated in ways which do not arouse defensiveness or fear of change, which are blocks to progress. In a similar vein, Sister Mary Corita of Immaculate Heart College has said that art takes things out of context, examines them for new values, then replaces them. Art rearranges elements from (or in) the environment, then rearranges them again when people have become accustomed to the change. Discipline comes from uncertainty.

Art and Science. The entire path of historical progress, the accelerating expansion of social development as related to that of nature, is led by, and based upon, two forces we now call science and art. Science is the skeptical and questioning search for knowledge and understanding of the world around us; art the search for creative decisions on new forms and arrangements, based on visions derived from that new knowledge.

Painters today seek new ways to express their reactions to the world. These reactions result from the impact of science and technology—the camera, the microscope, the airplane—the new vision, vision in motion, the new landscape. Sculptors and architects, too, produce unprecedented forms resulting from unprecedented resources and inspiration. Music searches for new forms and a broader vocabulary, hearing not only the classical tradition but folk and jazz, Asia and Africa, the streets and factories of the Western world. Poetry and literature react to the world in strange and shocking forms, but only because it is a strange and shocking world when we remove the wraps of convention and polite usage.

The fine arts, or even the fine and applied arts, or even the fine, applied, and mass arts, are only a fragment (the leading fragment) of our world of art. Art, as the dictionary says, is skill. We say skill, not for repetition of something learned, but for exploration of something sensed, for pushing back the boundaries of human experience and understanding, even as science pushes back the boundaries of knowledge. Art includes every creative act of man—and the creator, as long as he or she continues to produce. We have creative engineering, creative politics, creative medicine, creative law, creative agriculture, creative teaching, creative labor. We have also uncreative painting, sculpture, architecture, music, poetry. Art resides, not in the kind of activity, but in the creative spirit brought to it and the creative quality of its production.

The landscape which surrounds us continually in space and in time is a product of the constant interaction of art and nature. Art is both process and result. In the final analysis, it is an objective rather than a realization. Constant examination leads to constant refinement and to continuous exclusion of specific examples from the realm of art and their consequent return to nature (the world of nonart processes, human as well as nonhuman). Every new effort of man to improve the landscape is an effort, however weak or confused, to achieve art. These efforts meet the exclusive standards of a civilization which is not yet quite sure that Picasso can join Michelangelo.

The landscape, poised with us between past and future and sharing both, is in process rather than stasis, becoming rather than being. Who has not experienced the magnificent quietude of great mountains, the continuous power of great rivers, the sparkling serenity of woods and meadows, the joyous life of mountain streams, the impenetrable mystery of deserts, without sensing a continuity of meaningful process against which the clamorous anarchy of human construction often seems mere sound and fury, signifying nothing.

There was a time, in the sweet childhood of the human race, when man lived close to nature, and was an integral part of its processes. His skin clothing, grass shack, and stone ax were scarcely distinguishable from their natural context. The world of nature and the world of man were synonymous, and to man little more than a strenuous and exhausting pursuit of livelihood. Nevertheless, he found time, energy, and inspiration to paint on the walls of caves.

Man is curious, skeptical, busy. He cannot let well enough alone. Somehow he could not remain a simple cog in the machinery of nature. Skins led to textiles, grass to timber and masonry, stone to iron. Every step was a step toward art, the search for meaningful form, the constant production of new ideas, forms, arrangements, and relationships. Every step, once taken successfully, became a part of man's natural processes, hence again a part of nature. It is only man's creative urge, his imagination, restlessness, and dissatisfaction with the *status quo,* that lifts him constantly out of, and beyond, nature. And yet, because he is himself a part and a product of nature, every such effort, momentarily beyond nature, becomes almost immediately again a part of nature, part of the *status quo,* not subject to change until the next burst of creative energy. Man has become one of the primary evolutionary forces on the natural scene, and nature will never be the same again.

Man, in relation to the unguided evolutionary processes of nature, is a revolutionary force. He upsets the normal directions of natural development, inserts objectives and demands which were never before a part of nature. In the natural wild landscape there is a normal pattern of development, leading to a climax balance in which topography and drainage may be stabilized by vegetation which has reached the volume of growth possible within the local temperature-moisture limits. Major changes occur then only through geologic shifts, earthquake, fire, flood—or man. In agricultural landscape the elements of nature are rearranged and changed by clearing, draining, irrigating, selecting, propagating, and cultivating. Urbanization imposes much more major changes by gradually increasing construction until nature is crowded out altogether.

The development of the world as we know it today might be con-

but if any appear, it is either amended or discarded. FRED W. EMERSON[64]

First Step: Observing the Facts. . . . Second Step: Formulation of Hypotheses to Explain the Observed Facts. . . . Third Step: the Deduction of Further Facts. . . . Fourth Step: Testing the Hypotheses and Eliminating the Invalid Ones. . . . LOBECK[65]
This series of steps is remarkably close to the process of observation, analysis, and synthesis through which the solution of any problem in design must proceed.

The fact that the scientific investigator works 50 percent of his time by non-rational means is, it seems, too little recognized. There is without the least doubt an instinct for research, and often the most successful investigators of nature are quite unable to give an account of their reasons for doing such and such an experiment, or for placing side by side two appaprently unrelated facts. . . . And not only by this partial replacing of reason by intuition does the work of science go on, but also to the born scientific worker—and emphatically they cannot be made—the structure of the method of research is as it were given, he cannot explain it to you, though he may be brought to agree a posteriori to a formal logical presentation of the way the method works. He is no doctrinaire. A tendency is easily noticed in him to prefer not to discuss the working of the method, out of an expressed fear, perhaps, that if he knew exactly what he was doing he might not be able to do it. . . . Out of impulses which the investigator cannot understand and does not bother to examine introspectively, new experiments are born; facts which to all appearances have no connection are set side by side, the investigator cannot tell why, and illumination results; the mazes of technique are threaded by a sure instinct so that unisolatable substances are isolated and insuperable difficulties are overcome. JOSEPH NEEDHAM[66]

What then is the purpose, the social function, of science and art? Why are reared upon this mock world and this mock man a frigid but true image of reality and a phantastic but warm reflection of man's own countenance?
Both are generated as part of the

(a)

(b)

(c)

(d)

sidered a resultant of the interaction of three basic sets of forces: (1) those representing the *status quo* in both society and nature, resisting change except at their own rate, (2) the forces of curiosity, represented today by science, but always, since man began, by the skeptical, dissatisfied, restless, searching, seeking human spirit, constantly asking questions and pursuing answers, and (3) the creative forces of man, seeking not only answers to questions but decisions based on those answers—new forms, new techniques, new relationships, new ways to communicate visions of the world, as it is and might be.

Art, as the human urge to create and improve, is always at the forefront of change. Yet no sooner does it succeed in promoting an improvement than that change is taken over by the forces of the *status quo,* made a part of what is, The Establishment, and divested of its fire and trouble-making potential. Perhaps it was ever thus, at least since Plato first began to fear art as subversive. The scientist and the artist-designer represent change; society and nature represent the *status quo* resistant to change. Yet society in relation to nature represents change.

(e)

Art and design contribute many special forms to the landscape. The House of Parliament in Copenhagen (a), Watts Towers in Los Angeles (b and c), sculpture by Jacques Overhof (d and e).

43

Societies have varied in their commitment to change, and the United States is perhaps most of all committed to it. Yet our controlled changes are primarily restricted to certain areas of technology and production, leaving their by-products to fall where they may. While we rationalize that this is a result of inability to control the machine, it is really inability to control those who control machines, or to control irresponsible nondesign decisions by them.

We, as a society, are ignorant and afraid of art as a constructive social process, stultify it as entertainment or therapy, shunt it off into odd corners of life, frustrate and block it by writing vast reams of principles, standards, codes, regulations, ordinances, etc., all designed to bypass or evade the creative processes of art and design, and thereby we frustrate and stultify our total decision-making structure. The results are plain to see all around us, in our increasingly ugly and misshapen physical and social environments.

We applaud creative intuition in science, medicine, engineering, law, business, or military strategy. But when it is applied to our environment, we are suddenly fearful and skeptical. Music, painting, and sculpture are all right in certain special places at special times. Architecture and landscape architecture are all right as long as they do not make the job cost more than it might without them, and as long as they do not upset us with wild new ideas or disturb the pattern of sound return on investments new or old. The applied arts are all right as long as they make things more useful and cheaper. Mass communication is all right as long as no egghead messages get in. It is more or less the same with our social environment. Politicians, government planners, sociologists, and anthropologists all make us a little nervous. We are skeptical of their intentions and objectives and of the possibly disruptive changes they may bring to our lives.

Writers from Caudwell to Kepes[37] have concerned themselves with the relationship between art and science. Generally they agree that far from being unrelated or incompatible, these two are the main inseparable creative prongs of man's constant effort to improve his life in this world. Art is specific, subjective, intuitive, naïve. Science is general, objective, rational, knowledgeable. But this is completely true only at their centers. As we move toward the peripheries of each field, we can find artistic approaches to science and scientific approaches to art. Bertrand Russell says that modern science knows the world by inference, while art knows it by experience.[67] Albert Einstein says that the physical world is reality and that mathematics is a system for measuring, relating, and cataloging reality.[30] Science tends to view the world as a system of typical categories, while art views it as a collection of specific variables. Both views are important to full intellectual-emotional understanding, which is the beginning of control and improvement.

Both art and science must refuse to accept, except on a trial basis, arbitrary rules, preconceptions, dogma, mechanical approaches, and rigid positions. Both must live by trial and error, use hypotheses which must

social process: they are social products, and the social product whether material or ideological can have only one goal, that of freedom. It is freedom that man seeks in his struggle with Nature. This freedom, precisely because it cannot be won except by action, is not a freedom of mere contemplation. To attain it a man does not merely relapse into himself—"let himself go." Just as the spontaneity of art is the result of laborious action, so freedom has as its price, not eternal vigilance but eternal labour. Science and art are guides to action.

(1) Science makes available for the individual a deeper, more complex insight into outer reality. It modifies the perceptual content of his consciousness so that he can move about a world he more clearly and widely understands; and this penetration of reality extends beyond his dead environment to human beings considered objectively, that is, as objects of his action, as the anvil to his hammer. Because this enlarged and complex world is only opened up by men in association—being beyond the task of one man—it is a social reality, a world common to all men. Hence its enlargement permits the development of associated men to a higher plane at the same time as it extends the freedom of the individual. [Science] is the consciousness of the necessity of outer reality.

(2) The other world of art, of organized emotion attached to experience, the world of the social ego that endures all and enjoys all and by its experience organizes all, makes available for the individual a whole new universe of inner feeling and desire. It exposes the endless potentiality of the instincts and the "heart" by revealing the various ways in which they may adapt themselves to experiences. It plays on the inner world of emotion as on a stringed instrument. It changes the emotional content of his consciousness so that he can react more subtly and deeply to the world. This penetration of inner reality, because it is achieved by men in association and has a complexity beyond the task of one man to achieve, also exposes the hearts of his fellow men and raises the whole communal feeling of society to a new plane of complexity. It makes possible new levels of conscious sympathy, understanding and affection between men, matching

the new levels of material organisation achieved by economic production. . . . Art is the consciousness of the necessity of the instincts. . . .

This development of art and science is not the merely contemplative discovery of static realities, it is part of men's active relation with Nature. The phantasy of art, by the constant changes in organisation which it produces in man's ego, makes man conscious of the necessity of his instincts and therefore free. This is not an absolute freedom but relative to the means of change— the complex, rich, social ego against which man presses his own blind ego in the embrace of art. This social ego is in turn built up not of ideal stuff but of the real concrete emotions and aspirations that a man experiences from living in a real concrete society. . . .

Art and science play contradictory and yet intermingled roles in the sphere of theory. Science in cognition gives art a projected selection from external reality which art organises and makes affectively appealing, so that the energy of the genotype is directed towards imposing its desires on that external reality. Thus, attention, moving inwards from action, through art moves outwards again to action. Attention to change of externals causes the inward movement of cognition; attention to change of internals the outward movement of action. . . .

. . . Energy is always flowing out to the environment of society, and new perception always flowing in from it; as we change ourselves, we change the world; as we change the world we learn more about it; as we learn more about it, we change ourselves; as we change ourselves, we learn more about ourselves; as we learn more about that we are, we know more clearly what we want. This is the dialectic of concrete life in which associated men struggle with Nature. The genotype and the external reality exist separately in theory, but it is an abstract separation. The greater the separation, the greater the unconsciousness of each. The complete separation gives us on the one hand the material body of a man, and on the other hand the unknown environment. Spreading from the point of interaction, the psyche, two vast spheres of light grow outward simultaneously; knowledge of external reality, science;

prove themselves, and proceed from research through analysis to synthesis. Both art and science attempt to expand the boundaries of human experience—art in the area of sensation and feeling, science in the area of perception and knowledge. Both of these are essential to understanding. We cannot live well in today's world without either. Art can seldom function without a little science—painstaking research, penetrating analysis. Science can seldom function without a little art—inspired intuition, bold speculation, skillful improvisation. Art emotionalizes the intellect. Science intellectualizes the emotions. Together they bring order to nature and freedom to man. Both find previously undiscovered aspects or possibilities in nature and in man. Nature is a world of sensation, science a world of intellection. Art builds orderly connections between these. Life is composed of work and play. Work represents discipline and wear; play, release and reconstruction. Art is work with freedom and play with discipline. It represents the escape from the dichotomy of life. Science provides the basic knowledge and understanding which make it possible for us to combine freedom with discipline. Art provides the basic emotional adjustment and direction which make it possible for us to participate in this combination. Art and science are both concerned with relations between freedom and necessity. Art is concerned with quality and appearance, science with quantity and structure. Art and science depend on each other. Science finds internal order in nature. Art brings visual order to nature. Each depends on the other.

In the context of total learning and creative effort, if the three great branches are the physical and social sciences and the humanities, and if physical science treats the world around us, social science the relations between people, and the humanities the past and present accomplishments and potentials of people, then the intimate reciprocal relations between man and nature, with their great mutual potentials for construction or destruction, fall between physical science and the humanities. Also, the intimate reciprocal relations between individual and society, with their great mutual potentials for construction or destruction, fall between social science and humanities.

Design and Art. Design is an art process. Art is an expressive or communicative activity; and because form is essential to expression and communication, art is also a form-giving activity. Art is concerned with solving problems in a manner which communicates special and enduring values, sensations, or qualities to the user or observer. These values may well outlast the utility of the specific design solution. The success of art is measured by the number and/or importance of the people who respond to its message and by the continuity of this response in time. Design is the process which may produce art, in the sense of a solution which expands the boundaries of the problem, outlives it, and creates constantly widening circles of influence.

Designers employed by nondesign decision makers (executives) assemble and present alternative solutions and their recommendations. These decisions involve determining the essential components of the problem, the relevant resources which exist for solving it, and how to combine resources and components in the best solution. The best solution will be creative, that is, will go beyond its precedents. This applies to all of the problems and all of the decisions of life. Design is the problem-solving and decision-making process (every decision concerns a problem), and art is the creative segment of the problem-solving decisions. The noncreative majority of decisions, the run-of-the-mill hackwork, indicates individual and social failure to develop the potentialities of creative decision making. The questions of how far a decision must go to be judged creative, who determines its creativity, and who agrees are connected but we need not explore them in order to validate the central idea.

In many situations decisions may be creative for some of those involved and not for others. Creative merchandising, for example, may be creative for the merchandiser and exploitative, frustrating, or exasperating for the consumer. In such cases history will determine the general validity of the decisions. At times it may be that the scale of the problem may require a scale of decision making that is too great for the existing institutional pattern of society. Then problems are not solved but merely palliated, tolerated, or endured. In the past great civilizations have disappeared, perhaps because of this inability to match the scale and demands of new problems. Today it may be that some of our pressing problems are beyond the scale of effort and organization or reorganization that we are willing or able to undertake. Air pollution, juvenile delinquency, massive suburbanization, the nuclear prohibition of war as the final stage of political decision making—all seem to leave us floundering.

Design which sets out to produce art, using a specific problem as a vehicle, may so distort design procedures and concepts as to fail to solve the problem. Its art status may or may not outlive this design failure. This is a moot question.

The individualism of the nineteenth and twentieth centuries has very likely produced more concerted efforts at personal monument building (defined as "art") by designers and architects than any previous period in history. The dream of many designers—that they and only they know the truly correct form for every problem—grows out of today's unprecedented freedom. However, this freedom tends constantly to produce new sets of rules, established by the strongest and most aggressive practitioners, and new eclecticisms. Frank Lloyd Wright's work demonstrated the results of a life of extreme individualism, in the growth from the serene clarity of the Robie house to the pretentious genius of the Guggenheim Museum.

According to the dictionary, "plan" and "design" are almost synonymous. In common usage, the two words are apt to refer to different aspects or stages of one consistent process. "Plan" tends to refer to the more generalized, objective, basic, preliminary, analytic, diagrammatic, broad-scale, overall aspects, "design" to the more specific, subjective, detailed, finalizing, synthesizing, precise, aesthetic, refining aspects. Or, more often, the words refer to operations of entirely different scale:

knowledge of ourselves, art. As these spheres expand, they change the material they dominate by interaction with each other. The conscious sphere of the genotype takes colour from the known sphere of external reality and vice versa. This change—change in heart, change in the face of the earth—is not just a consequence of the expansion of the two circles, it is the two expansions, just as the flash of light is the electromagnetic wave group. . . .

Art therefore is all active cognition, and science is all cognitive action. Art in contemplation is all active organisation of the subject of cognition, and in action all active organisation of the object of cognition. Science in contemplation is all cognitive organisation of the subject of action, and in action all cognitive organisation of the object of action. The link between science and art, the reason they can live in the same language, is this: the subject of action is the same as the subject of cognition—the genotype. The object of action is the same as the object of cognition—external reality. Since the genotype is a part of reality, although it finds itself set up against another part of it, the two interact; there is development; man's thought and man's society have a history. CHRISTOPHER CAUDWELL[68]

The key to real freedom and emancipation from local dependence is through scientific method. Authors, painters and composers have exercised their imaginations from time immemorial. . . . Creation directly from principles, and not through the imitation of appearances, is the real way to freedom for an artist. Originality is the product of knowledge, not guesswork. Scientific method in the arts provides an inconceivable number of ideas, technical ease, perfection, and, ultimately, a feeling of real freedom, satisfaction and accomplishment. . . . I have succeeded in evolving a scientific theory of the arts. . . . This theory of art is not limited to the conventional forms but embraces all the possible forms that can be evolved in space and time, and perceived through the organs of sensation. . . . JOSEPH SCHILLINGER[69]

The evidence increases that we are in the midst of a crisis in the scientific community, and of a period of bewilderment, disagreement and anxiety about the role of science and the scientific method. These deep doubts and misgivings, first felt among the scientists themselves, have now spread widely. . . .

The increasing crisis of confidence does not stem from any lack of respect or recognition for science in its classic role, as the aspect of human genius by which we gain knowledge of the natural world; quite the contrary. The flowering of scientific creativity is generally recognized as the distinctive achievement of mind and imagination of our time.

The crisis of confidence has its roots in concern that scientists and other experts and specialists have more and more been seeking to use methods applicable to the physical world in areas of the world of men that are beyond the reach of such methods: human goals and purposes, human priorities, motivations and conflicts.

DAVID E. LILIENTHAL[70]

A "third culture" was rising to bridge the widening gap between the scientific and literary communities. A "mixed bag" of social historians, economists, architects, students of government and experts in psychology and medicine . . . are devoting their energies to the main problem—"the human effects of the scientific revolution." C. P. SNOW[71]

Science is value-free, though it is based on values, among which paradoxically enough, freedom from value judgments is one of the first; and life is directed by values. Science has shaped our natural and social surroundings and goes on doing so; without disinterested science, mastery over nature and history would be impossible. And science has no means to tell us what we are to do with this mastery, nor whether it is good or bad in itself. If there were an answer, it would establish unity; but it would not be given by science. Popular opinion is wrong when it looks upon scientists as the successors of the sages of old. To consider science as the universal measuring rod for values is an unscientific ideology: when a scientist answers a question in the field of values, he is speaking not as

a man of science, but as an ordinary believer, citizen, moral subject, although his schooling may—sometimes—help him to be more consistent and clearheaded than his neighbors. . . .

Science is a human activity in a world that man understands and understood before he tried to know it scientifically, a world he has lived in before, and while, creating sciences and methods. There are questions about this world, but our wonder (the first step toward science and universally valid knowledge, according to Plato and Aristotle) begins only when, in a world that is familiarly understood and trusted, something "goes wrong." We understand the world before we question it: understanding, in an anthropocentric manner, is older than science and more profound. It is an absurd wish to reduce understanding to science. . . .

When science renounces anthropocentrism, it is bound to be at the service of the most primitive interest, the acquisition of power. Our culture has developed a split personality, rent between its thirst for objective truth and its desire for power. And curiously enough, this schism results not through any fault of technology and applied social science, but through the fact that the most disinterested and purest form of science refuses to pronounce on questions which by their very nature are not "objective" because they concern ways of life. ERIC WEIL[72]

The most influential assumption of modern science is that the best and indeed the only scientific approach to the study of natural phenomena and of living organisms is to divide them into fragments and to investigate elementary structures and properties in greater and greater detail. . . . Although everyone recognizes that the very existence of natural phenomena and of living organisms is the manifestation of the interplay between their constituent parts under the influence of environmental factors, hardly anything is known of the mechanisms through which natural systems function in an integrated manner. . . .

Whereas science was at first a method to deal with the world of matter and of life as man perceives it through his senses, much of the scientist's knowledge is now acquired through technical and

mental processes which operate outside the range of immediate human experience. . . . discussions of matter in terms of mathematical symbolism, or of life and man in terms of disintegrated components, cannot be related to any form of direct experience. Specialists must return to the original human basis of their work if they want to converse with mankind.

Just as scientific knowledge is becoming alienated from human experience, so are its technological applications becoming increasingly alienated from human needs. . . . science and the technologies derived from it now often function as forces independent of human goals. . . . knowledge creates concepts that man cannot restate in terms of his experience; and increasingly technology creates services and products that man does not really need. All too often, knowledge and technology pursue a course which is not guided by a predetermined social philosophy. . . . it results rather from a political and social process which allows science to move blindly in the social arena. . . . many modern applications of science have nothing to do with human biological needs and aim only at creating new demands, even though these be inimical to health, to happiness, or to the aspirations of mankind. . . .

The Industrial Revolution, with mass production of energy and its rapid injection into all aspects of social life, is everywhere beginning to disrupt the great dynamic processes which have so far maintained the earth in a state compatible with human life. . . . Land conservation, water resources, urban development, the physiological and mental qualities of the human race are but a few among the immense problems created by the impact of scientific technology. It is therefore a moral obligation for the scientific establishment to devote itself in earnest to the study of ecosystems, both those of nature and those created by man. But ecosystems cannot be studied by the use of the oversimplified models which constitute the stock in trade of orthodox experimental science. RENÉ DUBOS[73]

The world we think about seems to be drawing away from the world we see and feel. Our manipulative understanding seems increasingly uncoupled

47

a city is planned; a chair is designed; a house or garden may be either planned or designed. The process involved in all three scales of problem is basically the same: program-analysis-synthesis; survey-plan-design; observe, digest, create; determine exact nature of problems, solve them in such a way as to improve on previous solutions.

The problems design sets out to solve are the result of relations between people and between people and nature. Design deals with specific problems in ways which may be creative. Its success is measured by the completeness with which it analyzes and solves the problem. Complete and sound design processes must determine the relationship between necessity and choice (objectivity and subjectivity) in each specific problem. Engineering is a design process which dominates certain types of functional problems (highways, bridges, dams), but design is the parent process which includes engineering and is larger than it. It is a design decision to determine when engineering must be subordinated (the engineer as consultant to the architect) and when it must dominate. One of the problems today is that those policy makers concerned with such decisions are seldom designers and are rarely even interested in the qualitative aspects of design. Thus we have problems of great complexity including large areas of choice in form and arrangement (drainage-basin planning, community planning, landscape design) reduced to oversimplified engineering projects (flood control, land subdivision, erosion control).

The relationship between objective engineering and subjective nonengineering design might perhaps be clarified by a change of language. It is not primarily a matter of professional boundaries. If design problems fall into three main categories—functional (what is it for?), technical (how shall we do it?), and sensory or visual (how does it feel?)—then the engineering approach to design tends to concentrate on the first two, assuming that the third will take care of itself with their solution, while the nonengineering (architectural-landscape-artistic) approach will either concentrate on the third first or solve the first two in order to get at the third as most important. These might be called the technical and the sensory approaches to design, regardless of profession. The technical approach has had a vast influence on modern design, particularly on architecture, to the point that sensitivity has almost gone out with eclecticism. Today we find minds limited to technicalities among the supposedly sensitive arts, and we find sensitive minds among the engineers. It is a difference of approach and outlook, rather than professional registration. Pure engineering without subjectivity and pure art without objectivity are almost nonexistent.

In order to solve problems, design must search for form, because we must give form in order to produce a solution. It is precisely in the area of form that the difference between humdrum and creative solutions is to be discovered. The difference will be found in the breadth and depth of integration of the technical, functional, and sensory aspects of the problem and its solution, and beyond that, in the existence and

from either physical enjoyment or spiritual satisfaction. . . . Durkheim's unhappy conclusion that the more men become capable of controlling the external conditions of life, the less interested they become in living [leads to] the disappearance of a sense of interdependence with the rest of society. . . .

How shall we set about developing the common scale? Largely it seems to me that we must look to the humanities and the creative arts. High culture may not have been very good at helping us understand how the physical world works, but it has been much better than science at making us feel its importance. Both science and art are concerned with giving some sort of order and form to our universe, refining our perceptions and putting them into some sort of order. . . . science has become more and more preoccupied with discovering or inventing order purely as a means of understanding and control primarily of the external world, whereas art has retained its original preoccupation with experience and its orderly expression as a means of cultivating the individual personality. In this view, art not only sharpens our perceptions and reveals an aesthetic order among them. By so doing it makes the world and its ambiguities and conflicts not only more understandable but more tolerable. . . .

Somehow the world science knows so well and so much more fully and precisely with every passing year does not seem fully satisfying. We seem to know more and more about how to live without finding out any more about why it is worth while to live. Even more disturbing is the thought that although the applications of science have abolished or controlled an astonishingly large number of the obvious causes of sorrow and tragedy, it is not obvious that the majority of men feel life to be any less sad or tragic than ever before. . . .

Because of this ability to endow ordinary human situations with a transcendent importance, art plays a significant part in the development of the ethical sense. . . .

The primary purpose of both revealed knowledge and of artistic knowledge is to make the individual feel better about the world as it is. The emphasis is on altering or enlarging the individual's experience of the world, not

48

on changing the world itself to serve man's desires. [Why not both?]

. . . [Our problem is] the difficulty we have in bringing into coherence the knowledge of the world we infer from the scientific method and the knowledge that comes to us directly through the senses. It is a gross oversimplification of the problem to hold that the fine arts and humanities are concerned with value problems while the sciences are not. . . . ROBERT S. MORISON[74]

The significant distinction in our culture, then, is not between the arts and the sciences, but between the limited technicians and the creators of images. . . . At the root of these problems is the preoccupation of twentieth century scientia with function and process, and with the nature of observation. . . . It has brought extraordinary progress in science and scholarship, and radical changes in the arts, but it has not sought or promoted solutions to the major dilemmas of human existence and behavior, nor even provided the means of assessing the value of its own achievements. JAMES S. ACKERMAN[75]

If we can decide what scientists want laboratories for and what artists want studios for, we will probably know the difference between science and art, between truth and beauty. . . .

Science tells us what the world is and art tells us how the world feels to one who lives in it. . . .

Thus the arts, by joining fact with value, unite what the sciences (in commercial society, anyway) appear to sunder; and, within their scope, they offer an account of the human situation more nearly whole. . . .

The reason for this is that although the brain in its higher centers thinks literally (that is to say, its language points directly to things and relations among things), the rest of the brain and the body thinks associatively—by pictures, images, and clues from rhythmic sounds. . . .

Every work of art displays a tension between the figurative and the factual, and the ability to distinguish these is essential to creativity and enjoyment. . . .

Thus, though the sciences, in merely stating facts, can get along without

strength of that spark, flash, or explosion of creative inspiration which keeps design alive and tradition growing. Louis Kahn, Philadelphia architect, in discussing the relationship between design and form before the American Institute of Architects in Los Angeles in October, 1960,[76] said that form is the character or quality of a solution or arrangement, and that it is unmeasurable. Design is the means for realizing form through the organization of measurable elements.

The search for form at community scale is much more complex. Design at individual-project levels will spare no effort to achieve maximum richness, individuality, and special character. But put into one design process the equivalent of fifty, a hundred, or more individual projects and what do we get? Standardization and regularization tending toward mechanization and sterilization. Pompous overscaled formal abstractions, experiments in technical virtuosity, or tortuous and contrived romanticism. Multiple individualism in single design projects may destroy the possibility of harmonious community landscape. But mass standardization in overall community design projects may destroy individualism. How do we solve this?

There are varying attitudes toward the search for form. With some, it is a lifelong search which is never completed to their own satisfaction, regardless of the material success they may achieve. "Creation is a patient search."[77] With others, school and perhaps a few years after are the time for searching; soon the demands of career and competition seem to force settlement into a personal style or adherence to a group style; thereafter, they can concentrate on production and on bringing in jobs.

Sometimes the search for status sidetracks the search for form. The designer is so eager to be fashionable, to set new style trends, to be a taste maker, to avoid mistakes, to be more original or more safe (or ideally both at once) than his competitors that he becomes unable to concentrate on that modest and open-minded search for relevant and meaningful form which is the essence of good design. The need to appear omnipotent and infallible makes it impossible to say that one just has not yet made up one's mind or to change it once made up. The scramble for jobs forces premature design decisions without benefit of adequate analysis or search. Some problems are so empty and frivolous as to frustrate a search for form at the beginning.

Further confusion arises in the relation between the satisfaction of the designer's sense of appropriate form and the satisfaction of his ego. With some, the form that is appropriate to time, place, and people, expanding their sensory frontiers and moving them forward a bit in the development of design tradition, is felt to be the goal. With others, the landscape is considered a gymnasium for the personal ego; every job must be a monument to genius and a landmark to remind the populace that the great designer was there. When this ego is associated with inadequate or mediocre talents, the results are apt to be farcical to the observer and tragic for the designer. When great ego and great talent come to rest in the same body, the result is a force to be reckoned with. In a society which glorifies the go-getter, modesty is a handicap, the search for new forms is a diversion of energy, and anonymity is suicide. In our disinterested society the armor provided by the big ego seems necessary to carry the designer through the long road to success. Modesty and a relaxed attitude are handicaps which may result in anonymity or being pushed aside by more aggressive colleagues. Salesmanship is often more effective than talent. Psychological research shows that arguments tend to be won by those voices which are loud and persistent rather than by those which are reasonable and persuasive.

The Personalized Anonymous Landscape. Among architects, landscape architects, and city planners, we have, in theory at least, two kinds of artists, or two extremes of attitude toward which such designers tend to move. One is the personal artist, all of whose work is his own expression, varying from day to day with his feelings, his stomach, his disposition, and the specific environment he happens to find himself in. This one accepts only personal judgments on values and ethics, operates on the philosophy of relativism, sees no social standards or scales, no cumulation of historical values and experience, and starts each experience over again from the bottom, fresh as a babe in the woods. He may be a genius or a hack. The other is the impersonal artist, who approaches his problems with an attitude of scientific responsibility, conscious of their nature, the materials available, the history of each particular kind of problem, general theory in his field as a cumulation of historical experience, the general and specific nature of the world around him, his relation to it, and so on. This one searches for rational social values which are based on general agreement and takes seriously the problems of the relation of the artist to society and the people and the relation of the people to culture in the arts of sound, words, and action, the arts of graphic and plastic form, the arts of spatial organization. He, too, may be a genius or a hack.

Few if any actual artists, architects, or planners gravitate completely to either of these extremes. Some approach one or the other rather obviously; most fall between, partaking of both. It is more difficult to be impersonal in those arts involving considerable freedom of choice in form, such as painting, sculpture, and landscape design, than in those arts concerned with strong and positive programs such as architecture, engineering, and city planning.

Most direct decisions about mass graphic art are made by the commercial interests in advertising, movies, etc., most decisions about mass building by commercial builders, most decisions about mass landscaping by nurserymen and gardeners, most decisions about land use by real estate men, and most decisions basic to all these by bankers; and the professional is left with the few scattered jobs which require special treatment of one sort or another and with whatever theories or ideas he wants to develop in the nonprofit homework of easel painting, paper projects, and theoretical writing. The personalized design which tends to result from the insecurity and irrelevance felt by the professional designer will

ethics, or at least are not immediately crippled by the lack of it, the fine arts have got some ethical content all the time. Presumably this is what makes them "dangerous." . . .

Now, a rational society would (almost by definition) be one which desired that all facts be accurately known and all values accurately judged. It would therefore wish to establish throughout its whole culture that principle which the fine arts already possess: the union of fact with value, of science with ethics. Clearly, we ourselves are yet at a distance from such a society. Nevertheless, we have in the fine arts a curiously civilizing power, which tells us not only how we fare in our happy-unhappy present but also how we will fare in an altogether-happy future. People have their gains and losses, social improvement comes as history permits; but at all times it is true of the arts that they must liberate or perish.

It is liberty which the arts confer, not license, not irresponsibility. . . . It has to do with a constant assurance that we and our fellows can become masters of a common destiny and so live together that everyone finds himself fulfilled in the fulfillment of all. . . .

Every success will be one more proof that human beings really can master their environment, and consequently will be one more incitement to do so. . . .

With artists alone, a nation cannot be strong, though it might be civilized. With scientists it can be strong, whether it is civilized or not. BARROWS DUNHAM[39]

On Form as a Language: The more I hear teachers talk about the meaning of poetry (by which they always seem to mean paraphrasable content), the more I suspect them of talking that way because they never learned to talk about form. I do not mean to imply . . . that poetry has no meaning. Meaning in poetry . . . is inevitable but secondary—still assuming, that is, that by "meaning" one means "paraphrasable content."

If, however, "meaning" is taken to mean the "intention" of a poem, then let it be added that the meaning is never in the subject content but always and only in the way that content is fused into form. Form is always first.

For the poem is not a statement but a verbal artifact. It exists as a painting or a piece of sculpture or a piece of music exists. It is a wrought entity. It is not simply a sequence of words and phrases. It has thingness. *It exists as a form.* JOHN CIARDI[78]

The modern sculptor's creed as it now stands, if I understand it rightly, would therefore read as follows:

1. Sculpture is the conversion of any mass of matter without formal meaning into a mass that has been given formal meaning as the result of human will.

2. Essential sculpture is sculpture which has the same kind of meaning as the sphere, the cube and the cylinder.

3. The meaning of naturalistic or romantic imitation, as Socrates said, is merely empirical and conjectural; and what is commonly called art is merely such empirical meaning expressed by skillful tricks of hand; but the meaning of geometric art is universal and everlasting.

4. Sculptural feeling is the appreciation of masses in relation.

5. Sculptural ability is the defining of those masses by planes.

6. Sculptural energy is the mountain.

7. Sculptural imagination is the power to organise formal energy in symbols for the universal analogy of form. WILENSKI[79]

We go into this fantastically expensive wasteful type of cut-and-fill conception of suburbia, only to find that because of the terribly high cost of the cut and fill, we must resort to the small lot; and the beautiful mountains and hills have now become the potential slums of tomorrow. . . . The ratio of land cost to the total cost of the project for a single family house is higher in Los Angeles than in any place in the United States. . . . It just costs so much to do this very unimaginative kind of work.

. . . Instead of a cut-and-fill form of mass housing in what people at the outset consider suburbia only to find themselves engulfed all around . . . if we took the hundred acres that you would ordinarily develop for 250 families at great cost and great destruction

persist until we have some larger programs of actual construction which are social in content—housing, planning, recreation—and sufficiently large, rapid, and demanding of quality solutions to sweep up and swallow up the energies of artists, planners, and designers in collaborative work larger than any individual.

Art is both personal and anonymous. As the sum total of creative human contribution to the landscape it is anonymous—only rarely do we credit a special building, garden, or other work of art to an individual. The general landscape, even at its peaks of quality in England, France, Italy, or Japan, is to us today an anonymous social product. And yet individuals have left their mark on this landscape, perhaps most notably Lenôtre and Hausmann in France. Curiously, these great strokes of individual expression became the basic vocabulary for the greatest system of worldwide landscape standardization, L'École des Beaux Arts. The comfortable anonymity of England, Italy, and Japan remains to us as a greater landscape legacy. Modern design is not impervious to the tendency to standardize.

The scientist strives to know, and the artist to communicate, a vision of the world as it is and might be. Neither is overly concerned with self-expression as a conscious object. Yet there is a persistent myth, borne out by the actions of certain monument builders, that architects, landscape architects, and others as artists seek to express themselves in the landscape. How true is this?

We must consider the relation between the normal healthy ego and the social context. Every productive person deserves, and seeks, credit. Self-expression is a natural by-product of strong convictions, strong visions, strong curiosity. It does not exist for its own sake, except in the commercial promotional approach so common in our times. In the optimum society self-expression would be normal and unobtrusive. With us, especially in the early stages of a professional career, we must express or perish. Of the various paths to success today most (save the social and political) seem to require us to make a personal splash in the landscape, hastily recorded in photography and distributed as widely as PR techniques can manage. Soon, if all goes well, there is a new school, people line up to buy our kind of design, and we are a success—as long as we can continue to make our personalized mark on the landscape.

We know that the landscape is one continuity of experience wherever we go and that ideally it would be so designed. Therefore we end with a conflict between the "controlled" (regimented) landscape, in which form and style are preconceived and personal variations are not allowed, and the "free" landscape, in which every designer does as he pleases, some well, most badly, and the end product is anarchy in which even the best is lost. However, in this phrasing both control and freedom are irrelevant to the serious artist, and without him society cannot produce a meaningful landscape today. Handicraft societies tend toward unconscious charm, industrial societies toward automatic ugliness. "Freedom" of self-expression is a pathological condition, without discipline, in which the artist is lost with only himself to express. On the other hand, "control" is a rejection of creativity, a negation of the vital forces of humanity, an effort to design by rules, codes, guides, principles—and now, computers. The sensitive design process, truly oriented toward the solution of problems within a natural-social context, needs neither "control" nor "freedom." It needs fundamentally to be an integral part of the processes of social decision, preceded by scientific fact-finding. Design processes locked integrally into decision-making patterns would demonstrate that "control" is only an effort to bypass design and "freedom" is only the cry of the frustrated designer excluded from decision making. While present-day nondesigner decision makers may scoff paternally at the realization that designers want to participate, they should think befor scoffing. The urge is not based alone on frustrated ego, but on the essential nature of design, in the broadest definition, as a decision-making process, and the only potentially creative process. The American landscape, shambles that it is, is littered with the results of decisions by nondesigners, and is in fact a monument to their ineptitude and arbitrariness, greed and opportunism. This is not a plea to substitute arbitrary design decisions for arbitrary nondesign decisions. It is a plea to recognize the fundamental nature of the sound design process as incapable of arbitrariness, whereas nondesign decisions are almost certain to be arbitrary.[80,81]

Sound design decisions will produce an anonymous landscape because they are organically interlocked with development processes. Efforts to personalize elements in the landscape, whether to demonstrate social-historical importance or the genius of the designer, usually demonstrate maladjustment between the demonstrator and his society. Such personalization is not necessary to real personal or social success, although it may help momentary commercial opportunist success. However, we must beware of confusing efforts toward personalization with the impact of genuine artistic genius or the individuality of times and events. Frank Lloyd Wright did not have to try to personalize the landscape. The full tide of his powers did this for him. And yet he was a product of his times—after an early struggle consigned to oblivion during his most potent middle years by narrow-minded journalism. Very likely this experience left him subconsciously determined to leave his mark on a blind and puritanical society. He was the last great rugged individualist. Design is always a result of interaction between designer and environment.

The problem is not exactly the personalizing of the landscape, not even its conscious personalizing for commercial or ego satisfaction. The latter comes from a social atmosphere, a national, slightly pathological fascination with personality manifestations, stemming perhaps from the Hollywood star system, journalistic and political distortions of the idea of individualism, what has been called the cult of personality.

The problem really lies in the effect of personalizing on our experience

of nature and let nature be and took the same people and located them on one acre, yet dedicating the original one hundred acres to that general purpose so that when you go through the gates of this hundred acre park, this beautiful product of nature that you have everywhere in the hills of Southern California, you have one water connection and one sewer connection and one road and one cut-and-fill problem to one acre, utilizing one percent of the hundred acres.

You build that one acre and you put on top of it a glorious building to house 250 families. . . . One sewer system; one water system; one road—perhaps two, if escape is required. . . . Having done that, you can afford . . . to give the occupants of this 250-family high-rise building tennis courts, riding trails, corrals, swimming pools, the sort of thing you cannot afford to do when you put all your money in this wastefulness and desecrating end result in the cut-and-fill technique. . . . By rising with the mountain and giving opportunity to cantilever construction for beautiful balconies perfect in absolute privacy, unlimited view, . . . all the things and advantages that come with communal living in the true sense of the word and yet each person's privacy more highly respected. . . . WILLIAM ZECKENDORF[82]

We can no longer tell the difference between the unique contribution of genius and its vulgar imitations. We encourage the seasonal novelties of the hucksters and allow the slow flowering of the hermit to pass unnoticed, or worse, to be denigrated.

Because we are rightly and wrongly preoccupied with art as a measure of our new humanism in our search for freedom for individual expression in an age of developing mass-culture, we are apparently doomed to go through a period of artistic anarchy, chaos, confusion, and proliferation. Cultural continuity is today very hard to come by. SERGE CHERMAYEFF[83] and evaluation of the landscape. When we see it as a continuous physical experience, in which the various parts and sequences are evaluated in relation to each other, and in terms of their direct effect on us, that makes possible reasonable and reliable judgment. But when the personality of the designer or developer is there, whether by his decision or ours, then our experience and judgment is warped by special attitudes toward that particular segment of landscape. These include our attitude toward the designer-developer as a person, his ideas, the school or group he represents, the effectiveness of his verbal or literary interpretation of the design, etc. No doubt this is one of the reasons why we say that we cannot finally judge contemporary art, being too close to its sources and too easily involved in the personal aspects of creation. But nevertheless we are forced to pass judgments on the landscape every day in all its parts, new and old. It is constantly developing and changing, and it is the environment in which we live, breathe, and move, as fish in water. If we do not participate in the development process, at least by commenting on what is there and what is proposed, we allow the design of our environment to go to others by default. It is precisely here that the conscious personalizing of the landscape becomes a bit snide and cynical. It is like the doctrine of *caveat emptor*—let the buyer beware. This is the slogan of social barbarism and irresponsibility, which says that I will take advantage of every situation to advance myself at others' expense unless specifically prevented. A responsible and civilized attitude, on the other hand, will consciously avoid overt personalizing of other people's environments, recognizing that this, like advertising, is an inexcusable invasion of privacy.

Of course the personalized landscape has a broad range, from the crudity of the worst signs, billboards, and commercial structures to the strength, delicacy, and refinement of the greatest works of architecture and landscape architecture. In the final analysis it is probably impossible to draw the line between the personalizing that results from strong conviction and sense of form and arrangement and overt personalizing for purposes of advertising, promotion, prestige, and the satisfaction of the hungry ego. Each designer knows, within his own heart, when this line is crossed, but no one else can tell.

We may say, then, that the good landscape is both personalized and anonymous. It is personalized by the impact of creative talents released to perform and by the credit due them from a grateful society. It is anonymous because in the final analysis all citizens participate in its formation; even the greatest geniuses cannot function without social support and a cultural atmosphere which sustains them, whether by nourishment or frustration. By and large the good landscape reflects the freedom and justice embodied in the society which produces and inhabits it. This is no simple platitude. We do not find a totally good landscape anywhere in the world today, not on either side of the negative and anticreative iron and bamboo curtains.[84]

The implications of design are more final and complete than planning. A city plan rarely reaches the design stage. However, if we assume for our purposes that design includes planning, we can then set down certain factors by way of final definition:

Design is a process carried on by certain people who are therefore designers, whether conscious or unconscious, professional, commercial, or amateur. Participation in the process does not guarantee competence or skill; it merely implies the responsibility. The object of this process is the making of certain decisions regarding materials, forms, arrangements, sounds, words, textures, colors. The decisions are required in order to solve certain problems which have been presented to the designer (perhaps by himself). These may be problems of communication—writing, theater, painting, music, movies, television. They may be problems of the organization of space and the improvement of physical environment—buildings, gardens, cities. Or they may be problems of the detailed furnishing and the equipment of buildings, gardens, and cities.

All of these problems require certain basic stages in the process of their solution. The problem must be clearly analyzed and studied to be sure that all its conditions, connections, implications, and possibilities are understood completely and thoroughly. The resources available for the solution—labor, materials, finances, technology, ideas—must be thoroughly surveyed and understood. Then the synthesizing, imaginative, creative faculties which primarily distinguish the human being must be brought to bear. To be completely successful, they must be brought to bear in such a way as to produce forms and arrangements from the resources which will solve both the immediate, limited, or obvious aspects of the problem, those which may have brought it to attention in the first place, and the long-range, future, or peripheral implications which may not be at all obvious to the casual observer, even the owner or sponsor.

Design varies in scale, in relation to human size. Some fields are concerned with objects or elements which are smaller than people and may be handled and looked at, whether functional or not. Even if larger, their nature is still such that we walk around and look at them. These fields include painting, sculpture, furniture design, industrial design, graphics, textiles, mechanical engineering, etc. Other fields are concerned with organization and control of the three-dimensional space within which people live with these objects and elements—architecture, civil engineering, landscape architecture, planning. There is, of course, a direct connection—object design is essential to the completion of the interiors of spatial design.

Still other fields are concerned with direct communication to people within and among these spaces and objects—literature, poetry, music, theater, radio, television, movies, etc.

Communication and improvement of the environment may be said to be two primary functions shared by all of these design fields. Emphasis varies—literature is primarily communicative, music and painting seek either to communicate or to improve the environment or to do both, architecture is primarily concerned with improving the environment. Yet literature can help in the latter aim, and architecture has a definite story for those who can read it.

Specifics

CHAPTER 5
Design in the Landscape

To design the landscape is to determine how best to develop a given program to suit a specific site or how best to develop a given site to suit a specific program. The process involves the making of all specific decisions as to physical form and arrangement, from the most generalized preliminary diagrams of land use, space needs, and circulation to the final, most minute detailing of each fence, walk, and flowering plant. To design the landscape is to decide the exact form and arrangement of everything to be seen or experienced by a given individual or group within a given area or movement zone.

The designer of a landscape must determine, among other questions, the following: What is the landscape with which he is to work? Is it the land within the site property lines? Is it everything visible on approaching or leaving the site? during a five-minute walk? a one-hour drive? a three-day trip? How do the people with whom the designer is concerned relate to this landscape? Do they live in it? work in it? play in it? like it? dislike it? help it? harm it? What are the basic elements and materials with which he must work? How is he to select among them those which are more or less important? How does he put these various elements together to form a comprehensible unity? What principles, attitudes, or approaches should govern their arrangement, their organization, their patterns?

The landscape in which we live today is a product of a constant flow of decisions on form and arrangement since man in his constructive-destructive form first appeared upon the scene some ten thousand years ago. This flow of decisions goes on around us constantly and ceaselessly—the landscape is a continuous project. The types of decisions which have been made in the past influence those being made today, and together these influence what types will be made in the future.

Design decisions are made within a framework of control. We cannot design what we do not control. Elements of communication or of visual art—stories, plays, music, paintings, buildings—have specific beginnings, endings, boundaries, dimensions. The designer always knows where he starts and stops. But the landscape has no physical boundaries (moun-

LEFT: The design process can bring art to the public landscape.

59

tains and oceans can be crossed, and even outer space will soon be pierced). Therefore, it has always been designed in fragments or segments of a size subject to convenient and practical control. This control is established by property rights, through real estate practices. Occasionally, autocratic rulers have controlled the landscape by executive order or fiat. This has seldom been more than skin-deep—Pharaoh, Caesar, and Louis XIV controlled the specific design of segments, such as Versailles; Hausmann cut boulevards through Paris without redesigning the segments between. Their design was concerned with very limited specific segments of the population. They had no need for, or conception of, that detailed relation between all local citizens and their surroundings which is, or should be, the essence of good contemporary landscape design.

Thus we have had two kinds of landscape design through history—detailed specific conscious design of controlled segments and the accumulation of multitudes of more or less conscious design processes into the general landscape. The latter, the accumulation, seldom achieves the overall high quality that art processes can produce. Occasionally, in a city or pastoral landscape, such quality has developed through fortunate combinations of conditions. Such scenes are celebrated in our culture.

This is the basic process of landscape design in the large sense: the production of a landscape, especially in more developed urban and suburban areas, compounded of many separate parcels of real estate and of all the multiple disconnected decisions made by different people at different times on these different parcels. The problem of how to unify and coordinate these multiple decisions so as to produce a harmonious community landscape has been the province of city and regional planning. Its approach has been primarily analytic, diagrammatic, legalistic, and advisory. Increasingly large segments of urban landscape are being tackled as physical design problems by combinations of public and private enterprise under the various community redevelopment and urban renewal acts and as urban design components of comprehensive planning. Such programs as these (which may expand to suburban and rural renewal), slum clearance programs, and expanded park, recreation, school, and hospital developments have a tremendous potential. They are leading to a filling of the broad gap between normal city planning procedures and normal architectural and landscape practices.

None of us is prepared adequately to fill this gap. This requires new thinking on architectural relations, urban design, all the multiple problems of specific three-dimensional design at neighborhood and community scale. As the proper relations between overall control and democratic processes are worked out more and more carefully, the community landscape will become more and more a recognized physical design problem. Its solution will require major reorientation by all the design and planning professions.

One hundred years ago there was little public control of the development of private land. The owner was free to create a shambles or a paradise as he pleased on his own land. As it became clear that in our high-pressure industrial society the results were more often the former than the latter, organized community pressure for control developed. Over the years this has produced an expanding pattern of restrictive covenants, building codes, zoning ordinances, planning departments, public housing programs, and their culmination in urban redevelopment and renewal legislation and programming. These renewal programs represent the broadest approach to date to the problems of slum clearance and the improvement or replacement of blighted areas by a combination of public and private enterprise. All of these developments have been resisted doggedly by those segments of society who think that what an owner does with and on his land is his business and his alone, who view every complaint against a messy front yard as the advocacy of socialism. Nevertheless the controls are here. Regardless of their quality or results, the precedent for organized community control of community environment has been established.

From our present stage it would only be a short step from urban *redevelopment* to urban *development,* a short step conceptually but a long step in its potential for positive community improvement. It has been a long road from the negative restrictions, piecemeal requirements, and overgeneralized scanning of earlier steps through the sterilizing qualitative timidity of most public housing programming to the positive action we now can take once blight and deterioration set in. Now we can conceive of urban development legislation and programming which would make possible the establishment of development agencies at municipal, metropolitan, county, state, and interstate or regional levels.

Such agencies could expand the coordinated teamwork between public and private enterprise which has already been established in various redevelopment and recreation programs. They could begin a process of coordinating and integrating the activities of many governmental bodies concerned with physical development—public works, building and safety, parks and recreation, schools and colleges, hospitals and libraries, planning and engineering.[80] Urban development agencies, properly founded and organized in relation to local political and power structures, could look long and carefully at the community structures around them in terms of specific detailed design as well as long-range overall planning. They could help us to escape from our fatal tendencies toward private wealth in the midst of public squalor and toward avoiding action until catastrophe is here. They could explore private as well as public resources, viewing the community as a unit. They could point out its needs and problems and program specific solutions, regardless of which social sector they impinged upon but with the cooperation of all sectors as much as possible. They could show us the way to community landscapes of a visual magnificence equal to those celebrated in older parts of the world, landscapes in which everyone would live well in terms of environmental standards and public wealth would render the struggle for private luxury less relevant. One may hope that the new Federal Department of Housing and Urban Development will move in such a direction.[81]

Landscape design today begins with back yards and front yards and all the miscellaneous open spaces left over by building, street, and utility construction, within the preconceived patterns of standard subdivision and land planning practices. It expands from these problems into larger planned open spaces—parks, school and college grounds, other institutions, parkways and freeways, country clubs, golf courses, etc. Now landscape design is becoming synonymous with the unified design of the humanized landscape. The basic vocabulary for this includes ground forms, buildings, trees, vehicular circulation, pedestrian circulation, green open spaces, paved open spaces, and water forms. The secondary vocabulary includes all the multiple detailed furnishing, equipping, and enriching elements of the man-made world and the world of nature. Thus landscape design begins with the common or garden variety of local landscaper and ends with the merging of all the space-planning professions and all other fields of design concerned with improving our world. There are many forces converging on this field of landscape design. They might be grouped under these headings: architecture, nature, history, society.

Architecture is important to landscape design because it is the primary expression in the landscape of human creativity and control of nature. At best it represents the highest level of human imagination, the broadest connection between abstract conception and concrete reality, the greatest steps toward production of a completely humanized environment. This is the positive expression of the human mind in the physical world. The ugliness and inhumanity of most of our cities result from failure to use the best architecture has to offer.

Nature is important to landscape design because it is the world of forces and processes within which we live and work, the world of which man and all his works are an inextricable part, no matter how broad the contradiction may become between his efforts to control nature and to preserve it. Climate, vegetation, soil, topography, and water movement are all fundamental to landscape design thinking. Although very often landscape design appears to assume the role of defender of nature against the destructive attacks of man, its true constructive role is the establishment of connections, relations, and adjustments, both physical and visual, between buildings, sites, and their surrounding landscapes, that is, between people and the total landscape around them. It is, of course, often true that landscape design must endeavor to save man from his own folly in order to make such good relations possible. In the final analysis landscape design is direct physical liaison between man and nature. This may take various forms. It has been said that the English built gardens to draw nature to the house, the French to keep nature away.

History is important to landscape design because it represents the entire background and tradition from which we begin. William Appleman Williams says that history is a way of learning and a way of breaking the chains of the past.[15] All our thoughts and actions begin as reactions to thoughts and actions which have gone before. Modern architecture began as a reaction to the eclecticism which failed to recognize the new world produced by the Industrial Revolution. The history of landscape design is an integral part of the history of human culture and human society in general. History might be called a continuously growing stream of tradition and expression, shaped constantly by the actions of multitudes of people. The forms of the past cannot be used to solve the problems of the present. But they can help to inspire new solutions.

The dominating presence of historical monuments, which has been so influential on art and architecture in the Old World, has been less relevant in the New. The influence it has had has been through the memories and pictures of colonists, immigrants, and travelers rather than through physical presence. The need of people for traditional monuments connecting them with the stream of history has been evidenced by the persistent New World efforts to build up precedents—colonial, classical, mission. While the modern revolt of the past fifty years has apparently won a victory over the forces of historical eclecticism, it has not eliminated the need for contact with history. Indeed, it has begun to build its own eclecticism, and bits of history and romance are creeping back in. One must confess an expanding respect for the ancient peoples of the Mediterranean, Central Asia, and China, whose courage and imagination, with little precedent to work from, established basic cultural prototypes which still bear heavily upon us. Those who are first on any scene seem to find the greatest opportunities. Perhaps we become more conscious of history, and more intimidated by it, as we accumulate more of it behind us.

Society is important to landscape design because it presents problems for solution and opportunities for production. The humanized landscape is the expression of social forces on the world of nature. For thousands of years landscape design officially solved problems for a minority of the population—private parks, estates, villas, palaces. Central Park in New York, built in the nineteenth century, initiated a new and unprecedented phase of landscape design in which the general public became the client. The fact that these new park problems were solved largely with forms developed by the romantic movement in the eighteenth century should not obscure the importance of their impact upon the general landscape. There has been an increasing and gradually accelerating democratization of design processes ever since. The private estate is no longer the only problem the landscape architect will deign to touch. A whole new school of design has grown up in California around the problem of the small middle-class garden. A large proportion of landscape graduates go into public service. Irrespective of the detailed quality of work produced, the potential of these facts is for a broad improvement in the general quality of the landscape in which we all live. An unprecedented world situation in which general war has become impossible, in which we must choose between coexistence or no existence, impels us toward an unprecedented concentration upon the arts of peace.

Yet the physical landscape of the United States today expresses great activity but little culture. Some might call it a playground for speculators. Except for a few isolated buildings, parks, and islands of Old World urbanism, and the rural and wilderness areas which have not yet been overrun, we live in a world of gigantic gridiron subdivisions, clumsy practical buildings, and neurotic advertising. One is reminded of Joseph Conrad's phrase, "the age in which we are camped like bewildered travelers in a garish, unrestful hotel."[85]

The primary fact in the development and maintenance of American land and buildings is rampant speculation. Speculation is buying for less in the hope of selling for more. While few do it full time for livelihood, it is, like prejudice, a national disease to which all of us are vulnerable. How many of us would question the intentions of the purchaser who offered us twice what we paid for our house? The existence of a best seller entitled *How I Turned $1000 into a Million in Real Estate*[86] testifies to the durability of this dream. The mass rape of agricultural land, old estates, and large gardens by subdividers and developers throughout the country testifies to the enormous power of undirected economic forces.

Speculation has implications of gambling, with overtones of heroism. The legal gambles of American enterprise are considered great games for high stakes. However, as free competition has shrunk and monopoly has grown, speculation in land and building has been carried on more and more with other people's money and always with landscapes which the speculator will not inhabit. Government subsidies and guarantees have tended to eliminate the gamble from the outlook of all but the consumer. As the primary quadrangle of banker-realtor-builder–materials producer has consolidated in organization and grown in scale of operation, short-term speculation has been paralleled by long-term investment, with built-in guarantees of reliability and durability. Decisions on the shape of things to come are made at larger and larger scale by fewer and fewer people, and their results are built to last longer and longer. Such guaranteed security can only be based on control of the conditions which surround the investment. Otherwise it is merely long-term speculation. The controls necessary to guarantee long-term investments in American land and buildings tend to become political, the partnership of private enterprise and government as in urban renewal, and to be outside the traditional patterns of democracy and free enterprise. In that peculiarly American pattern, the parallelism of political democracy and business autocracy, hybridization begins to appear. This leads us to wonder which parent is apt to produce the dominant genes. While there are well-known examples of large-scale investment

Real estate is booming. The face of America is being lifted by . . . that new titan of America, the real estate speculator. . . . These men have been able to gain enormous wealth and power essentially because the building industry in our society has become a favored industry, depending on tax and other benefits. . . . What is taking place is a shift of emphasis from land speculation—the purchase and resale of ground—to the leasing of land for purposes of building—a tactic which the tax structure has made far more profitable. . . . Today all the devices available to the real estate millionaires— building on leased land, accelerated depreciation, capital gains, and syndicate operations—have combined to set in motion a wild spiral of construction and speculation. . . .

How about the buildings themselves? What are they like to live and work in? The answer, unfortunately, follows straight from the pattern of the real estate market I have just described: the cheaper the product, the higher the return. . . . It has become so apparent that builders are intent on covering every possible inch of New York with construction that when rare exceptions occur—such as the Lever Brothers and Seagram buildings on Park Avenue— the news hits the front pages of the newspapers. . . . even the most superficial observer cannot fail to be struck by the amount of architectural mediocrity the building boom has already created in New York. . . . The few worthy and interesting new buildings in the city have been put up by billion-dollar corporations as showplaces for their home offices. And even these are plagued by the problem of the setting in which they are placed. . . . It is difficult to judge the extent to which better building could be commercially possible for speculators in the present state of affairs. . . . As long as predatory cunning and acquisitive lust pass as social virtues, the real estate speculator and shoddy buildings will be ·with us. . . . there is no question that changes must be made before it is too late. . . . It would be foolish to be optimistic about the chances of these reforms to succeed. DANIEL FRIEDENBERG[88]

developers who are cultured and humane, most of the results of urban renewal, insurance housing, and similar large-scale projects have been quite terrifying to date. The guarantee of tenure on the land, with its potential for long-lived construction and tree planting, is itself no guarantee of a good landscape.

It is obvious that neither the politically democratic nor the economically autocratic parent of the forthcoming American hybrid can be eliminated from the scene. Our problem is how best to influence genetics to emphasize the democratic, and reduce the autocratic, elements in the offspring. It is how to plan and design for people first and profit second; how to concentrate on warm, real, living human values and minimize cold, hard, abstract dollar values; how to relate people more to nature than to property, more to cooperation than to conflict, more to culture than to corn.

The concept of a unified landscape has been made difficult for us to grasp by our national concentration on the production and exchange of commodities. Throughout our history we have been traders—Yankee traders, slave traders, horse traders, or what have you. Merchandising is our business. Shopping is one of our chief forms of recreation, and the shopping center, downtown or outlying, often seems to be the true American cultural center. All things are commodities to us. The chief quality of commodities is salability, which means alienability—they must be completely separate from each other. Objects are easily alienable, and we shine in the production of objects, gadgets, gimmicks, and what-nots.[87] Real estate operations require the subdivision of the unbroken surface of the land and the continuity of landscape which it supports into a collection of alienable commodities—lots and parcels of real property, buildings, and other facilities. Every element which goes into the makeup of the single landscape around us must be separable from it. Buildings cannot be detached from their sites without great travail and blocking of traffic, but we have produced house trailers of remarkable dimensions. This commodity consciousness affects our entire psychology about our landscape, atomizes it, puts merchandising spectacles over our eyes, makes it difficult or impossible for us to see the landscape as one unified and controllable experience of space and materials wherever we go.

While some may rationalize that this is merely the physical expression of American restlessness and mobility, we must ask whether our restlessness and mobility are cause or effect. Do we like to spend our lives in motion? Or are we perhaps looking for something? a better life in a better landscape? Today we spend our lives running from pillar to post. Wherever we go within the continental United States, we find, except for variations in nature and in what history has left, the same standardized and monotonous anarchy, the same organized irresponsibility, the same destruction of both nature and urbanism in a flood of mass-produced claptrap and junk. This is not, as some would have it, the machine running wild in Frankenstein fashion. It is only the mid-twentieth-century expression of the single-minded and wholehearted pursuit of the honest dollar.

The house trailer, once considered our prime symbol of mobility—even our houses were becoming mobile—has now grown back toward the size of a real house, and is taking on once again almost the same stability. Trailer livers travel from trailer to trailer; when trailers are moved, it must be by special truck. The mobile home is becoming more and more stabile, symbolizing the fallacy of the easy theory of mobility as a desired way of life.

Another factor which conditions the quality of the community landscape is the relationship between resident and absentee ownership and tenancy. It is a truism of property management that the resident owner takes best care of his property and that property which is rented is apt to deteriorate. Large rental properties—apartments, offices, shopping centers—can be subjected to sound management-maintenance procedures which will keep up the quality of their appearance—if they have any to begin with. But the millions of small holdings scattered through the central areas of our cities, between downtown and suburbs, are subject to little such control or interest. When neither tenant nor landlord takes any pains to maintain the physical quality or appearance of a property, it is bound to deteriorate. This is one of the components of blight.

The search for a truly humanized landscape, at all levels of scale from back yard to metropolis, is conditioned by relations between certain fundamental forces. The program, compiled by owner-client and designer-planner, is a projection of needs and desires within the scope of their joint outlooks. The budget is the owner's ultimate control over the scope of the work. The spread between budget and resources is variable, and may sometimes be narrowed (at least in the private sector, which may include public philanthropy) by artful persuasion from the designer. Program and budget are limited by the life experience, both literal and figurative, of owner and designer. Their experience, in turn, is limited by the structure, mores, prohibitions, and permissions of the social culture which surrounds them. Thus a society which views land and building as primarily vehicles for buying and selling, wheeling and dealing, and other more subtle and complex forms of speculative maneuvering is apt to view the concept of the total humanized landscape as something of a menace. And yet nothing is total in these United States—for every two who would like to turn their thousand into a million by real property manipulations, there may well be one who would prefer to turn our urban and suburban jungles into places of joy and beauty by real design organization. And it has yet to be demonstrated conclusively whether good design and reliable profits are or are not compatible. In truth, it seems that sometimes they are and sometimes they are not. Subject to research is why they are, when they are, and

John Galbraith states the problem with classic simplicity:

The final problem of the productive society is what it produces. This manifests itself in an implacable tendency to provide an opulent supply of some things and a niggardly yield of others. This disparity carries to the point where it is a cause of social discomfort and social unhealth. The line which divides our area of wealth from our area of poverty is roughly that which divides privately produced and marketed goods and services from publicly rendered services. Our wealth in the first is not only in startling contrast with the meagerness of the latter, but our wealth in privately produced goods is, to a marked degree, the cause of crisis in the supply of public services. For we have failed to see the importance, indeed the urgent need, of maintaining a balance between the two.[8]

William Appleman Williams speaks of . . . *the paradox of plenty without purpose.*[15]

why they are not, when they are not. Not subject to research is the matter of which gives way when there is a conflict of interest.

Our schizophrenic approach to private and public development is reflected in professional design work as a free license for richness and fantasy in private work and a limitation to mechanical functionalism or pompous and sterile formality in public work. Parallel to these reflections are the contrasting concepts of people as the most important elements in the landscape and as a necessary evil in it. Parallel also is the popular notion of the relatively superior competence of those in private enterprise as contrasted with those on the public payrolls.

The architects Eleanor and Morton Karp return man to nature in the ecological city.

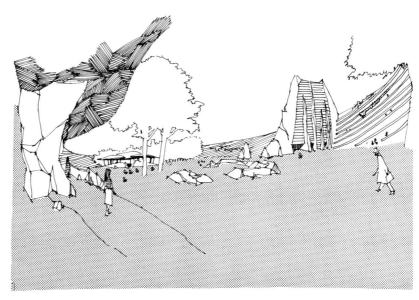

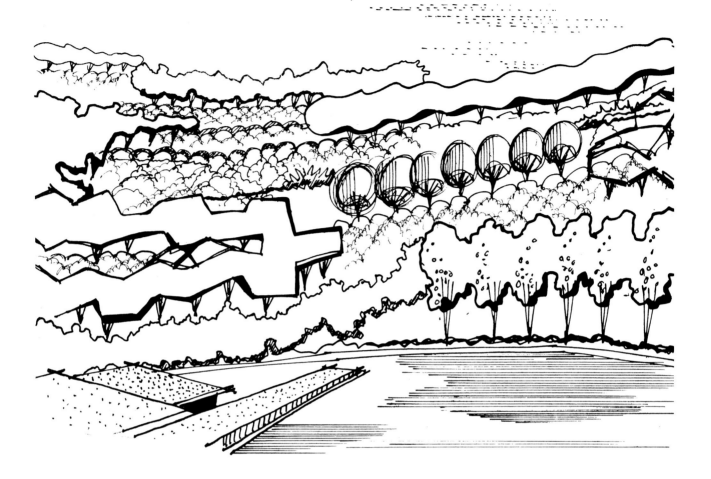

Design professions exist to solve the technical, functional and aesthetic problems in the landscape.

CHAPTER 6
Design Professions

Landscape design as a process occurs whenever the landscape is changed, "developed," or "improved." One of man's functions is to change the landscape for his own greater convenience and comfort. The function of the design process is to guarantee that this change brings real improvement. All design tends to produce fragments of landscape at different levels in scale—furniture, cars, billboards, gardens, parks, buildings singly and in groups. All designers affect the landscape somewhere sometime and therefore have responsibility to it.

Landscape design begins as handicraft and grows through amateur, commercial, and professional stages as technology, wealth, culture, and civilization grow. The principal design professions affecting the landscape are planning, engineering, architecture, landscape architecture, interior design, then the other visual arts. Sometimes the gaudy multiform production of the auto industry or the tasty folkways of the billboard enterprises disturb this order of importance.

Professional design today is primary as a source of theories and ideas. Historically handicraft and folk art were basic, with professional design as an end product. The Industrial Revolution, in separating the worker from the results of his labor, separated him from his normal standards of taste and judgment. We have been left with no general social standards for design, and the leaders of our culture have done little to fill the gap. The burden of maintaining standards has thus fallen on professional designers. The span of ideas, from nonobjectivity to social realism in painting, from technological concentration to personal expression in architecture, expresses the impact of this responsibility upon them. Designers have been unable alone to produce such standards.

Professional design processes, which today are the prototypes for all design processes, proceed through preliminary studies of variable length to final designs which are acceptable to both client and designer. These may be developed into presentation drawings and models in order to confirm their acceptability. Sometimes the pressures of competitive promotion reverse this process: presentation precedes and conditions design. Thereafter the designs are converted into precise working drawings and specifications, the language by which the designer conveys his exact intentions to those who will be responsible for the physical production of the designs. Almost always, direct supervision of the production process by the designer is necessary in order to guarantee the proper interpretation of the drawings and proper adjustments to unforeseeable contingencies.

A plan is a horizontal section (slice) through a three-dimensional development which exists mostly in the imagination of the designer. It is common practice, particularly in landscape plans, to show more than one horizontal section in the same plan; thus the paving pattern and the tops of trees may both be shown. This, plus the fact that there are usually apt to be more changes in surface outside buildings than inside, tends to make landscape plans appear more complicated than they actually are. A line of the same weight on the plan may indicate merely a change in paving, as from brick to concrete or blacktop, a change from paving to grass or ground cover (still on the ground plane), or the vertical face of a structural division which may be anything from a curb 6 inches high to a wall 10 feet high. Where planting, whether regular or irregular, is indicated on the plan, the great reduction in scale from actual size, plus the convenience requirements of an easily readable plan, produces a simplification or abstraction in which the plants tend to be drawn as circles or groups of circles. It is obvious that these plants do not have continuous circular outlines in actuality, and many draftsmen spend much time developing more complicated delineations of planting. If these are diagrammatic complications, that is, if they indicate actual differences in the quality or importance of the plants, they may make the plan more readable. Otherwise they merely confuse it. It is possible and desirable to render plans, that is, to weight the delineation, so as to suggest on plan the actual strength of the various elements in the actual space form. This is an entirely different thing from the Beaux Arts rendering, whose purpose is to become a beautiful pattern or work of art in its own right, often covering up a paucity of plan ideas in the process. But such diagrammatic delineation would also have to be differentiated from working plans, whose purpose is to convey the desired results to the workmen on the job in the most complete and understandable manner.

To be sure there are plans and plans. There is the precise and lovely paper geometry of the formal school, and there are the romantic soft-pencil squiggles of the informal school. But these are not plans: they are projects in paper design or rendering. The lines and shades on paper have no balanced reference to actual elements in space on the ground of the site. By plans we mean horizontal-section drawings in which every mark on the paper has a specific reference to a specific element or arrangement on the job, and in which, if there is any weighting of lines or shades, it is a diagrammatic presentation of the actual weight or proportionate effect of those elements in the overall space relations projected on the site. Purported plan drawings in which the poverty of

Without plan there can be neither grandeur of aim and expression, nor rhythm, nor mass, nor coherence. Without plan we have the sensation, so insupportable to man, of shapelessness, of poverty, of disorder, of wilfulness. . . .

A plan is to some extent a summary like an analytical contents table. . . . it contains an enormous quantity of ideas and the impulse of an intention.

The plan carries within itself the very essence of sensation. . . .

But the sense of the plan has been lost for the last hundred years. The great problems of tomorrow, dictated by collective necessities, based upon statistics and realized by mathematical calculation, once more revive the problem of the plan. When once the indispensable breadth of vision, which must be brought to town planning, has been realized, we shall enter upon a period that no epoch has yet known. . . .

LE CORBUSIER[60]

ideas and of understanding of the problem is covered up by a display of dexterity with compass and T square or Eagle drafting pencil are irrelevant to our discussion.

Planning. Planning has grown from zoning ordinances through subdivision codes to master planning, and from a no-man's-land sporadically invaded by engineers, landscape architects, and architects to a recognized specialized professional field with its own schools, organizations, and employment opportunities. Following on the heels of successful campaigns to pass registration laws for landscape architects in California and other states (placing them on a legal level with architects and engineers), efforts are being made to pass similar laws for planners.

Beginning with action to eliminate or isolate land uses found unhealthy or dangerous by the neighbors, planning has grown to a comprehensive and complex process for the control of community development. Functioning within the political framework of city, county, and state, it uses the basic tools of zoning, subdivision control, and master planning. The master plan developed as a rationalization for the expansion of the other two procedures. It has now come to dominate them, at least in theory, and to use them as means for implementing its projection of community pattern. The master plan proceeds through inventories of physical structure, land use, and social and economic factors to an understanding of the beginnings, growth, prosperity, natural character, and changing nature of the community.[89]

It is clear that planning is an established process through which it is possible for citizens to control the physical development of their communities if they can agree on the objectives of that development. Plans, ordinances, and codes are general, diagrammatic, legalistic controls rather than specific designs. They establish areas of use and lines of circulation which frame and control future design processes within variable limits. Skyscrapers on Manhattan Island have been shaped quite specifically by setback controls; hopeful overzoning for commerce helps to produce the shoddy anarchy which lines so many miles of our main streets and highways. But in general the visitor from Mars will not be able to tell from a perusal of city planning documents what the city may look like; he will have to go out and see for himself. Houston and Los Angeles are similar in character, although the latter has zoning and the former, until quite recently, did not. We might perhaps say that planning makes it possible to improve the physical quality of the community but does not guarantee it. It is an essential and inescapable first step. The proposal for a community design plan and program put forward by the Joint Committee on Design Control of the New York Chapter of the American Institute of Architects (AIA) and the New York Regional Chapter of the American Institute of Planners (AIP) is a wholly commendable effort to expand the area and impact of planning procedures.[90]

Engineering. Within the framework established by planning, the precise subdivision of the land for use and circulation and the design and

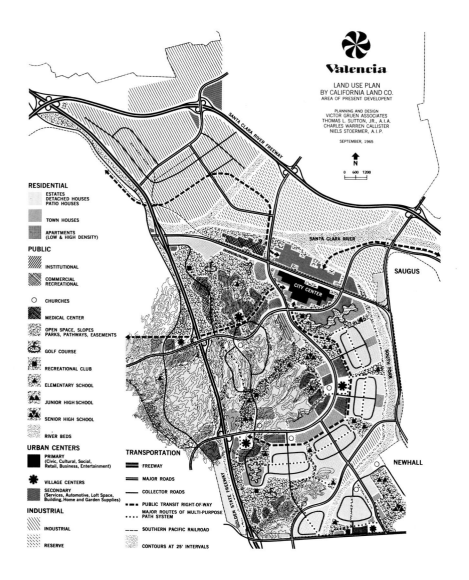

Valencia

LAND USE PLAN
BY CALIFORNIA LAND CO.
AREA OF PRESENT DEVELOPENT

PLANNING AND DESIGN
VICTOR GRUEN ASSOCIATES
THOMAS L. SUTTON, JR., A.I.A.
CHARLES WARREN CALLISTER
NIELS STOERMER, A.I.P.

SEPTEMBER, 1965

N

0   600   1200

RESIDENTIAL

ESTATES
DETACHED HOUSES
PATIO HOUSES

TOWN HOUSES

APARTMENTS
(LOW & HIGH DENSITY)

PUBLIC

INSTITUTIONAL

COMMERCIAL
RECREATIONAL

CHURCHES

MEDICAL CENTER

OPEN SPACE, SLOPES
PARKS, PATHWAYS, EASEMENTS

GOLF COURSE

RECREATIONAL CLUB

ELEMENTARY SCHOOL

JUNIOR HIGH SCHOOL

SENIOR HIGH SCHOOL

RIVER BEDS

URBAN CENTERS

PRIMARY
(Civic, Cultural, Social,
Retail, Business, Entertainment)

VILLAGE CENTERS

SECONDARY
(Services, Automotive, Loft Space,
Building, Home and Garden Supplies)

INDUSTRIAL

INDUSTRIAL

RESERVE

TRANSPORTATION

FREEWAY

MAJOR ROADS

COLLECTOR ROADS

PUBLIC TRANSIT RIGHT-OF-WAY

MAJOR ROUTES OF MULTI-PURPOSE
PATH SYSTEM

SOUTHERN PACIFIC RAILROAD

CONTOURS AT 25' INTERVALS

construction of streets and utility systems are generally considered practical problems subject to engineering control. Professional planners may design subdivisions, but even when architectural or landscape design considerations are recognized, engineering principles tend to remain dominant. Civil, structural, mechanical, and electrical engineers have probably had more direct effect upon the quality of our physical environment than all of the other design professions together. Engineers design solutions for problems technically complicated in nature—structural and mechanical problems, utilities, earthwork, bridges, dams, highways. This is a kind of design which bulks large in a technologically advanced, highly industrialized culture such as ours. It is a kind of design which produces magnificent forms and daring solutions when the objective functional portion of the problem bulks large and can be readily defined, analyzed, and programmed and when the scientific and mathematical analysis of structural relations and the properties of materials can be relied on to determine the forms and arrangements in which they are used.

Of the five general branches of engineering—civil, mechanical, electrical, chemical, and mining—it is primarily civil engineering which comes within our definition of space organization. Including as it does transportation engineering (railways, highways, waterways), structural engineering, hydraulic and irrigation engineering, surveying, and the engineering of urban problems such as sanitation, heating, and ventilating, civil engineering obviously bulks large in the process of determining the form of our spatial environment.[91] Civil engineers undoubtedly do more actual land planning of streets and subdivisions than any of their space-organizing colleagues. Electrical engineers, too, in the course of designing large-scale light, heat, power, and communication systems, have a major effect on the landscape in which we live. The magnificent treillage of high-voltage transmission lines and stations, long viewed with alarm by nature lovers, is in truth a major expression of the creativity of man. When we come down to the scale of the power and telephone lines in the ordinary residential community, however, the lyric quality seems to disappear and the problem of their effect on the landscape becomes acute. Mechanical engineers often seem to find it necessary to contribute substantial bits of industrial sculpture in unexpected portions of the landscape.

CHAPTER 7
Architecture

Architecture is many things to many people. Potentially and often actually, it is the highest art of building—a component of total building, contributing an indestructible unity of function, structure, and space. It is a product of the construction industry. Its function is to give leadership to that industry in solving the shelter problems of society. Architecture has always been man's most creative and inspiring contribution to the humanized landscape. The primary new conception which it produces on each site is basically an abstraction, something new in the world, an improvement on what has gone before. The solution of direct problems of shelter from the elements has led to the production of great lyric statements in space and structure. Architecture has a great tradition of bringing magnificent order out of manifold complexities, of putting great quantities of highly variable members and elements together in such a way as to give the result a new and special identity, greater than the mere accumulation of parts. It provides liasion between technology and human needs, guiding the former to serve the latter.

Every new building makes a qualitative change in the landscape into

LEFT: Architecture spans almost a century at the Neighborhood Church in Pasadena, California.

RIGHT: Designers propose a terraced base for the church.

which it is introduced. This change is small if the building is a repetition of what is already there, large if it is different. The change may be for better or for worse, depending upon one's point of view, but it cannot be avoided. From this fact stem many of the battles between conservatives, to whom change is anathema, and freethinkers, who feel that change is demanded by the times. Architecture is a radical force in the landscape; landscape design is a conservative force building harmonious coexistence between the new and the old.

Architects design buildings—structural enclosures of space, with social and aesthetic content. Historically, particularly in the great formal periods—Hindu, Moslem, Renaissance, Baroque—architecture has produced complete concepts of overall site form and organization, including considerable architectural definition of garden and park space. The informal, or naturalistic, reaction to this formality, as it became excessive, produced the landscape gardening movements of China, Japan, eighteenth-century England, and the American park designers—movements existing by contrast with architecture, in defense of nature and the beauty of natural elements, plants, rocks, water, the good earth. The modern architectural revolt, cutting its way out of the jungle of eclecticism, was so concerned with the reanalysis of structural form and space organization, the production of its own concept of a twentieth-century architecture, as to have little energy left over for the extension of its aesthetic into outdoor garden space. Yet such an extension was implicit in, and essential to, the whole modern concept of open plan, free wall planes, and glass walls facing the outdoors. It was projected on paper and occasionally realized on the site by leaders of the revolt—Wright, van der Rohe, Le Corbusier. However, their primary concentration on structural design and on the complications of actual realization of the building on the ground, plus a certain tendency to consider planting as a decorative setting for the architectural *objet d'art,* prevented full realization of this potential. This remains partially true today, with the modern revolt won and the forces of historical eclecticism routed, in spite of much collaboration between architects and landscape architects and much good work by the latter. Consider how many buildings published in the architectural press show landscape environs of any importance or interest.

The difficulty may perhaps be traced to some natural and unconscious arrogance on the part of both architects and landscape architects, in which one's own sphere of activity tends to assume primary importance. Architecture moves toward greater refinement and daring in structural design, "the new sensualism," a new eclecticism, and expansion into urban design concepts which remain primarily structural. Landscape architecture endeavors to reconcile the traditional and obviously necessary defense of nature as complementary to structure, with the urge to complete the projection of spatial patterns begun but rarely completed by architecture. The building wall, solid or transparent, remains a

See Lewis Mumford's critique of the new Paris UNESCO complex in *The New Yorker.*
It has the effect of turning the site into an esthetic void . . . unrelated . . . structures and scattered objects of art . . . disposed at random.[92]

boundary between differing concepts and processes instead of becoming a design element in the center of a unified site space. The difficulty may perhaps be traced even more to the economic climate of ordinary daily work for both professions, in which the scramble to get jobs out and keep up with the telephone leaves little time or energy for projecting new relationships. This leads us to place our primary hopes for the development of integrated design thinking in the professional schools.

The context and background for the design of earth, rock, and water forms is geology. The context and background for the design of planting is plant ecology. The context and background for the design of structural elements in the landscape is architecture, in its narrower building sense. *But* the context and background for the design of space for people to use, out of doors as indoors, is architecture in its broadest sense, as the functional-aesthetic organization of space for living, at the scale of neighborhood, city, and region. This is true because architecture, whatever its failings or inadequacies, is central to the problem of improving our habitat, central in theory and central in practice, and from its projections of spatial and urban aesthetics come the primary impulse and inspiration for the brave new world. However, this truth will only materialize if architecture collaborates or merges with landscape design or assimilates from it certain contrasting elements of scale, flexible form and arrangement, relation to nature, use of plants, and so on.

Architecture and the landscape live in a state of constant reciprocity. The landscape provides site and setting, material resources, inspiration, discipline, and responsibility. Architecture provides searching imagination, the impact of the human search for a better life, and positive spatial concepts with unavoidable effects upon the form and character of the surrounding landscape. The natural landscape is the great reservoir of strength and inspiration to which people and their architecture return when human insight and imagination seem to fail. But the structural and spatial intuitions of architecture set in motion forces which change the face of nature. There is a clear path traceable from Greek temple and Roman Forum to Renaissance gardens, baroque parks, and their reaction in eighteenth-century English romanticism and nineteenth-century American naturalism. A somewhat more complex path can be traced through centuries of cultural history in China and Japan, culminating in the classical Japanese house and garden. In general, the function of architecture at its best has been to bring order and reason into the landscape, and those who have resisted such order and reason have tended to be antiarchitecture. At its worst, succumbing to the "practical" pressures of economics and technology, architecture tends to clutter the landscape with shelters and their conveniences. When the pursuit of order overwhelms reason and results in the sterile regimentation of formal classicism or just plain overbuilding, the resurrection of reason then requires a strong dose of romanticism as an antidote to the excessive pursuit of order.

77

Most landscape problems—except parks—are intimately involved with buildings, that is, with architecture. The relations between these two design processes are constant and unavoidable. But as practiced, landscape architecture and architecture differ in certain very important aspects:

1. Material: Architecture uses the complex variety of construction materials. Landscape architecture uses some of these, but primarily the materials of the natural landscape—rock, earth, water, plants. These are also complex in their variations.

2. Discipline by technique and function is usually less in landscape architecture than in architecture. The parts of a garden do not hold each other up, and a garden may have no other function than to provide a pleasant experience for those who are looking into it or passing through it.

3. Scale: The scale of architecture is a compound of human scale and structural economy, often reflecting the site scale. The scale of landscape architecture is a compound of human scale and site scale, often reflecting the scale of the surrounding landscape.

4. Continuity: Architecture tends to produce buildings which are complete and self-sufficient works of art, however carefully they may be related to the site. Landscape architecture must almost always establish relations or connections between building, site, and surrounding landscape. Therefore it tends to establish continuity between them, must relate itself to their forms, and hence can rarely be self-sufficient. Of course, when architecture involves groups of buildings or adds to existing groups, it also becomes concerned with continuity. But this is usually a continuity of prime building concept rather than of open-space design. The difference is in whether one views the development as an expanded architectural work of art on a neutral base, as a street-plaza-park work of art with a neutral background, or as a balance of both.

Material, discipline, scale, and continuity are today measures of difference between two space-organizing processes. Tomorrow they can become unifying elements within one. The well-known concept of pure architectural urbanism (Piazza San Marco has no trees; why do we need them?) may be an escape for architects from the problem of relations to nature, as the concept of parks as pure natural breathing pores is an escape for landscape architects from the problem of relations to architecture. Balanced relations between buildings, trees, open spaces, and circulation elements are perhaps the highest objective of the truly humanized urban environment. Of these, trees are most often neglected or sloughed off. Trees and low-rise buildings are about the same scale designwise, and they work together in the organization of space. But if you judge by most architectural design drawings, trees are not taken as seriously as buildings. If you say that trees and buildings are equal partners in design, this is not recognized in fact, because the buildings are very carefully worked out in detail and trees are shown as though they are all alike. There is a great variation in trees. They run from 15 feet high to 70, 80, or more—that is seven or eight stories—and they have great differences in form, structure, texture, color, and seasonal effects. An urban design cannot be complete until the trees are organized as carefully as the buildings. And when you come to a one-story scale, a suburban scale, the trees are really superior, and can create the suburban landscape. Indeed, they are about the only means for giving scale and variety to the suburban landscape.[93]

Architecture is the *pièce de résistance* of the humanized landscape. The people, who must humanize the landscape in order to live in it, who cannot live in it without humanizing it, give architecture its *raison d'être*. This eternal triangle—landscape-people-architecture—sums up the cultural landscape. It is of special concern to geographers, planners, architects, landscape architects, engineers, politicians, aviators, military men, realtors, promoters, developers, investors, bankers, landowners, and farmers; it is of general concern to all the people who inhabit it.

Architecture may be of the landscape by people. More often it is on the landscape, by people. This is because it tends to be of people more than of the landscape. People came from the landscape; architecture comes from people. One great problem for designers and planners is how to take architecture back to the landscape, how to save the landscape from architecture, how to save architecture by reconnecting it with the landscape, how to save the people by helping them to develop a world for living, in which architecture and the landscape are in harmony, proportion, balance, organic integration—*simpatico*.

Architecture in the landscape represents the injection of a new force into an existing structure. It produces technical, functional, and visual problems whose solution requires adjustments in the surrounding structure. These solutions must recognize:

Difference in scale between new force and existing structure.

Proportions of nature and man in existing structure.

Proportions of improvisation, design, and art in new force and in existing structure.

Relations between precedents and new ideas.

Chronological pattern of existing structure.

Relations between perception and understanding in the people who will be involved.

Mass and void, solid and opening relations between new force and existing structure.

Form, space, and material relations.

Relations between people in new and old structures.

Historical relations which have produced them.

Relations between space scale and connection needs.

Detailed intimate relations at human scale.

Relations between architecture and building, or between conscious and unconscious design.

Relations within architecture: Degrees of consciousness, of timidity or boldness, of recognition of landscape, of design skill; schools of design represented; objective forms produced by subjective theories.

Landscape needs of new force.

Architectural needs of existing structure as seen by architect, landscape architect, owner, general public.

Architecture is the central, most important and dominant art in most humanized landscapes, with the general exception of pastoral, or rural, and park areas. Wherever man builds to stay, the geometry of construction appears in nature. However, architecture is not the only art of the humanized landscape, nor is it complete. The establishment of harmonious relationships between the new building, the disturbed site, and the surrounding landscape breeds a host of delicate problems. Those in the technical and functional areas are generally objective and relatively easy to solve agreeably. Those in the visual and economic area become entangled in subjectivity and are correspondingly more difficult to solve. While the landscape budget in normal construction programs may run from 2 to 20 percent of the total, who can say what percentage of visual importance that landscape development will play in the total picture five years later?

Each new building sets up contradictions with the existing landscape, especially when it ignores it or when it embodies technical, functional, or aesthetic concepts which are new in the world. Where space permits, these contradictions may be resolved within the site boundaries by a landscape design process which endeavors to establish convincing relations between building, site, and surroundings; to establish connection, contact, continuity; and in the process to tie up any loose technical, functional, or aesthetic ends which may have been left trailing. Buildings are rarely complete and self-sufficient in themselves. Technical, functional, and aesthetic forces and needs protrude from them in all directions, with unavoidable impacts upon the site. Construction in itself is a messy operation which of necessity takes up and destroys more of the site than the building area. Only full prefabrication or exhaustive care can eliminate this mess and the resultant cleanup and repair problems. The general contractor's tendency to clear the site of such obstacles as trees and rocks is a result of this need for space in which to work. No matter how completely owner and architect may agree on the idea of intimate relations between building and site, especially if the latter has natural charm and beauty, a whole series of landscape problems produced by the construction process require solution.

Landscape forms developing and refining the meeting of forces extruding from the building and from the elements of the site and surroundings may solve technical, functional, and/or visual problems. Technical problems inherent in climate, site, and construction processes can be measured and defined accurately. Functional problems may vary from a minimum of direct access to the building to a maximum of full outdoor living in mild climates. Although these functional problems may be expanded with more resources and desires (which tend to go hand in hand), there are limits beyond which people cannot use space directly. But visual problems exist wherever the human eye can reach, along all circulation routes into, out of, or through the property, in and out all doors and windows, in all weather and all seasons.

Architecture in the Landscape. On the single site, buildings usually dominate the landscape, as well as their own interior design. But general broad landscape design must dominate buildings, which become a kind of interior design for landscape space.

There are, in general, three basic types of landscape in which new buildings may be developed: primeval, rural, and urban. The primeval, or wild, landscape is that in which the forms and processes of nonhuman nature remain undisturbed in dominant quantities. The rural, or pastoral, landscape is one which has been so changed and developed by agricultural processes as to lose most of its original wild character and take on new qualities which are a compound of natural plant and animal growth processes and human organization. The urban landscape is, for our purposes, any section in which human construction has concentrated sufficiently to dominate the landscape and crowd out nature and agriculture. It is the architect's field of great opportunity; the city has been the center of creativity, culture, and civilization throughout history. Quantitatively, the urban landscape is primary in producing new architecture—but qualitatively its clamor and congestion fill us with nostalgia for primeval and rural surroundings. In them we feel able to get at the roots of desirable relationships between buildings and the world around.

At the scale of landscape experience architecture is a primary space former. This is especially true at larger scale when it becomes a collection of objects arranged within the landscape and usually its principal elements. When the concentration of urbanism produces wall-to-wall construction and the running together of masses of buildings, larger and less orderly objects result. They are less orderly because they are composed of a number of elements originating separately in time and society, stuck together without previous thought about their relationships, by main force and awkwardness. Almost every block on Manhattan is such a structural object, visible as a continuous, however undigested and discordant, entity from the streets and miscellaneous open spaces around it. With rare exceptions the individual work of architecture is lost in this jumble.

Outdoor experience stems from a continuous pattern of solids and voids, varied not only by arrangement and proportion but also by the variable density or spatial quality of the solids. These variable solids, mostly buildings at the urban centers, become mostly trees and topography as we pass out through suburbia to more open country. Buildings and trees, solids at general landscape scale, become smaller-scale patterns of solid and void themselves as we approach them, passing from macrocosm to microcosm.

Architecture is discussed in two ways, and these are often confused. It is a body of existing buildings, scattered about the national and world landscape, whose origins extend from last year back into past history, and whose inclusion in, or exclusion from, the list is debatable, more so as the origins become more recent. On the other hand, architecture, like all design, is a process, the process of searching for the right form or combination of forms to solve a specific given problem of shelter development. As a process, it tends to cease or to shift focus to other problems when the current problem has been solved, i.e., when construction is complete. The building then becomes part of experience, personal or historical, to be returned to for information or inspiration from time to time by various architects, other designers, students, or general cultivated public in quantity determined by the influential force of the building. Thus there are constant reciprocal relations between architecture as design process, the search for form, and architecture as a collection of buildings which have resulted from past foci of this search.

The experience of landscape architecture, whose work is never done because plants are obviously living, growing, and changing, suggests that design does not really end with completion of construction. Maintenance is a continuation of the design process, by others who may think they are also designers, as in the obvious example of some gardeners, amateur or professional. Many things may happen to buildings, too, after the architect leaves—interior decoration, exterior decoration (landscaping), graphic design (signs), repainting and other maintenance adjustments (moving parts must be adjusted, repaired, or replaced), remodeling resulting from changes in program or from faulty program analysis during the original design.

Structural design includes architecture as its most vital and leading component. The constant interaction between structural design and the surrounding general landscape is the principal process conditioning the quality of that landscape as environment for people. (Structural design also includes engineering—structural, civil, mechanical, electrical.) This is true in the center of Manhattan, an almost totally structural landscape changing more rapidly and constantly than any natural scene. It is also true as we move out from such centers through rings and patches of gradually lessening structural concentration, through suburbia and exurbia to that ultimate architectural dream, the isolated gem in the pastoral or primeval setting. Always the structures, the buildings and roadways and utilities, which are primary necessities to shelter the most fundamental activities of personal and social life, are visually the strongest and most inspiring (or depressing) expressions of man's genius for bringing new forms and arrangements out of the storehouse of nature. Landscape quality results from structure and the relations it creates or eliminates with open space and natural elements—earth, rock, water, plants—in any given locality. Architecture does not produce a series of isolated *objets d'art* which exist in a vacuum, with or without decoration. It produces the most highly refined nuclei in a network of interdependent technical-functional-visual relations which is continuous throughout the total environment.

As structures decrease, open space and/or natural landscape increases, and it is possible for us to get away from buildings more and more. This is the dream of all park lovers, suburbanites, exurbanites, and country-life and wilderness lovers. Buildings have become associated with the ugliness and the evils of urbanism; therefore the fewer buildings, the better life we have. The whole American park movement, beginning with Central Park, has been founded on the notion that urbanism and construction are inherently and automatically ugly and unhealthy, saved only by the introduction of natural green breathing pores. This unsophisticated idea still lingers in many minds, including those of some architects. Opposed to these, of course, are those lovers of architectural urbanism who say, again, "The Piazza San Marco has no trees; why do we need them?" These voices never mention the pleasant green garden between the Procuratie Nuove and the canal. Surely this is an integral part of the piazza complex.

Architecture is the prime mover, the central force, in refined conscious design of the humanized (urbanized) environment. Always and everywhere the geometric necessities of shelter construction are obvious in the landscape. Above the most primitive level human life centers increasingly in buildings, and a great deal of that life experience involves going into, out of, and between buildings and other structures. This began with the first straw, mud, or ice huts, when productive life was mostly outdoors, and continues today, when productive life is mostly indoors. This will remain true until we reach the science-fiction ultimate of the enclosed and air-conditioned city. Current shopping-center mall developments suggest that even that ultimate will only change the technology of landscape work. All planting will then be indoor planting.

Today ultimate downtown urbanism produces a concentrated structural landscape from which the elements of nature have been eliminated, except in the occasional small park. Here the buildings represent the solids and the voids are the streets, the parking lots, and traffic elements such as circles and interchanges. Here indoor-outdoor patterns are intense and continuous, particularly at rush hours. Here, where people and their environmental problems are most concentrated and most intense, there is the greatest tendency toward standardization of experience. All spaces, indoors and out, tend to become similar in character and in scale. Central Park is the great symbol of urban relief, but Robert Zion's recent excellent proposal for many small downtown parks, in the AIA *Journal*,[94] is closer to the need.

As downtown concentration thins out and we approach the more open suburban scale which characterizes most of the area of most Ameri-

Roofed shopping malls are a preview of the air-conditioned city of tomorrow.

can cities, the proportion of void (open space) to solid (building) becomes higher and includes expanding areas of planting, workspaces, stockyards, and waste and vacant land, in addition to vehicular areas. Population density is lower, especially during the day, and indoor-outdoor patterns are correspondingly less intense. Nevertheless they are primary and continuous in the experience of those who are there. In older sections and institutional areas trees and other vegetation may reach a scale which obscures or conceals large percentages of the structures. At their best these areas achieve a variable balance of structure, open space, and planting which we show off as our best environmental efforts to date. With less luck or skill the remaining open spaces are largely misused, carelessly developed, or sheer waste space. Whatever the quality or relative proportions of building and open-space development, the fact of regular transitional experiences between them for most residents remains constant.

Beyond the suburbs are the vast open spaces of the continent, apparent from the air, inhabited by a lucky few in affluence and an underprivileged minority in poverty—exurbia, the country, the wilderness. Here, where people are few, are our great landscapes, our rich environmental experiences, our revitalizing contact with the processes of nature and of agriculture. Here, too, the processes of extracting mineral wealth from the earth go on, leaving their scars and tailings. Here come the hordes of weekending and vacationing urbanites, escaping the strain and smog of the city, distributing beer cans and cigarette wrappers from coast to coast. Here were the great architectural design opportunities of the twenties—the country estates, the institutions, the monasteries, the palaces for retired monarchs. Here, too, will be many great design opportunities of the late sixties and the seventies—new towns and housing developments, decentralizing industries and research parks, universities and colleges and other institutions. These opportunities are great because they offer greatest scope for imaginative integrated architectural-landscape conceptions. If not seized with vigor and insight, they may produce a greater debauchery of the landscape than we have yet known. But they are not our greatest problems. These are where the most intense and pressing confrontations between people and landscape take place—in our cities and metropolitan areas.

What is the essential nature of this constant reciprocal interacting process which goes on between architecture and landscape? How does it affect each, and how might it affect them if it were subjected to exhaustive design scrutiny?

Buildings are objects of varying size, form, density, and quality. They vary in size from the country shack to the metropolitan skyscraper and larger industrial and military agglomerations. They vary in form from pure cube, cylinder, or pyramid to the formless complexity of some romantic institutions and metropolitan blocks. They vary in density from the castle and the air-conditioned concrete cube to the Park Avenue glass house. They vary in quality from the most refined products of architectural genius to the most humble practical expedients, with an increasing inventory of commercial nightmares and monstrosities demonstrating that something has gone wrong with the mutation process. Perhaps the atom bomb?

In ordinary landscape experience most buildings are compounded of rectangular planes, with superimposed pyramids of hip and gable roofs symbolizing home and mother. The walls of these buildings are pierced by various openings. Some of these are doors through which we can walk, others are windows through which we can see and light and air may circulate. Some doors allow vision through, some do not. At times windows expand to become entire walls or cubes of glass. But the most recent architectural tendency seems to be toward less glass and more structure.

These openings are the principal but not the only connections between building and landscape. They create two-way patterns of visual and physical circulation, extrusions and intrusions of a network of interlocking forces and desire lines. (Desire lines connect points of origin with desired destinations.) Physical circulation patterns connect building, site, and neighborhood. They require recognition in surfaces which will stand the traffic and make it comfortable and convenient. Otherwise we have paths worn through grass, ivy, and shrubbery and over or under barricades, with accompanying bad language from gardeners.

Circulation is the means for that continuity of sequential space experience which is the fundamental vocabulary of architects and landscape architects, expressed so neatly in Halprin's space-notation system.[95] We

85

move physically as far as time, energy, and mechanization will carry us. We move visually as far as we can see, aided by imagination, memory, and the stimulus of what we see. The traditional principles of unity and variety, rhythm and balance, proportion and order, continuity and accent, harmony and contrast, applied so often to paper plans and elevations, take on their true complex and subtle meanings in the real four-dimensional world.

The system of extrusions and demands which relates architecture to the landscape has many forms. There is a technical system which interlocks with the atmosphere above and the earth below. The earth connections are the world of foundation and soil engineers and geologists. But they expand beyond the foundation lines. Changes in contour and in profile demand adjustments around the building that may extend to, and at times beyond, the property lines. These may begin with engineering demands—drainage patterns, angles of repose, percentages of compaction. But they speedily become interlocked with problems of physical and visual circulation. When these are not solved, we are left with the clumsy oversimplification of much engineering construction and earthwork. When property lines interfere with desirable forms projected by relations between building and topography, we are forced sometimes to use arbitrary walls and slopes that are too abrupt. The subtle and intimate relations between bedrock, subsoil, topsoil, vegetation, and atmosphere cannot be resolved by the engineering approach. Yet these are fundamental to the convincing completion of earthwork. The problem of the basic contradiction between foundation demands for firm, dry, sterile ground and plant demands for loose, moist, fertile soil is solved usually only by improvization and the adaptability of plants. The relations between floor levels, wall openings, and topography are probably the most important factor in the quality and character of indoor-outdoor relations. The building on a concrete slab 6 inches above grade is totally different in feeling from one with a wood floor 2 feet above grade. Consider each with extremes of open to solid walls and extensions or retractions (indoor planting) of floor plane. Then tilt the ground plane at various angles so that half of the building is pushed further and further into the slope, while the other half is raised higher and higher above. Then add floors vertically up to ten (maximum tree height) and beyond to maximum structural height. With each additional floor we have different structural and foundation problems and changing relations to the diminishing site and the expanding landscape around. These are familiar and obvious relations which architects must consider, but their impact on site and neighborhood development is much less carefully considered. Architectural discipline still tends to stop a few feet beyond the foundation lines, while landscape disciplines approach these as a frontier. Actually the foundation line is the vibrant center of the total zone of interlocking indoor-outdoor relations which is a truly successful work of architecture.

Above ground the building rears its head into the complex world of weather and atmosphere, climate and meteorology, sun and wind, rain and hail, dust and snow. Here again much has been done to solve such problems within the limits of the building shell, sealing it with increasing tightness on the outside, controlling the climate more and more precisely within. As mechanical engineering and heating–air-conditioning techniques improve and expand, less and less is done to solve climatic problems in the site space around the building. The glass cube, tinted and conditioned, sits serenely and self-sufficiently in open country or urban clutter from Phoenix to Fairbanks, from Chicago to Calcutta. The more extreme the weather without, the more shocking the transition from the changeless perfection within. Permanent climate and permanent plants lead us hand in hand toward the brave new world, to the enchanting strains of Muzak. Perhaps we are halfway between the completely natural life of caveman, tree man, and Bushman and the science-fiction world of air-conditioned cities under geodesic domes. But today the increasing climatic self-sufficiency of buildings tends to destroy not only regional quality in architecture and landscape but the fundamental design process by which man has historically linked buildings and site with functional-aesthetic patterns of earth and water and vegetation.

Perhaps we should rejoice that with every advance in building technology, the gap between our "best" (most advanced) buildings and most existing buildings grows larger. There is still great scope for the time-honored historical processes which use trees, water, and ground forms to break wind, capture breezes, filter, exclude, or welcome sun, change local temperature and humidity, divert storms, and generally make the world more livable. We can hope that the ancient Chinese art of geomancy will remain relevant for years to come. In the West we have yet to determine the proper relations between nature and technology.

Not only is the building adjusted, in one way or another, to the weather which surrounds it, but it creates new microclimates around it on the site. Its south side is warmer by reflection and reduction of air movement, its north side cooler through constant shade nine months of the year, half shade the other three. The east face is warmer in the morning, cooler in the afternoon, and vice versa for the west face. These microclimates are simplest if the building is a cube, more complex and special if it has projections in various directions. Most difficult of all are those planting spaces so dear to modern architecture, under the building on pilotis or the 20-foot cantilever on the north side. Here, without overhead light or moisture, it is a rare plant which will not look sad and frustrated.

Functional demands by building on site are expressed in terms of circulation and area usage. Circulation patterns originate and focus on doors and the larger openings created by sliding panels, solid or glass.

Complications arise when such panels are planned for ventilation only, because their circulation demands are visually obvious. The same was true of the old wall of French doors. Such modes of traffic, pedestrian or vehicular, must be connected more or less directly with desirable areas on the site, circulation through and around it, and points or zones of access on its periphery. Design of areas for use or experience in relation to these circulation patterns involves problems of space organization analogous and complementary to those inside the building. These are the bare bones of the functional relations between building, site, and neighborhood, often complicated by inadequate space and excessive problems, such as parking, which cannot be solved within the site. But, even as in architecture, the sensitive three-dimensional design of volumes adequate to these demands, plus the visual potential of the total situation, is the heart of landscape design.

Technical and functional demands may at times determine the entire form of site response to architectural forces, especially when coverage by building and vehicular surfacing (parking) is high. But on most sites where such coverage is less than 80 percent form does not emerge easily from technical-functional demands alone. Here we come face to face with the heart of architecture-landscape relations, the formal, visual, sensory problem. This problem includes and must recognize all other problems, limited as it is only by physical and visual motion potentials. We must come to grips with physical and psychological facts—the actual form of building, site, neighborhood, and region, the actual nature of the human user-observer. The building, over and above its technical-functional demands, extrudes formal visual forces which demand recognition. Historically the range of vocabulary for such recognition is broad, from Renaissance geometry through romantic naturalism to Oriental refinement of nature and geometry. Modern architecture and landscape architecture, barely halfway through their first century, are still experimenting with variations on these themes.

Structures in the open framing stage are analogous to trees in their landscape impact. They extrude no directional forces; rather, they make focal centers to which we are drawn. Their only directional force is by accumulation in rows or groups, as with trees, or by extension in length of one structure. It is when they are closed in with walls, skins, shells, or facades that they become masses with extrusive force in the landscape.

The simple structural cube, without fenestration, extrudes in planes which are extensions of its sides, plus diagonals from the corners. Complications in such simple forms—multiple cubes in rectangular or angular relations—produce complications in such extension patterns. Pyramidal forms are centripetal, and the primary emphasis is on the vertical axis expressing the force of gravity linking earth and sky. The reverse pyramid (Niemeyer[96]) throws us out into free space. Hip, gable, and mansard roofs have fragmentary pyramidal forces determined by their extent—

two-way or truncated. Semispheric dome forms are more centrifugal than centripetal and are also vertical in emphasis, as are cones. Larger segments of spheres become more and more centrifugal, radiating repulsive forces in all directions. Buildings which are round in plan with horizontal planes in elevation—like a hatbox or cylinder—radiate horizontally in all directions equally. They too are repulsive and difficult to approach. Plan forms of more than four sides and angles larger than 90 degrees—pentagons, hexagons, octagons—seem to radiate perpendicular to each plane rather than parallel, and from the points bisecting each outside angle. Triangular buildings with angles of less than 90 degrees radiate primarily from the points bisecting the outside angles. Asymmetric shed-roof slopes carry us up at the high edge and down at the low.

These are all simple geometric extrusion patterns derived from buildings abstracted as uniform masses. They are true of solid-walled buildings—castles, factories—and partially true of glass-walled buildings, modified by see-through and reflective qualities. Beyond these, however, as soon as we begin to introduce doors, windows, and sliding panels, and design facades with modulations of surface and changes of material, we complicate and change the pattern of extrusive forces. Take again our solid cube. Place in one face one window. Through this there now radiates a horizontal pyramid of visual forces, centering on the eye of the observer within at the angle which it makes with the window frame, but not exceeding the approximate 60-degree angle of perception and comprehension. This pyramid is as variable in position as eye and head movement can make it, but it rotates around the central perpendicular horizontal projection. It stops only at solid objects—its extension is infinite, to the farthest stars.

Now put in the same side of the cube a solid door at ground level. This becomes the center for a horizontal fan of potential circulation lines, strongest at the perpendicular center, weakest at the parallel sides. Each line represents a tunnel through the landscape, 3 feet wide and 6 feet high. In the selection and development of this pattern of circulation we begin to resolve the relations between forces extruding out from the building through the door and forces focusing in from site and neighborhood on that door. Should the door be of glass or have a pane of glass in it, we then have another horizontal visual pyramid superimposed on the circulation fan. This however is a moving pyramid, a sequence or collection of them. It moves as the people who project it move, in and out of the building and along the circulation lines. As the people move, the pyramids rotate with the movement of their eyes and heads, scanning the total landscape around.

If we multiply doors and windows to a normal or typical pattern, we get a multiplication and overlapping of these extrusive forces. If we expand the scale of openings to strip windows, glass panels, and sliding doors, we expand the scale of pyramids and fans. In the ultimate glass-walled building the pyramids merge into one the size of the building wall.

So far we have assumed the building wall to be a single-plane surface. If we now give it relief, modulate it in and out three-dimensionally, we produce a smaller-scale multiplication and complication of the patterns described for building masses. Vertical modulation in rectangular sections will produce extrusions of extended vertical planes. Horizontal modulation in rectangular sections will produce extrusions of extended horizontal planes. These two are apt to come together—bay windows, balconies, etc. Modulations in other geometric sections, as semispheric or octagonal pilasters, will project more complex radial patterns, on into the ultimate complexity of freely curved, plastic, sculptural, baroque undulations.

Materials too have varying extrusive forces. Fine textures, as stucco, are weakest. Coarse textures, as stone or block, are strongest, and stronger as the scale of units increases. Colors have force—black, white, and primary hues strongest, becoming progressively weaker with mixing and graying. The patterns in which material may be combined in a building wall will determine the ultimate strength of their forces. Large walls of one material will tend to be strongest. As the wall breaks up into patterns of two or more materials, their combined forces may be stronger or weaker. Sometimes they cancel each other out, as in some baroque buildings of many different marbles, and the forces become distorted and entangled in confusion. At other times, as in the English half-timbered house, combinations of wood, plaster, and brick become abstract patterns which transcend the nature of their materials and take on a new and specially forceful life of their own. This leads us, of course, to the marriage of art and architecture, as in Indian temples or Juan O'Gorman's library at the University of Mexico. In such works the force of the wall and the force of the art become united and further transcended into the strongest and most demanding statement a building can make. The commercial building with one wall converted to a billboard is a gross vulgarization and exploitation of this fact.

This is not a discussion of the design of buildings or building walls. It is a discussion of the impact of that design on the site space immediately around the building, the neighborhood around that, and the region as far as the building can be seen. This impact is a resultant of the forces we have described radiating from the building, countered by similar forces radiating toward it from other structures or elements around it. It is the function of the design of the site space to receive both sets of forces and resolve them into a harmonious organization of physical elements which will interlock the entire complex and give it visual and functional equilibrium.

In the classical case of castle or manor house in open country the problem is relatively simple. The strong and obvious forces radiating from the building meet the more subtle and diffuse forces radiating in from the natural or pastoral landscape around. Ground forms radiate from basically pyramidal, conical, semispheric, or single-slope forms. Dense trees are radial in plan and horizontal, radial, or vertical in elevation, with constant emphasis on the vertical central trunk. Other vegetation is similar without the trunk. Quiet water is level with direction resulting from its horizontal form. Moving water carries us in the direction of its movement—flowing or falling down, jetting up. All of these forces are multiplied by size and scale (apparent size). Landscape forms may be developed which are extensive enough to satisfy the demands of the architectural forces and absorb the impact of their meeting the forces of the landscape, as in the great country houses of France and England. These landscape forms can be simple and readable, as they represent the interlocking of a single building with nature.

Such isolated buildings or groups in open country, wild or pastoral landscapes, represent the ideal situation for production of high-quality architecture in the most flattering settings, without the competition and responsibility of uncontrolled neighboring buildings. Nature (including pastoral and garden settings) and architecture have ideally complementary and supplementary relations. Architecture brings the landscape to life by injecting the highest form of human imagination into it. The landscape receives and resolves all of the multiple forces extruded by the building in the simplest, most direct and satisfying centrifugal pattern. This is not, however, a one-way relationship. The landscape makes demands on the building, through such elements as views (good or bad), topography, sun, rain, snow, wind, vegetation. The building may recognize these and adjust itself with care and sensitivity in the regional, natural, poetic, or romantic way. Or it may ignore them, in whole or in part, or force its own forms on them, as most Renaissance and international-style work, setting itself up as a self-sufficient entity, the cube in the meadow or the architectural garden, and leaving the landscape to solve its own problems of adjustment to this uncompromising new form. This merely transfers the area for resolution of conflicting forces from one which includes the building to one which is totally outside it. If we call the latter approach the classical and the former the romantic, then the classical requires more space around it in which the forces of architecture and landscape can meet and resolve themselves in designed interplay. The romantic solves these problems within a more limited area by solving many of them within the form and detail of the building itself. Our romantic category includes not only architectural concepts of FLW, Gaudi, Richardson, medieval, and folksy persuasion but anonymous, handicraft, peasant, agricultural, and native forms as well.[97] Our classical includes not only Roman, Renaissance, and international-style concepts but present-day technocratic and engineering approaches which ignore biology in favoring mechanical solutions, and commercial attitudes which view the environment as a subject for exploitation.

In the reverse case, of the powerful building with congestion of other construction and inadequate space around it, as most European cathedrals or downtown skyscrapers, we have a much more complex situation. The forces extruding from the major building are met and canceled out by competitive forces produced by the miscellaneous construction around, and the space between is not large enough to resolve the meeting of these forces. The result is confusion, although, as we know, great architecture can transcend and force itself through any such encirclement. I am well aware of the detailed analyses that have been made of the intricate spaces around medieval cathedrals, of the virtues of surprise, sudden vistas, etc. These spaces are organic physical expressions of the social patterns which produced them. I am not here making an effort to set up a new and inflexible system which will say that all cathedrals should have great plazas cleared around them. But they and their environments could be reanalyzed in terms of extrusive and conflicting forces. Certain adjustments in their more or less accidental environments might then be made.

It is when we put two or more buildings together that the plot thickens, particularly when the two buildings are designed at different times by different people. Two or more adjacent buildings designed by the same person at the same time will very likely be harmonious. But when they are not so integrated, they may or may not be harmonious. Of course there is the multibuilding project, designed in deadly unity and harmony, whose monotony sends us shrieking back to the anarchy of the city streets. The answer must lie somewhere between these extremes. There has been much architectural discussion centering on such questions.

Buildings in groups of any size, as in rural, suburban, and urban areas, each radiate their own set of extrusive forces, as I have described. Pushed together with party walls on city lots, groups or blocks become single complex buildings, with equally complex radial patterns meeting their counterparts within the narrow street canyons. The street, bearing its own problems of people, vehicles, and street furniture, is unequal to the task of resolving conflicts in these forces when they differ much from each other. Quiet and urbane streets in many famous cities testify to the possibility of achieving a harmonious balance of unity and variety along such two-dimensional spaces.

As soon as we separate individual buildings by spaces wide enough to walk through, we complicate our problem by the addition of another dimension. Each face of each building now extrudes forces which meet in the space between and are either resolved and harmonized or cancel each other out in anarchy and confusion. Resolution and harmonization may come about through landscape elements, through sculptural or minor architectural elements, or through sheer open space of adequate dimension and flooring (Piazza San Marco). The greater the differences in form, scale, and detail among buildings, the greater the problem of resolution by design or by absorption in space. On the other hand, buildings all alike place no burden on the spaces between save that of developing their own self-sufficient identity within neutral backgrounds. This was one of the important contributions of the international style to landscape architecture.

As we move from urbs to suburbs and beyond, the spaces between buildings become larger. At a certain horizontal dimension, different for each building, the forces which it extrudes will be absorbed by the open space around it. There will then be no possibility of architectural structure, continuity, tension, or harmony between buildings. They become isolated objects in a sea of landscape (or asphalt). Either isolation or interlocking tension may be architecturally productive in the landscape. Worst, no doubt, are the amorphous in-between situations—buildings neither close enough to interlock with force nor far enough apart to achieve isolation. Detached suburban housing is usually too far apart across the street and too close together in the side yards to achieve meaningful structure even with the aid of trees, fences, and other landscape elements. Improvements are beginning to occur (town houses, clusters) in subdivision and tract housing circles, usually for other reasons. (See also Sitté.)

Relations between buildings of great variety in form and detail have the highest potential and the lowest production in terms of architectural-landscape relations. When older buildings of Renaissance, romantic, or other persuasion meet sleek new modern forms, tensions are set up of a power and intensity not possible in any other way. Yet the relations must be just right. Too much of one or the other will be overpowering, too equal portions confusing and tiring by strength of contrast. The persistent drive to replace the old with the new tends to render such discussion academic. The proportions are changing as we talk. With adequate control we might capture some of the potential.

Reciprocal relations between buildings and between buildings and landscape are conditioned by many variable factors in the buildings themselves. Scale, proportion, precision, simplicity or elaboration in form and detail, natural or synthetic materials, and relations between solid and void are all factors which can connect or separate buildings and landscapes, increasing or decreasing the space needed to resolve the mutually extruded forces. From straw hut to steel factory, from glass cube to romantic sculptured form, architecture is a primary force in the landscape. Preindustrial patterns which produced similar forms in given areas over an extended period of time tended to resolve their own relationship problems naturally. Postindustrial cosmopolitanism, in which all forms are known and used in all areas, creates the monstrous anarchy which surrounds us, particularly in newer cities. From this stem delicate problems of architectural control. Can and should we have it? Can it control form and placement as well as detail? Should control by areas be by style, form, material, color, size, envelope, or what? When does control in the interest of order and harmony become monotonous regimentation which destroys architectural freedom? Efforts by Le Corbusier in Paris and Frank Lloyd Wright in Venice to introduce new forms into stabilized, controlled, and highly valued historical areas represent an attack by free creativity on repressive tradition to some, an effort to disturb a harmonious and beautiful urban landscape to others. Certainly few man-made landscapes can remain fixed and static for long. The forces of change will out destructively if they cannot follow designed constructive patterns. Construction of Corbu's dynamically sculptural Carpenter Center in the midst of Harvard's Georgian elegance is perhaps the latest and most extreme example of the impact of change. Is this the beginning of the end? or a new beginning? Is it possible to resolve even such dramatically contrasting forces if there is an adequate amount of space between?

The most obviously successful pattern for continuous resolution of relations between buildings and landscape was the Roman-Renaissance tradition finalized and codified by L'Ecole des Beaux Arts. However, success breeds sterility, and rules breed regimentation. This particular strand of Western culture has become a vast and growing burden for living designers to bear. Like the Old Man of the Sea, it rides quietly and bides its time. Ultimately, when we have had our fling with revolt, modern space, and the nature of materials, there it is back on our shoulders as strong as ever, as is apparent in the work of many architects and landscape architects today. This is not necessarily bad, even though we who began in revolt cringe in hypersensitivity at symmetrical plan, quarter-circled corner, or terminal feature. A return to sources—Villa Adriana, Villa d'Este, Villa Lante, Villa Medici, Villa Gamberaia, Vaux-le-Vicomte, Rambouillet, Sceaux, Marly-le-Roi, Paris itself—will demonstrate that they were strong and vital; only their imitators and measurers were weak. Certainly a jury concerned with structural continuity in the landscape would never have awarded first prize to a vertical solution on a diagonal axis of Washington's central composition in the Franklin Delano Roosevelt Memorial competition.

London, Rome, and Japan demonstrate that architectural-landscape harmony can be found by more flexible and subtle means. Naturally irregular growth patterns can produce a sense of form as great as the axial. Centuries of growth can be linked together by color, material, and intimate placement. And architecture designed in sympathetic response to nature can have a greater refinement and elegance than any monumental palace. When all is said and done, the actual quality of the physical landscape depends upon relationships among four kinds of elements:

Structures: Buildings, parking lots, streets and roadways, utilities.
Open space: Free for safe pedestrian movement and relaxation.
Natural elements: Rock, water, earth, plants.

Furnishings: Signs, furniture, *objets d'art,* cars, decorative elements, mechanical and electrical elements.

It is difficult to establish the best possible relationships between these elements when their design is handled by different people with different backgrounds at different times. That is the task of urban design, or true landscape design.[98]

Garden and campus typify the expanding scale of landscape architecture's response to the pressing problems of the environment.

CHAPTER 8
Landscape Architecture

The normal province of landscape architecture has been the open space between buildings, streets, and other engineering construction, on the one hand, and undeveloped land, on the other. In developing these open spaces, it has endeavored to establish continuity, connections or relations between building, site, and surrounding landscape. This landscape may be almost anything. It is seldom pure nature, pure agriculture, or pure architecture; usually it is much more complex and confused. Therefore landscape thinking and feeling has had to be flexible and ingenious, while rotating around the primary effort to create space within the limits set by building, site, and surroundings. In general, such design must work with forms and materials derived from both the specific structures with which it works and the specific sites and landscapes which surround them. It is in the combination and interrelation of these diverse forces, in many complex patterns ranging from complete integration to complete contrast, that the vitality of the art lies. It is thus an art of continuity, of connections, of relationships to existing forces, more than an art of pure original conception, as architecture.

Today landscape architects are becoming more and more involved in site-planning, urban design, recreation, and regional problems. Neither the Renaissance idea of forcing architecture on nature nor the romantic idea of forcing nature on architecture can solve such problems today. The function of landscape design is to establish the best possible physical relations between people and the world around them. The landscape architect is concerned with relations between people, buildings, sites, landscapes, trees, ground forms, water forms, and a multitude of detailed elements. He is concerned with relations between public and private spaces and between green and paved open spaces, with great variability in problems and solutions. He must understand not only the physical and sensory potentials of the landscape but also the physiological and psychological facts and potentials of people. Landscape design tends to become the connecting link between the other space arts and the world in general, the continuity of the total landscape.

97

Landscape architecture is the design process which makes it possible to control completely the quality of our gardens, parks, neighborhoods, communities, and regions. Planning provides a diagrammatic control of land use and circulation; architecture and engineering provide the structural network of buildings, utilities, and trafficways which house the most detailed and refined social processes; landscape architecture organizes all the open space between and immediately around these structural elements, ties up the loose functional ends trailing from them, completes the three-dimensional pattern and continuity of our physical surroundings, and establishes a direct re-creational relationship between man and nature. In doing these things, it helps to produce the complete cultural expression of our society in the physical landscape and to provide a home for the work of the allied arts.

Landscape architecture is the art of improving people's use and experience of outdoor space. It may also be called the art of improving direct physical relations between man and nature. It works through jobs—land development problems which are presented by a client or group of clients. Each such problem involves a specific piece of land, with fixed boundaries and established topography. On it there usually is, or is intended to be, one or more buildings, and there may be various other structures, trees, rocks, water. This site will be surrounded by a landscape of specific character—urban, suburban, rural, primeval, or as Victor Gruen has said, cityscape, technoscape, transportationscape, suburbscape, etc.

On new projects the building tends to separate from the landscape development. On most sites it is the core of the problem, the primary objective, representing most of the anticipated expense. Client resources are seldom able or willing to take on the entire burden of appropriate site development at once. Therefore, in practice we tend to concentrate on the building and to sweep other problems under the rug until such time as we feel able to cope with them.

Nevertheless, in the landscape too the client will have various needs, desires, and economic resources, and these together constitute a program. The needs and desires may be vague—"a beautiful garden"—or specific—a swimming pool or tennis court. It is a peculiar expression of the drives inherent in the American standard of living that the resources are almost always inadequate for the realization of the program. This is the heart of most landscape problems.

In addition to these more or less formal elements, there are many others which may not be pointed out by the client but which the designer must determine for himself in order to do a good job. These include:

Personality and attitudes of clients or their representatives. (Sometimes these show up too late.)

Technical problems: Local construction, soil, climate, drainage, and vegetation patterns and possibilities. Problems produced by grading—loss or burial of topsoil, exposure of raw rock, steep hard cuts, long soft fills, compacted ground, change of level around trees, changes in drainage patterns. Problems produced by construction—relation of finished grade to floor levels; increased runoff from roofs and paved areas; reflection, glare, shade, cold dark dry corners under overhangs; washing windows; need for protection from wind and sun.

Functional or use problems: What relations between people, structures, site, and surroundings are established or implied by the conditions presented to the designer? How does one get in or out of the project, afoot or on wheels? What goes on inside the building? What will be seen out of each window? Who can look in each window? What specific activities are desired outdoors on the site? What do they require in terms of surfacing, enclosure, shelter, furnishing, or equipment? How will maintenance work be carried on? What good or bad views exist around the site? Are there privacy problems in relation to the neighbors? Or are there problems of improving physical connections with them? How will the project be managed and maintained? This kind of analysis is required by every piece of land—primeval, rural, or urban; tract lot, large estate, school, hospital, park, complex of public buildings, or any other.

Aesthetic problems: Careful technical and functional analysis is basic to every landscape architectural process. However, this alone can seldom produce the final solution. These objective factors of landscape development are rarely strong enough to determine precise forms, although they are strong disciplinary controls. It is the careful analysis of all these objective factors which has distinguished contemporary design in California during the past thirty years, by contrast with a former tendency to rely on the forms of tradition and precedent. However, we have found no new, safe, ready formulas for successful design; rather, we have complicated our problems by throwing open the field of choice. Shall the paving be brick or concrete? Shall the enclosure be fence or shrubs? Shall the shelter be structure or trees? Shall the plan patterns be rectangular, reflecting the building? irregular, reflecting the site? angular, circular, or more complicated? What do these patterns of lines on paper actually mean on the ground anyway? And finally and most important, how are all these solutions to drainage and soil management and outdoor living and wind and sun to be put together in a unified arrangement that will be consistent, orderly, harmonious, beautiful, fanciful, or romantic? What are the overall disciplines for landscape design?

Landscape architecture is most successful when it produces recognizable units or continuities of outdoor space or volume with special characters and proportions. The definition of this space is accomplished by the placement of buildings, trees, ground forms, shrubs, rocks, water bodies, ·ground surface patterns, fences, walls, and shelters in such a manner as will not only solve the technical and functional problems but also impress the user or observer with the special quality of the space between and among these elements. This is the third dimension of landscape design, more important than patterns with flowers and paving, foundation planting, or pretty pictures out the windows and inclusive of all of them. It is subject to endless variation in conception and execution, even as painting and sculpture, to which it is closely allied. Great feats of landscape ingenuity have been called forth by the general anarchy of our landscape: the creation of special worlds as escapes—the patio, the cloisters, the tea garden, the private or public park, the horticultural paradise. A more orderly, balanced, and humane landscape might call forth greater design and less ingenuity.

In the search for further background and inspiration, the landscape architect must explore the world which is behind him in time and around him in space, the world of nature and the world of man, and the new forms which the interaction of these worlds can produce. Any rich rural countryside is an encyclopedia of forms and arrangements produced by the joint action of man and nature. History is important, but not in the old copybook sense. The allied arts are important, because each produces refinements and specialized concepts which can inspire the landscape architect. With all this background, the primary sources of landscape inspiration lie in specifics—the specific character of the individual site, the specific nature of the people involved, the specific nature of the materials available, and the specific possibilities for the creation of outdoor space.

Typical landscape problems are small, medium, and large gardens; estates; schools, hospitals, churches, clubs, community centers; shopping centers, colleges and universities, public building complexes; housing and community development and redevelopment; small, medium, and large parks. These can be boiled down to typical groups: private gardens, public grounds, parks, and public recreation spaces. In addition landscape architects are moving more and more into large-scale site, neighborhood, community, and regional planning.

Private gardens make up a large part of the total area of humanized landscape and are greatly variable in the detailed relations between house and site, the broad and intricate play of individualized creativity, personal expression by choice and whimsy, family life, and the range from visual pleasure through outdoor living to active gardening, from utility gardens through living gardens to show gardens. They also involve the greatest concentration on detailed human scale and intimate livability. It might also be said that the majority of private yards never become gardens at all. Residential design is the most intricate, specialized, demanding, responsible, and frustrating field for designers. This is true because of the infinite variability in sites, houses, and people, when the design is done at individual-unit scale. Group-built housing is quite another matter. It merely bypasses the individual problems and passes them on to someone else—the buyers or tenant in single housing, the manager in multiple housing. The pattern of young designers beginning with residential design (because there is least money for the most effort and smaller units) and later graduating to larger and "more important" (more money for less effort) jobs is really the reverse of the demands of the problems. Residential design should pay more per hour rather than less. The whole problem of individual versus (or plus) group environment is implicit in this relationship.

Public grounds are front yards, whether for houses or city halls. They are spaces to look into rather than to use, and their primary functions are to provide settings for buildings and to impress the passerby. In doing this, they have a potentially great contribution to make to the community landscape. The suburban streetscape is an endless continuity of private front yards. This potential contribution is rarely realized, through failure to make use of the full possibilities inherent in free arrangements of trees, shrubs, flowers, ground cover, and grass. Maintenance problems are also an inhibiting factor, basically through inadequate budgets. When public grounds are adequate in size, a good sense of outdoor space can be created. Too often the penurious land use created by real estate speculation produces public landscape which is merely planting beds between buildings and walks or parking areas. This is exterior decoration, the plantsman's nightmare, rather than landscape design in the sense of creating space.

Parks are sections of green outdoor space large enough to be used for circulation and relaxation by the general public. A "keep off the grass" sign will convert a park space to a public grounds space, to see only. Parks are pure, positive humanized landscapes with a primary potential for saving communities from speculative constructivism and the auto. They are not raw land waiting for development. We should all live in parks rather than having to go to parks. Parks embody the greatest opportunities for free landscape design with elements derived largely from nature and a minimum of construction. When, as in New York City, large parks become unsafe because of active thugs, hoodlums, and delinquents, the sickness of society has reached a new critical stage which man, not nature, must cure.

Active public recreation spaces and facilities are specific and positive in their requirements. Playfields, game courts, playground areas, and community buildings tend to be treated in a mechanized functional manner, without grace of conscious design; the result is that many of them are about as attractive as a parking lot or a warehouse. When these active programs are merged with passive park spaces, the latter may lose more visually than the former gain functionally. However, sensitive design control can take advantage of the more dynamic patterns which result, with multiple variations in combination and contrast. New forces are at work in these design backwaters, as illustrated in *Recreation Places* by Wayne Williams and *Creative Playgrounds and Recreation Centers* by Alfred Lederman and Alfred Trachsel.[99]

On Being a Landscape Architect. The landscape architect is a designer and supervisor of outdoor development and a consultant on such problems. The landscape architect is also quite often site planner, land planner, recreation planner, and/or urban designer. In these cases he may determine the relations between architecture, engineering, and nature, in collaboration with them. In the past, before today's specialization, landscape architecture was the source of much of the theory and practice of city and regional planning.

To be a designer, one must learn how to understand problems and how to search for the form of their solutions. Problems are not always what they appear to be or what the client thinks they may be. Form does not come from rules, regulations, standards, principles, schools, know-how, tradition, history, or precedent—even your own—although these all influence form. Form comes from an intense and everlasting interest in people and the world around them and in the possibilities for improving it, plus the release of the creative imagination which is man's unique power. This is the power to produce unprecedented improvements in existing situations—to add 2 and 2 and get 6, 8, 10, or 50, to produce experiences, values, comforts, and pleasures undreamed of by others viewing the same situation. The total of true progress in art, social organization, and material and cultural production is a direct result of creative imagination. To release this, we must be open to experience and to our own thoughts and feelings. We cannot resist them, limit them, or be afraid of them or their results.

However, we must reserve the power of judgment. Everything is not right just because it happens. There are forces and directions in both nature and society which are not good for people and therefore must

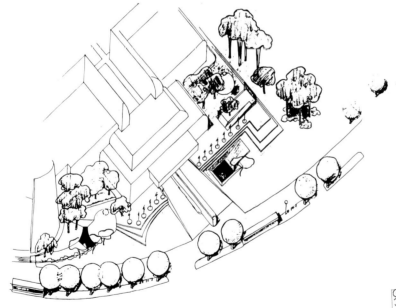

Typical early studies from a series done for Norman Bel Geddes's General Motors Building (LEFT) at the 1939 New York World's Fair. Similar ground sculpturing ideas cropped up again thirty years later in a design for an industrial building (BELOW) in San Jose, California.

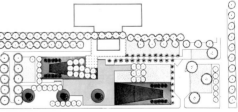

P L A N

E L E V A T I O N

102

be resisted or blocked. There are values, derived from the structure of human relations, which must guide and control the results of free experience, thought, and feeling. If we find the latter leading us into attitudes or acts which are antihuman, antisocial, antinature, or antiself, we must stop and retrace our steps to find how this happened. Then we may be able to establish a better relation between freedom and responsibility.

Creative design is a constant balancing of fantasy and practicality. We must not avoid even the wildest hunches or notions, but we must immediately project these into the realm of practical application to see what the results may be. We do not abstract and categorize the world as does science. We are concerned with direct, everyday, physical reality—with the infinite variety of a world in which no two phenomena are ever exactly alike, with similarities, analogies, comparisons, and relations which may be "merely" visual. We are concerned with the relations between words and facts, between pictures and interpretations.

To be a supervisor of the direct physical installation of designs is still another problem. Here finally we cannot avoid encountering direct physical and social reality, and if the design process has so far failed to make sufficient contact, supervision will be rough. The nature of the site, of available materials and technical resources, of the client,

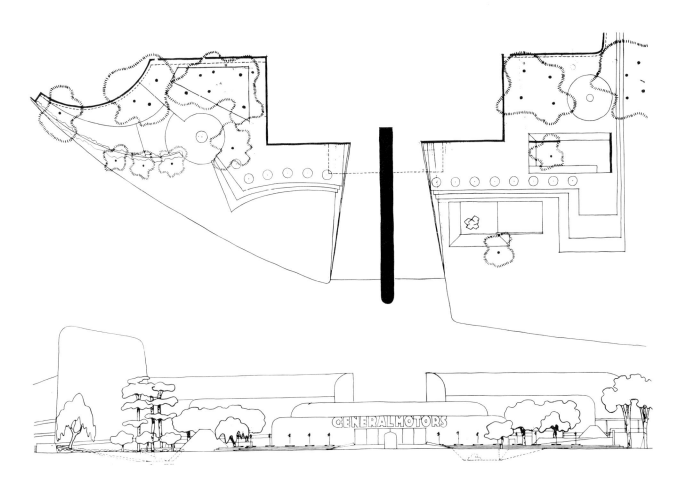

and of contractors and workmen will become elements of hard reality, against which the strength of the design must be tested. Supervision is a problem in human relations, because it involves direct work with people in laying out, interpreting, and adjusting the design on the ground. Supervision is also an extension of the design process, because paper plans and working drawings do not necessarily complete it. Working on paper is a convenience, a convention, a tool. It makes it possible to visualize the problem as a whole, to project its multiple relationships, and to produce integrated concepts for its solution. Plans and working drawings are a language for precising the ideas of the designer and transmitting them to the client for approval and to the contractor for development. But they are a language for which we pay a price. They have strong influences on design. The Japanese garden cannot be designed on paper, nor does it read in plan. Plans and working drawings function well for geometric structural design but less well for irregular natural design. A patio garden of paving, walls, fountains, shelter, and seating may be built from a good set of working drawings by a good contractor with little or no supervision. Earthwork, planting arrangements, rock groupings, and irregular water forms may be projected on paper, but they can only be finalized successfully by direct supervision on the ground. Since the ideal objective of landscape design is a careful balancing and integration (by interweaving or contrast) of structural and natural forms, it follows that we must additionally learn how to balance drawing-board design on paper and field design through supervision.

The other area of professional practice encompasses the consultant, critic, and teacher, who talks and writes about design, with occasional demonstrations, rather than actually doing it. This is an important and influential area; in fact, with the dependence of America on wordsmanship and salesmanship, it may be more important in impact on the landscape than actual design and supervision, if combined with it. But then it must be said that it is rarely possible for anyone to have much qualitative success in this verbalizing area unless he has had considerable experience at actual design and supervision, and unless he returns to such experience periodically to renew his forces and inspiration. Otherwise the verbalizing tends to become superficial and uninspired or merely sensational, leaving actual production for those who have fewer words but more inspiration. Of course those who have both words and inspiration are most influential.

Consultation precedes or follows design; if it precedes, it may never get as far as design. Problems of human relations, or communication, and of perceptive analysis by the consultant bulk large. He must be able to isolate the essential elements of the problem and determine whether they are primarily technical, functional, visual, economic, or social—or whether the client merely needs entertainment or psychiatry. Then the consultant must determine how far he can go in solving the problem—or in proposing solutions. He must know whether he needs help from other disciplines and how they should be brought in. The consultant's skills must be verbal as well as graphic, social as well as technical.

How do we produce designers, supervisors, and consultants? Obviously by education and by experience. But which kind of each? Separate schools for each profession or coordinated departments in colleges of environmental design? Work in private offices? public offices? commercial enterprises? How does the modest, patient, open-minded search for form relate to the pressures and demands of competition, promotion, and survival in our status-ridden economic jungle? or to notions of taste, fashion, and style, conservatism and radicalism, public service and private opportunism? How does this search relate to the requirement that we never make mistakes yet always be farthest out in design? to the requirement that our answers be infallible and our exploration continuous? that we express the imaginative order of man without destroying the wild free beauty of nature? that we produce landscapes of maximum charm and minimum maintenance? that these continuously beautiful landscapes provide a comfortable home for the great game of speculation in land and building, otherwise known as the pursuit of the honest dollar?

Certainly in our schools and offices we must begin to prepare designers, of whatever discipline, who are able to look at the environment as a whole, a single continuous related experience for each resident. They must understand the scale and properties of regional, community, and neighborhood landscapes as a total complex of man-made and natural elements. But it is not enough to think big and make large gestures. We must also remain human and think small enough to see this landscape through the eyes of each ordinary citizen. We must visualize constantly the daily, weekly, and annual patterns in the life of this citizen, from home to work, school, or shopping, to recreation and various social and cultural services, to weekend and vacation trips. Amid much large talk about the structure, functions, and needs of communities, we must not forget that their basic function is to house the lives of the multitude of typical citizens.

One question which most practitioners must sooner or later face is how big can a landscape architect (architect, designer, planner) become? Obviously there are no limits to the potential expansion of the individual professional reputation. Soundly based on design talent and technical competence and expedited by careful or lucky public relations, this reputation may become national or international in scope. Long lines of affluent and cooperative clients may indicate their willingness to wait months or years for their own plan to leap from the master's drawing board. But this is only the simplest part of the problem. How much creative work can a single landscape architect produce in a day, a month, a year, or a lifetime? How much can he expand this productivity by taking on associates and assistants? When does such expansion divorce him more or less completely from the design process and leave him as primarily organizer, promoter, administrator, director, critic, and contact man?

From the point of view of promotion, business, and technique there are no limits to the potential size of professional practice and professional organization. Tried and true administrative procedures and techniques exist to back this up, and many substantial firms in various design and contracting fields demonstrate the possibilities. It is only the sticky little question of "Who does the design?" which persists to obstruct the American dream of unlimited expansion.

Some say that design is a process dependent upon individual inspiration. They are right. Others say that design is a social process. They too are right. The individual and social processes go on together all of the time throughout the human effort to improve the environment. They go on together in varying proportions and relations, depending upon the size and complexity of the problem being worked on. Your patio garden will be shaped by private inspiration, but the first man on the moon will have been put there by the coordinated inspirations of thousands. The social process of design is the combining or fusing of several or many series of individual inspirations. As these grow in number, the problem of adjusting and weaving them so that the best inspirations dominate the process, without influence by personality pressures, becomes rapidly more complex. We tend to end up with the well-known bureaucracy (public or private), which evades the problem entirely in favor of getting on with the job and muddling through, or with the organization dominated by one or more prima donnas or empire builders who take credit for all inspirations produced within it. These lead us by reaction back to small-scale individualism, and the whole circle begins again. This is not to say that public agencies may not provide a good home for design inspiration, or that "big names" may not have constructive and fruitful relations with their associates and assistants.

The young designer begins his career as a one-man organization in which he does everything. As his practice expands, he is able to take on mechanical or personal help for the more routine aspects of his work, thus freeing himself for greater concentration upon his primary design and supervisory functions. So far so good. It is when the practice continues to grow to a point at which he can no longer personally attend to all of the design and supervision that he comes to the crossroads. Shall he remain an individual designer, or shall he become an organization? Shall he take on partners and divide up the work? If so, are they equal to him in talent and scope (design and supervision)? Or in a specialized world do partners specialize too, in promotion, business, design, technique, office, or field? If this is a partnership of equals, how similar must they be to remain partners, or how different can they be and still remain partners? If the partners specialize and divide the labor, what becomes of the educational ideal of the complete landscape architect? Then, too, there may be junior and senior partners. Seniority may come through age, talent, and competence or through sheer energy and aggressiveness.

If we are afraid of partnership, which after all is almost like marriage, being easier to get into than out of, do we go to the currently popular associate structure? This has certain advantages for all parties. The associate, halfway between partner and employee, can take on more responsibility than the latter without disturbing the prime position of the principal. Thus a more durable and flexible team is built, it is possible for people to remain longer and with more satisfaction in the organization before they venture forth on their own—in fact, they may never leave—and everyone is happier. When they do leave, there are few complications. However, the problem of "Who does the design?" is rendered more diffuse and complex, depending on the relative talents and energies of principal and associates.

We must recognize that while these questions are asked as though all landscape architects were alike, actually they are not. The ideal complete landscape architect is very difficult to produce in practice, even with the best experience and education. Therefore the various relations between principals, partners, associates, and assistants are important in providing spaces in which various kinds and amounts of talent can function. Nevertheless, while recognizing human frailty, we must pursue the complete ideal in order to bring out the most of the best in everyone.

Relations between principals, partners, and associates, who may participate substantially in design processes, and assistants, who participate less if at all, will vary considerably according to the type of practice. In an office devoted primarily to private gardens almost every drawing and field decision is concerned with design in that it has intimate influence on the physical result. In an office concerned with large-scale land planning, regional-scale park work, or the like, there is apt to be so much discipline by institutionalized rules and regulations, precedents, and preconceptions as to form and arrangement that much of the work in the office becomes routine, mechanical, and technical in nature. Design decisions are apt to be of a policy-making nature at the beginning, after which the staff is turned loose to produce the drawings. However, as we work in various intermediate scales between these extremes, we come to realize that rules, regulations, precedents, and preconceptions are not substitutes for design, and that if as community and nation we relied upon the design process as we should, there would be a consistent demand for inspiration at all levels, and a vast burning of all codes, ordinances, standards, principles, and rules which purport to render design unnecessary.

When all is said and done, there are no final moral rules or regulations about these questions of "How big can we become?" and "Who does the design?" There are too many complex variations in the talents and capacities of specific people and between the extremes of individual and organization, bureaucracy, prima donna, empire builder, and so on. Nevertheless, design being still a product of individual inspiration, it must be said that there are two basic directions which any professional career can take. One is toward concentration on maximum participation by the principal in each design assignment, with the implied limitation on total number of jobs at any one time and with qualitative selection among jobs as they come along. The other is toward unlimited expansion, taking on all attractive jobs as they come along, expanding to handle them by taking on partners, associates, assistants, or consultants as needed, delegating responsibility while hopefully retaining critical control, building an organization which may have one or many offices, heads, etc. Aside from normal personnel relations problems, perhaps the only moral question involved in such organization is the proper allocation of design credit to those who make the principal contributions toward determining the form of the of the solutions. This is especially important to those who are not principals in the organization. (Aesthetic exploitation is as serious as economic exploitation in the design fields.) It is also important to clients, who may need to know whether the actual designer of the work they have seen and liked will be working on their specific project. And it is important to the principals in the firm, who may as time passes become more and more divorced from design, more and more enmeshed in promotion, business, administration, and consultation, while scarcely realizing what is happening to them.

Of course another interesting question is whether expansion is promoted actively by the principal or forced on him by the demands of a constantly growing body of eager potential clients. The quiet designer with the small office may debate the question of expansion intellectually, but let him suddenly be offered seven large university campuses to plan and design. Will he expand, or will he select two and turn the others over to colleagues?

I have said that a landscape architect is a designer and supervisor of outdoor development. This may be at any scale from the back yard to the total community, for after all, buildings are outdoor elements until we go inside them. If the landscape architect is more than a technician, he must concern himself with increasing seriousness with the nature of the relationship between people and their environment. The pursuit of the ultimate and no doubt unattainable truth about this relationship might be considered his ultimate objective. The actual practice of design and supervision is essential to the major early part of his pursuit, even though it may end in talking, writing, and teaching. If the landscape architect is sooner or later diverted from actual practice into promotion, business, or technical activities, he is likewise diverted from this fundamental investigation.

The landscape architect stands in a position of fundamental and special relevance to the question of relations between people and environment. These are basically relations between man and nature, or the world around him. All designers, all planners, all architects and engineers are concerned in some way with man-nature relations. But only landscape architects are involved directly, specifically, as liaison agents, in detailed relations at every scale between human construction of processed materials and the rock, water, earth, and plants of the natural landscape. Although the landscape architect must be human in the deepest sense of the word, he should also have a better understanding of the processes and products of nonhuman nature than any other designer. The crying need in our urbanizing environment is precisely for more careful and balanced relations between elements which retain the quality of nature and those which are wholly changed by human processing, between geometry and biology, organization and free growth—relations moving toward human living patterns which are as well adjusted and easily balanced as those in the nature from which they came long ago.[100]

Everyone will agree with such generalized statements. But when we come to applying them to the day-to-day problems of the urbanized environment, a certain ambivalence creeps in. We are a technological constructivist society, fascinated with gimmicks and how-to-do-its. Among the physical arts, architecture is probably more expressive of the spirit of the times than is landscape architecture. We in the latter field represent the voice crying in the urban wilderness, trying to save technocracy from its own folly. Architecture is quite willing to have bits, or substantial segments, of landscape and nature among its building and parking areas if the urban land economics allow them. But the latter are sacred. When they say no, the trees go, and we are left free in our affluent asphalt desert. The reaction in some segments of our profession is to compete with the architects. We too will offer expanded service; we too will do site planning, land planning, or city planning. We will demonstrate that we are not mere plantsmen or nature boys by building constructivist landscapes that will compete with architecture in fantasy and photogenic quality. In fact, we really do not know much about plants; the boys in the back room do the planting plans. This attitude helps to preserve an old type of landscape architect, not recognized by the American Society of Landscape Architects, who is purely exterior decorator, plantsman, rock man, mound man. He is quite willing to leave all of the site planning and structural design to the architect, putting in the plants in the spaces determined by his planning. The new expanded service landscape architect continues to compete. And so the circle grows, and the search for a balanced and humane environment finds itself lost between professions and factions.

Set Design. Set design for theater, movies, or television is an art of intensified space organization in which all relationships are painstakingly calculated, all lines of sight from audience to stage or from cameras to action are worked out precisely. This is an art in which the environment for live action is designed directly for its exact needs and to express its quality. There are interesting analogies between the predominantly one-way design of theater stage set and typical private rear garden and between the multidirectional design of movie and TV sets and public open spaces.

Divine Comedy set by Norman Bel Geddes.

Object Design. The multiform spaces produced by architecture, engineering, and landscape design are furnished, equipped, and made intimate, warm, functional, and livable by the work of the many kinds of fine and applied art and design we have called object design.

Some architects design furniture and control the interior design of their buildings. In practice the landscape architect tends to control the detailed enrichment and furnishing of outdoor spaces somewhat more consistently. Functional collaboration between civil, mechanical, and electrical engineers is common. But the rich potential for collaborative production by teamwork between the space and object-forming arts remains largely untouched. Professional boundaries, misunderstanding, failure to communicate, competitive jealousy, conflicting theories, and general social isolation all tend to inhibit such teamwork. Modern architecture, which for years was antiart, when it recognizes painting and sculpture tends to convert them to a decorative function which destroys their integrity and potential positive contributions. In our times contrast and competition between the arts seem to be essential to development toward a larger unity. Landscape architecture, after years of placing sculpture *in* landscape settings, has by reaction produced a Noguchi who designs gardens as integrated sculptural conceptions. "Efforts to integrate sculpture with man and nature led me to attempt the designing of gardens."[101] The sculptural, painting, or object design process, taking up where space formation tends to leave off but without too much break in the continuity of thinking, can produce much greater enrichment and refinement in form and detail. Participation in the space-organization process will give easel painters and pedestal sculptors a wider and perhaps more inspiring field of action, greater opportunities for contribution to broaden human experience. Sculpture, which has never seemed as happy on its pedestal as has painting on its easel, can again become a direct and functional element in the real world. (See the work of Malcolm Leland, Claire Falkenstein, and Jan de Swart in southern California; see also Gyorgy Kepes in *Daedalus,* Winter, 1965.) Furniture and equipment design, instead of being in conflict or competition with the design of the spaces in which it must function, can become a more coherent and integrated part of spatial design.

Urban Design. Urban design is the latest concept for solving complex environmental problems. What do we mean by it? Urban design gives form to urban areas. In order to give them form, we must understand what they are and where they are going—or rather, where they think they are going and where they might be persuaded to go. The designer must always know when to lead and when to follow his client. In an urban area he must also know who his client is. Is the client all of the people? some of the people acting for all of the people? or some of the people acting for themselves?

Urban design is not the design of specific urban facilities by themselves. Residential, commercial, industrial, educational, health, cultural, recreational, and transportation developments in themselves are normal

RIGHT: Sculptor Jan de Swart produced this structured sculpture for the Fresno Downtown Pedestrian Mall.

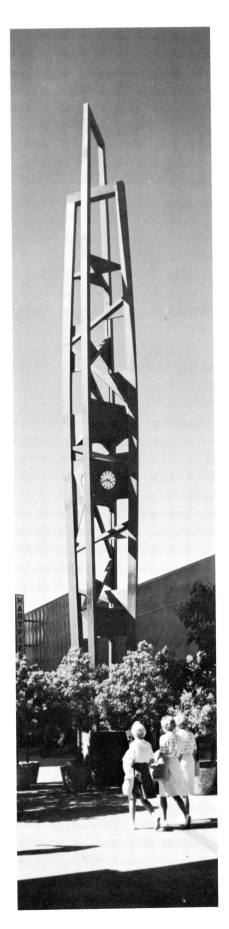

design problems assigned to one or more of the established design professions, unless the developer thinks he can do it himself. Urban design is the design of the *relations between* these facilities, their interconnected reciprocal arrangement in space and time. In designing relations, the design of the facilities is likely to follow smoothly and fittingly, for there is no telling where one stops and the other begins. This is the difference between city planning and urban design. Planning establishes master-plan patterns of land use and circulation, buttressed by zoning ordinances and subdivision codes, then leaves the design of actual physical development to others. This is, of course, our traditional way of doing things. But urban design says this is not enough, that we must think about how the development is going to look and feel, what precise form the development will take. The automatic charm of the handicraft environment has been replaced by the automatic ugliness of the industrial-commercial environment. Therefore, in order to protect ourselves and our progeny, we must think consciously about the end products of all physical development, in terms of quality as well as quantity. Design is the conscious search for quality through form.

The urban landscape, like any landscape, is composed of everything that we see or sense wherever we go within it. Produced by a long and complex multiple series of disconnected decisions, beginning with the subdivision of the unbroken continuity of the natural land and ending with the fractional division of labor among the various design professions, this landscape is nevertheless one single experience for each observer each time he is there or passing through. Buildings and trees, streets and ground forms, shrubs and signs, autos and people, street furniture, water and rocks—all are inescapable elements in the picture. Urban design must recognize, understand, and deal with all of them, in interrelationships rather than singly. This requires remarkable design objectivity. Urban design cannot be biased toward structure, nature, graphics, fine arts, or any other special elements. It cannot have preconceptions as to whether or not urban plazas need trees. It must first absorb the local situation like a receptive sponge after long drought, then search for the right balance of forms, elements, and relations as relentlessly as a weasel in a hen house.

Urban design is not concerned only with central business districts, fascinating and rewarding though they may be. It is concerned with the urban complex as a whole or with any segment of it large enough to include a reasonable cross section of the necessary facilities. It is concerned with the entire range of urban patterns, from downtown congestion to exurban scatteration (which nevertheless must have shopping, school, country club, and so forth). All of the various degrees and mixtures of life, work, and play, all of the complex contrasts between various land uses, old and new developments, fragments of nature or agriculture, waste land, engineering elements, and special facilities, are part of the concern of urban design.

Urban design is not a new field of design endeavoring to preempt an area covered by existing fields. It is a new field of design produced and required by problems of a scope and complexity not solved by existing processes. It embodies a way of thinking and of feeling about the physical environment that is essential to counteract the fragmentation of facilities and of design disciplines which exists. When you separate residential, educational, recreational, health, cultural, religious, commercial, industrial, and agricultural facilities completely from one another, treating each as an independent entity afloat in the limbo of our three-dimensional gridiron, you destroy the possibility of meaningful and constructive life for most residents. No amount of freeway construction or even mass transit (see New York) will rebuild this possibility. Only the reintegration of these facilities into organic urban complexes with Jane Jacobs's diversity and vitality can do this. That is a job for urban design.

This will be design for real human living rather than economic abstractions. It will design not only houses but the gardens which relate to them, the relations between neighboring houses and gardens, and their relations to vehicular streets and pedestrian walks, to school, park, church, and shopping, to the facilities needed and used by the principal daily residents of home neighborhoods—wives, children, grandparents. It will promote variety by controlling density rather than type of construction. It will expand its thinking and feeling from neighborhood through community to metropolis and region, always concentrating on specific human need and experience. It will design workplaces inside and out, in terms of those who work there as well as those who pass through. It will design the relations between workplaces and between them and homes, not relying on the auto *or* mass transit to solve the problem. It will design centers for secondary and higher education, for culture, for health, for administration, and for all of the other multiple facilities of the community, always in terms of their specific requirements, their physical-visual relations to neighboring development, and their social relations to those who will use them. Always the continuity of the landscape, in lively harmony, and the basic patterns of ordinary living, the central triangle between home, work, and play, must be the primary considerations.[102]

The objects of urban design:

1. To improve relations between dwelling, work, and recreation—therefore, between them and services including circulation.

2. To improve relations between enclosed and open space—indoors and outdoors.

3. To improve relations between open space treated structurally (street and squares) and open space treated as landscape (planted).

4. To improve relations between town (as concentrated structure) and country (as generalized open space).

5. To improve relations between urban, rural, and primeval open space.

6. To improve relations between ground forms, water elements, structures, open space, and trees.

7. All of these in order to improve the relations between man and his environment, in order to promote fuller development for more people—i.e., the expansion of democratic ideals and processes.

The Image of a Place. "Image" is a much-used and -confused word. It refers to the concept, picture, or memory associated in people's minds with a noun, proper name, trade name, or place. In relation to physical development over a substantial area, there are essentially two ways to approach the question of the image. These are not mutually exclusive.

One is by way of the graphic symbol (two- or three-dimensional) and the written and spoken word, the normal public relations procedure. The other, more difficult, more subtle, and requiring more time to develop, is by the creation of environmental quality, the sense of place which raises a picture and a feeling in us when one says "Paris," "London," or "Copenhagen." This is a product of the cumulative organization and arrangement (urban design) of all of the component elements of the place—buildings, streets, open spaces, topography, vegetation, water, rock, vehicles, street furniture, signs, people and the social ambience which they develop.

By neither of these do we mean the development of a "theme" or "motif" in the standard commercial sense—not a Tyrolean or Polynesian village. Such catchwords are temporary evasions of the fundamental problem of producing a durable and meaningful image through the development of sound and constructive public relations and urban design processes.

Public relations can sharpen, enrich, forecast, and prepare the atmosphere for the urban designer's concepts. Urban design will make the public relations stories and symbols come true, producing environment of a quality and kind which cannot be visualized save by the process of creative design.

Primary contributions to the image of the place will come from the elements of greatest magnitude and continuity, offset partially by qualities of placement, brightness, sparkle, contrast, or color in smaller elements. In approximate order of importance these image-creating elements are:

Building: The primary space-forming and environment-creating forms, particularly in a highly urbanized area. Architecture is the central, though not the only, art in the urban design complex. By creating an envelope prototype, in which the approximate size, form, and position of all major buildings are established, we can project the primary relations between buildings, streets, and pedestrian open space. However, fragmentation of the ultimate design of the area among various developers and their architects will probably mean that there will not be much control over the detailed design of individual buildings. Therefore their relationships of scale, material, color, or texture will be unpredictable, beyond the persuasive good relations we may be able to establish with individual architects.

Streets are next most important to visual experience, because of the quantity and continuity of paving, curbs, gutters, sidewalks, and street furniture and because of the rivers of vehicular traffic which flow through streets, isolating block from block. The physical components of the street are the most completely standardized of all those in the urban scene. Therefore any specializing that could be accomplished would immediately be a large step toward the creation of a special image. I recommend the investigation of the following:

1. Colored asphalt: To individualize all streets in the project area; mark transition from outside streets; delineate pedestrian zones, traffic lanes, and other special functional areas.

2. Special curbs, gutters, and sidewalks: Colored concrete, textured concrete, terrazzo, tile, brick, stone, wood blocks, wood or metal decking. Consider varying the slope and level of sidewalk as it relates to the street.

3. Street furniture: This element includes all of the multiple miscellaneous elements that accumulate in our streets—hydrants, alarm boxes, signals, signs, mailboxes, newsstands, seats, lights, etc. This requires a special study to determine, first, those elements with no choice as to form, second, those with some choice of available forms, third, those subject to redesign or new design as prototype or special element. Thereafter the grouping of all of these elements in the street space needs detailed study recognizing the spacing requirements of each but seeking the most agreeable combinations and relations. From this apparently complex effort could emerge a street scene as different from the ordinary as a professionally decorated living room is from one thrown together by chance.

4. Pedestrian bridges, steps, and plazas: These elements, interlocked as they may be with required parking structures, have a great potential for creating a special new image while also bringing pedestrians back to their rightful dominance of the streets. Second-story continuity of foot circulation and variable plaza and roof garden spaces, rarely visualized outside of world's fair "visions of tomorrow," can truly make tomorrow's city today.

5. Trees and other vegetation: A high-density downtown urban area with substantial amounts of vegetation and green open space throughout contains in itself the seed of a special image. Mere quantity of planting will not be enough to produce a convincing scene. A carefully studied master planting plan for the entire area, including its public and private sections, could produce an urban landscape of unprecedented quality. Particularly the selection and arrangement of kinds of trees, enough to give variety while maintaining unity, will make or break the planting scheme. On a sloping site I am suggesting, to emphasize the change of elevation in both topography and buildings and the Acropolis character of the future upper plaza, the zoning of trees in three levels. Hori-

zontal umbrella forms will dominate the lower levels, intermediate irregular or round forms the middle levels, and upright or vertical forms the higher levels. Within this basic zoning, continuities and contrasts of form, color, and texture will be woven together.

6. Open-space furniture: Basic to questions of visual design will be the desire to make all open space as comfortable and livable as possible. Good seating, informal circulation, adequate trash receptacles, rest rooms, recreation areas, overlooks, fountains, pools, canals, shelters, flower beds, mounds, and rock arrangements will all contribute to the feeling of livability, comfort, and relaxation which could be a key element in the new image.

7. Fine art: Mural, mosaic, sculpture, pottery, and other arts, carefully integrated with architectural and open-space design, can bring an air of culture and urbanity, a new level of richness that will make a new development stand out from its more pedestrian contemporaries.

8. Signs: The special impact of the printed word and its accompanying artwork requires special attention to all graphic work, public or private, from small street and traffic-control signs through billboards of all sizes to major identification and prestige signs designed as integral parts of buildings. A sign-control code should be written, defining and controlling all aspects—size, forms, color, typography, artwork, position, elevation, moving parts, lights—of all signs within the project area. Signs, normally more disruptive for their size than any other urban element, could become more enriching and refining components of the image.

SIGNIFICANT PERCEPTUAL ELEMENTS

THE IMAGE OF THE CITY

Accent and continuity
  Too much accent is anarchy
  Too much continuity is monotony
General structural elements
  Site form—topographic units
  Circulation system and facilities
    Street system
    Highway connections or intrusions
    Railway, bus, or air facilities
    Pedestrian patterns
    Bicycle or horse patterns
    Paths, edges, nodes
  Open-space system—green or paved
    Viewpoints
    Panorama that should be protected
    Urban squares
    Malls
    Parks
    Schools, public and private
    University
    Steep hillsides
    Drainage elements
    Groves of trees
    Golf courses and country clubs
    Cemetery

Districts or areas of distinctive character
  Continuity in texture—buildings, signs, cars
  Relations between buildings, streets, topography, and trees
Panorama from above
Skyline
Community furniture
  Signs and billboards (private)
  Public signs—directional, street, traffic
  Benches
  Rubbish-collection system
  Streetlights and traffic signals
  Utility elements—power lines, hydrants, transformers, vacuum breakers, valve assemblies
  Mailboxes, trash cans, newsstands, kiosks
Special elements
  Significant structural masses
    Architectural
    Engineering—as gas tanks or bridges
    Functional—as warehouses

Significant landscape features
  Specimen trees
  Groves, groups, or continuities of street or boulevard trees
  Water bodies
  Large rocks, outcrops, or ledges
  Special topographic elements—canyons, steep hills
  Vistas—by enclosure, as streets, by terminal feature, or both
Landmarks
Lookout places
Special places—nuclei
  Civic center
  Cultural centers
  Commercial centers
  Historical centers
  Religious centers
  Production centers
  Education centers
  Recreation centers
  Health centers
Special access ways
  Divided highways
  Landscaped roads
  Freeways

115

CHAPTER 9
Building—Open Space—
Automobile—Pedestrian

This six-way relationship (building to open space, building to automobile, open space to automobile, etc.) is the heart of the problem of physical environmental design at all scales, from private home to metropolitan region. When we view the landscape from architecture, open space becomes the receiver for visual and functional forces extruding from buildings, and it returns to them light, air, and some counterforces of its own. Relations between automobile and pedestrian movement are an increasing topic for discussion in planning and design circles. The general direction of such discussions is toward controlling or disciplining the movements of autos in order to expand the potential for pedestrians. Such direction has not yet made much impact upon the tremendous industrial-governmental complex which now represents the vested interest in constant expansion of motorized rubber-tired vehicles and their attendant ribbons and acreages of paved surfacing. This complex includes the auto and oil industries, substantial segments of the construction industry,[103] all of their suppliers of parts and raw materials, all governmental agencies concerned with streets, highways, and traffic, auto clubs, and all of the engineering professions which serve them. There is no such complex concerned with the needs and desires of pedestrians, in our commodity-oriented society. (Some say thing-oriented, but we seem only interested in things which can be bought and sold.)

Relations between buildings and autos are constant, intimate, and accepted as a necessity by most of us. It is now normal for most buildings to be surrounded on most if not all sides by a sea of asphalt, sometimes speckled with islands of forlorn planting, and filled some or most of the time with row on row of automobiles. The occasional special building, home, or institution which escapes this fate, i.e., pushes the auto storage away some distance, is considered special enough in content and resources to justify the necessity of *walking* an extra distance and the cost of the extra land involved. In the centers of cities, where land

LEFT: Once buildings dominated circulation. Now circulation dominates buildings.

117

costs are high, we are now putting our buildings *on top* of multilevel parking structures, above or below ground, so that we are in the building before we leave the car.

Relations between open space and pedestrian are simple, direct, obvious, natural, and yet fighting a losing battle in our urbanizing environment. The auto intrudes constantly between the two. It is rare that pedestrian and open space can come together without paying tribute to motorized transport. This matter is of concern to health, planning, design, park, recreation, and conservation professions and their supporters, who somehow remain a defensive minority in the face of the high-powered motor-car complex. Most of us, who would really like to be able to take a walk in the park in safety without first driving for an hour through traffic, remain helpless on the sidelines.

Relations between buildings and pedestrians are still fairly safe and comfortable, once we have found our way from the auto through the parking lot or structure to the building proper. This is becoming more and more complex and difficult. Architecture's careful attention to function and comfort, within buildings designed for pedestrians, has not yet been extended to pedestrian experience within care storage areas or structures. But buildings do remain the last refuge of the pedestrian. He may not walk far within them—good design minimizes circulation—but he can at least stand or sit within his air-conditioned, glass-wrapped fortress and watch a world gradually taken over by motorized monsters and their asphalt and oil excreta. (See *Rhinoceros.*[104])

Relations between autos and open space are obvious and melodramatic. The auto, the ogre, now holds open space, the maiden, in thrall. We can only reach open space by use of the auto. Yet somewhow as the auto approaches, open space shrinks, blanches, shrivels, and disappears. This is because the auto brings with it its own new-type open space, asphalted, oily, smoggy, and littered with evidence of mechanical casualties. Four hundred square feet per car in the parking lot becomes nineteen hundred on the 70-mile-per-hour freeway. No amount of rationalization can reconcile the fundamental incompatibility between automotive and pedestrian open space, yet the need for transition elements or spaces between the two has rarely entered the consciousness of designers. This is true everywhere, from downtown parking lot to fast-eroding national park. (It is interesting that the same word is connected with green open space and with auto storage space. Parks for people and parks for cars, inextricably intertangled.)

Open Space and Building. As urbanization mushrooms and spreads with frightening acceleration, there is growing alarmed concern with the present and future status of our close-in open-space resources. The current California State Development Plan includes a special study of open space within a 40-mile zone around all urban-metropolitan centers.[105] Other states are conducting similar studies. The Federal government has shown increasing interest in the problem. A large bookshelf on the subject can be assembled from all levels of government. It is becoming increasingly clear that open space has a positive function for relaxation, recreation, conservation of wildlife, natural and agricultural resources, and scenery (the total landscape), and the shaping and control of urbanization. This new consciousness runs head on into the traditional Western view of the landscape as an endless resource, with new acres over every horizon, and the standard commercial-exploitative view of open land as a raw material waiting for development to its highest and best use. In this view the highest and best use develops with 100 percent structural coverage of the land.

Any airplane flight will indicate that there is still plenty of open space in both the East and West—even in most metropolitan areas. The trouble is, close in, that our patterns of land use and development, in all but the dense urban centers, fragment the land so thoroughly that the open space becomes a series of bits and scraps of front yards, side yards, and back yards. There is no diversity of treatment, no variety in scale, no major confronting of building and open space in substantial units. We just do not seem to know how to organize ourselves and our use of the land so that we will do the most for each other.

To solve open-space or other community problems, where there is a will there is a way. Without the will any number of ways will be useless. It is primary, therefore, to develop a community will toward the preservation, development, and control of open space. Essential to the development of this will is understanding of the function and potential of open space in the physical and social structure of the community.

If, for instance, we were to establish a planning rule of thumb (an optimum around which practical variants would swing) to the effect that every unit (room) of indoor structurally enclosed space should have a complementary unit, perhaps twice as large, of outdoor space enclosed or formed primarily with natural materials, we would be rephrasing density and coverage standards and measuring the inadequacy of most existing environments. If, furthermore, we were to say that these units should be immediately adjacent and continuous, rather than connected by transportation lines, as are city houses and public parks or town and country in general, we would be attacking a fundamental problem of urban design.

Open space may be planned diagrammatically and legalistically in city plans, zoning ordinances, and subdivision maps. It may be programmed functionally in terms of active and passive areas and specific facilities, by recreation planners and other experts. But it only becomes open space with physical and visual meaning when it is designed, constructed, installed, and arranged on the ground. Too often planning and programming are unaware of the full meaning of this.

The only way to develop real control of community open space and the real will to that control is to begin to plan as though we expected good design rather than bad (to get over the doctrine of original sin) and then to demand good design lot by lot, block by block, area by area. Good design cannot be legislated, although good designers could be produced by legislatively created demands. Good design does not come from rules, regulations, standards, codes, ordinances, covenants, or any other mechanical or verbal procedures. Good design is a process of examining problems to determine their real content and eliminate irrelevance, of examining resources to determine their real potential for solving the problem, and then of combining the two to produce solutions which truly solve the problem in forms which meet all of its functional, technical, visual, and expressive demands. Design is the decision-making process essential to development, the process of deciding what form and arrangement it should take. Good design is this process with imagination and sensitivity, unrestricted by arbitrary preconceptions or rules.

Planner Samuel Zisman summarizes three types of open space: open utility (water supply, drainage and flood control, aircraft movement, production); open green (parks and recreation, greenbelts and green-ways, building entourage, natural and scenic protection); and corridor space (for movement, transportation, and passage). These include a multitude of forms and uses, hierarchies of scale and use, and the potential for urban open-space systems following historic prototypes in Cook County, Cleveland, Westchester, Boston.[106]

At first thought, open space is land not yet cluttered with construction. This does not necessarily mean no construction, but not so much as to destroy the sense of openness. It becomes a matter of proportion, or of amenity, as the British say. ". . . amenity is not a single quality, it is a whole catalogue of values. It includes the beauty that an artist sees and an architect design for; it is the pleasant and familiar scene that history has evolved; in certain circumstances it is even utility—the right thing in the right place—shelter, warmth, light, clean air, domestic service . . . and comfort stations."[107]

Space is air, the atmosphere in which we live like fish in water. Land is its bottom. It is only tangible and comprehensible when defined by physical elements—buildings, trees, topography, traffic elements, water. "Open" means freedom of movement, physical or visual, with no obstacles, either fixed or moving—or no continuous obstacles. This is a matter of proportion. Freedom is neither complete vacuum nor complete license.

The natural wild landscape is continuous open space—save for dense vegetation, steep topography, rock formations, water without boats, wild animals. Primitive man lived integrated with this open space. Agriculture begins to break it up. The land may remain open visually but access is restricted. (Consider English fox hunting.) Density of population remains low, and there is no congestion. Urbanization begins the final destruction of open space—but also its final appreciation. The more buildings and traffic and the more subdivision into private parcels, the

Taking possession of space is the first gesture of living things, of men and of animals, of plants and of clouds, a fundamental manifestation of equilibrium and of duration. The occupation of space is the first proof of existence.

The flower, the plant, the tree, the mountain stand forth, existing in a setting. If they one day command attention because of their satisfying and independent forms, it is because they are seen to be isolated from their context and extending influences all around them. We pause, struck by such interrelation in nature, and we gaze, moved by this harmonious orchestration of space, and we realize that we are looking at the reflection of light.

Architecture, sculpture and painting are specifically dependent on space, bound to the necessity of controlling space, each by its own appropriate means. The essential thing that will be said here is that the release of esthetic emotion is a special function of space.

. . . ineffable space [is] the consummation of plastic emotion.

. . . Architecture, sculpture, painting: the movement of time and of events now unquestionably leads them toward a synthesis.

He who deals with architecture (what we understand as architecture and not that of the academies) must be an impeccable master of plastic form and a live and active connoisseur of the arts. Now that the architect assigns to the engineer part of his work and his responsibility, admission to the profession should be granted only to persons who are properly endowed with the sense of space, a faculty which psycho-technical methods seek to reveal. Lacking that sense, the architect loses his justification and his function. To keep such candidates away from building, then, is a service to social health.

[We have] . . . an incessant desire to take possession of space by bringing into play architecture and city planning, sculpture and pictures, all capable of achieving that purpose through the never relaxed pressure of a continuing inventiveness. LE CORBUSIER[108]

Open Space: Unbuilt-on or *low-intensity predominantly non-structural use, such as agriculture, tree farming, cemetary, military reservation, watershed, flood basin and certain institutional uses* with *Reasonable permanence of use assumed by ownership (governmental or institutional) or appropriate controls.*

. . . any undeveloped or predominently undeveloped land in an urban area which has value for (A) park and recreational purposes (B) conservation of land and other natural resources, or (C) historic or scenic purposes.[109]

As *Architectural Review* says:

The landscape gardeners of the 18th century founded their theory of landscape on the close analysis of Nature's "accidents"—the accidents of contour and planting—and forged therefrom an art of what might be called the deliberate accidental. . . .[110]

Concentrating on the scale of the country estate and the public park and with a most naïve conception of architecture, the theory has revolved around the concept of the meadow surrounded by woods. Thus Olmsted says:

The park should as far as possible complement the town. Openness is the one thing you cannot get in buildings. Picturesqueness you can get. Let your buildings be as picturesque as your artists can make them. This is the beauty of a town. Consequently the beauty of the park should be the other. It should be the beauty of the fields, the meadow, the prairie, of the green pastures and the still waters. What we want to gain is tranquility and rest of mind. Mountains suggest effort. . . .

And again:

We want especially, the greatest possible contrast with the restraining and confining conditions of the town, those conditions which compel us to walk circumspectly, watchfully, jealously, which compel us to look closely on others without sympathy. Practically, what we most want is a simple, broad, open space of clean greensward, with sufficient play of surface and sufficient number of trees about it to supply a variety of light and shade. This we want as a central feature. We want depth of wood about it not only for comfort in hot weather, but to completely shut out the city from our landscape.[111]

There is the basic theory in a nutshell; it has been carried on consistently ever since, through the many words of Hub-

less openness. Yet with more density of people there is more need for open space as relief from crowding in construction.

Perhaps open space is noncompulsive. More than light, air, or specific dimensions, it must offer freedom of choice as to movement or stillness, physical or mental activity, thought or feeling. Utility and corridor spaces are only open for nonparticipants. Streets are compulsive for drivers and pedestrians. Agricultural land is compulsive for farmers. School yards and athletic fields are compulsive for participants. In all of these their openness is a by-product.

Open space is traditionally green, but not necessarily so. Consider Piazza San Marco, Trafalgar Square, Red Square, the desert and semi-arid regions of the world. Open space is traditionally unroofed, save by treetops, but not necessarily so. Consider proposals for downtown El Centro, Midway Plaza in Rochester, New York, and La Galleria in Milan. In the future city roofed completely with geodesic domes there will still be an open-space problem.

Why must we control open space? To prevent the development of compulsions—compulsive development, compulsive construction, compulsive activity, or compulsive nonactivity. Control means knowing for sure that these cannot happen from now on. This means acquiring ownership in whole or part. There are many variants. They include:

Direct acquisition of the land when funds are available or can be acquired by loan or Federal grant or when donation can be arranged.

Zoning, a traditional but weak tool, subject to deformation or reversal under pressure from powerful private or public interests.

Acquisition of development rights to private land, by donation, lease, or purchase, to maintain its open character.

Dedication of rights-of-way by subdividers or private owners.

Private purchase for future public acquisition.

Dedication of parks in subdivisions.

Improvement of existing public and private holdings.

Special conservancy districts.

Compensable regulations.

Tax concessions—exemption, deferral, partial rebate, and classification.

Guaranteed-value scheme.

Official-map principle.

Variations in acquisition procedures beyond direct purchase or donation—purchase and leaseback, purchase and resale with restrictions, suburban development districts, conservation easements, aesthetic easements.

There is a good deal of literature available on these procedures and proposals. See "References and Acknowledgments."[112]

The preservation of open space, which means the preservation of control, is a more extended problem. It is one thing to establish control, another to maintain it. Control is by the community through its elected representatives. Preservation is against the pressures of expanding urbanization—expanding both horizontally and vertically. It is to prevent the development of compulsions and the loss of freedom of action—or inaction.

The best preservation of open space is through full development and maintenance as an indispensable experience. Who would dare encroach on Central Park, Yosemite, or the Piazza San Marco? Development may mean completely new form and arrangement on raw land or the preservation intact of something inherited from nature or history or any combination of these two. Decisions on development are made through planning and design processes. Planning decides where and how much; design decides how; both must understand why.

Planning and design are, or should be, interlocking parts of one continuous process. Planning cannot proceed without concepts of desired qualitative results. Design cannot occur without adequate quantitative opportunity. These relations vary from region to region. Planning which preserves woodland or meadow in humid climates has already achieved qualitative results. The same area preserved in desert regions may be merely raw land waiting for designed development.

The basic components of the urban pattern are buildings, streets, and open spaces. The tendency to consider the last a negative by-product of the first two leads to most bad urban patterns. In rebuttal we may say that the open space is the positive internal space of the city, shaped by negative buildings and served by streets. This, of course, is equally inaccurate. The good urban pattern is a balanced relationship between buildings, circulation, and open space for pedestrians and planting. We design buildings and streets not only for themselves but for their joint function in shaping open space.

From both the small-scale view of individual experience and the large-scale planning approach it would help us to develop a concept of the city as a continuous pattern of structures and open spaces. Civilized life begins with the construction of buildings to shelter its activities and products. Community life begins with the grouping of buildings for mutual aid and protection. Every building makes demands upon the open space around it, for light, air, view out, outdoor functions, circulation, access. When groups first begin, at an exurban scale, they are far enough apart to have no conflict between these demands. As density increases to suburban and urban levels, there is increasing overlapping of outdoor demands. Suburban scale reduces side yards to a token; urban scale eliminates first side yards, then front yards, then rear yards. Thereafter the only open space for most buildings is the streets and alleys. Quantitative relief is provided by special efforts or programs—parks, schools, neighborhood commons, other institutions, parking lots. Their quality is variable. This experience has taught us that we cannot build good communities house by house, block by block, or even tract by tract. We can only build them by designing the relations

bard and Kimball, in Forest Park in Cleveland by A. D. Taylor, even to South Park in the Amsterdam *Boschplan.* Woods and meadow are elements basic to the humanized landscape; it is only with subjective limitations on arrangements that we quarrel. We must also avoid the naïvete of thinking the physical pattern of the town responsible for setting man against man. The reverse is more true. Mr. Olmsted would perhaps be shocked to know how unsafe Central Park has become.

Under the pressures of technical advance and population concentrated in preferred places, our problem today appears to be more to produce environments which induce non-movement rather than facilities which encourage useless motion between nowhere and nowhere. SERGE CHERMAYEFF[83] between buildings and open space continuously, unit by unit, within the framework of comprehensive land use, community design, and circulation planning. This planning must grow more specific and conscious of the physical results it is promoting, even as detailed design thinks continuously beyond the boundaries of each individual problem. Ultimately the two come together in urban design, giving form to comprehensible units, areas, or groupings within the city. Higher density does not necessarily mean that buildings must merge and destroy open space. They can go higher and preserve it. But this requires a different level of organization, technology, and design conception.

Streets are open space taken over by vehicles. Parking lots are open space demanded by vehicles. The automobile demands constantly larger portions of the fixed land area of cities, covering them with asphalt and smog. These open spaces are not good for people. We have now to revise our simple concept of the city as a pattern of buildings and open spaces. We must say rather that it is a pattern of structures, including buildings and all areas surfaced for vehicles—streets and parking lots—and of open space for pedestrians. This presents a truer measure of livability, though not yet of visual quality. An asphalt school yard is little better than a parking lot.

When we examine our cities as patterns of structure and pedestrian space, it becomes obvious that the latter is inadequate in all areas of concentrated construction. In suburban areas there is more space for pedestrians, mostly street sidewalks, but too few of them to use it. Development is so dispersed that all objectives are too far apart, with the result that everyone drives everywhere. Suburbs, like cities, are designed for cars, not for people. When automobile congestion becomes impossible, mass transit may expedite circulation, but it does not necessarily make the city a better place to live. We vacillate between extremes of centralization and decentralization, designing neither properly and therefore continuing to vacillate. The occasional happy median condition—Radburn, Baldwin Village—makes no apparent impression on general development activity. Energetic reform programs for the conservation of open space in 100-acre or larger parcels within 40-mile one-hour zones outside urbanized areas are necessary and indispensable palliatives.[105] But they do not solve the problems of cities and suburbs as living environments.

There is an unavoidable relationship between housing and open space. The latter provides light, air, free movement, free play, outdoor living, contact with nature, social contact, and organized recreation and culture. In the good American suburb (a minority) every garden provides some of these, often all but the last two or three. Social, recreational, and cultural relations have been designed out of the normal American neighborhood. They then have to force their way back in like private citizens, buying lots and developing them. When we think of redesigning neighborhoods as social complexes with open-space skeletons, we begin to think of reducing lot and garden sizes, moving toward row housing. We do not want to eliminate private gardens or patios altogether; they are too firmly a part of our expectations. Their elimination symbolizes a capitulation to overcrowding and poverty. There is, no doubt, a happy optimum range, perhaps from the detached house with lot big enough for private patio space, next to neighborhood park, through the row house with similar patio-park or -square relations, to the multilevel apartment with ample balconies, set in park space. The worst obstacle to this thinking today is old-fashioned restrictive zoning by building type. New concepts of planned unit or area zoning, based on density controls, make possible the more imaginative housing designs—clusters, town houses, mixed types—which have moved from professional theory to private building practice within the last few years.[113]

Neighborhoods make up most of the area of most cities. They are the center of focus of average family life. The family sees the city from its neighborhood. What is this neighborhood? You and the people next door and the people next door to them. A cluster of housing focusing on various facilities—school, park, shopping, church. Normally this is a miscellaneous scatter through a gridiron of streets, with accidental boundaries. This contrasts with the ideal cellular structure of professional theory. Many planners now question the validity of the neighborhood as a planning unit, feeling that cities are bigger and looser structures. They feel that larger districts are perhaps more natural and effective units. At any rate we have residential areas—the place where I live, from which I go to work, to shop, to school, to recreation or culture, to health care. The quality of these landscapes is primary in all of our experience. This quality results from the basic pattern of structure and open space and the detailed development of this pattern.

The impact and character of open space come from its relation to tangible elements—buildings, trees, streets, ground forms. In a crowded city any vacant lot, even a parking lot, is an instant relief from the density of construction. But this, like getting the new house built, is only a temporary thrill. We soon begin to think of furnishing, treating, designing, or decorating the space to give it more meaning and more function. Then the problem begins. The buildings around may give it form, but what form? How high are they? how continuous? how regular? or irregular? Of what materials, colors, and finishes are their walls? How might this space be used, and how do we furnish it, equip it, surface it, shelter it to promote such use? If the architectural enclosure existing is inadequate in some way, how do we supplement it, complement it, balance it? With more structures? trees? ground forms? water? How do we go beyond function and enclosure to give the space richness, meaning, symbolism, fantasy, inspiration—using a vocabulary such as Halprin gives us?[95] How do we put all these things together? That is the essence of the open-space design process.

The design of open space begins with enclosure, definition, boundaries or continuities, the determination of what distinguishes it from nonopen space inside buildings. Rural country is all open space. A vacant city block in a detached-house neighborhood will feel more like waste space than open space. The same block surrounded by three-story row houses will feel more comfortable and usable. In designing the vacant block, we will tend to shape it as something to itself, with trees and park structures. In the row-house block we sense reasonably adequate enclosure and proceed more quickly to questions of detailed internal development.

With enclosure and/or boundaries more or less established, with all of the worldwide vocabulary of open-space elements at hand, with program for facilities determined, what do we do next? We must consider circulation, slopes, drainage, facility areas, total experience. Circulation consists of desire lines of varying strength from point to point and of the possibilities for persuading them to detour from straight lines in order to improve the organization of the total space. Slopes complicate circulation and the arrangement of facility areas, and drainage complicates slopes. Facility areas may be plastic and variable passive spaces for relaxation, or they may be rigid active-game areas with fixed dimensions and orientations. The basic pattern of open-space organization will derive from relations between circulation patterns and facility areas. These are conditioned by topography and the nature of enclosing buildings or boundary elements. However, the strength of the search for total experience will determine whether the process is one of creative or mechanical design. Consideration of this equation will lead to a concept of the nature, scale, and arrangement of three-dimensional elements—trees, sculpture, shelters—needed to give the pattern meaning. It is this 3-D concept plus its reaction on the entire plan, which changes the design from a paper exercise in arbitrary patterns to a projection of meaningful space.

The range of open-space elements runs from the classical all-paved square including only architecture or sculpture to the neighborhood park of grass and trees, with diversions into romantic fantasies, Japanese gardens, horticultural gardens, special-use areas, children's playgrounds, and the like. The range of pattern vocabulary runs from Beaux Arts geometry, in which everything, including people, must conform to arbitrary preconceived formal notions, to romantic naturalism, in which the problem of form is evaded by sentimental references to Mother Nature. Beaux Arts geometry is an oversimplification and vulgarization of the strength and freedom of classical and Renaissance prototypes. Romantic naturalism is a vulgarization and oversimplification of the strength and freedom of natural prototypes. Both divert the design process from the fundamental search for meaningful relations between form and content. The modern revolt, which seemed at first to have discarded this academic dichotomy, appears lately to be returning to it.

Form for its own sake becomes arbitrary, self-conscious, and self-seeking. Content cannot exist without form, but it may be weak or strong, confused or clear. The content of open space may be specific functions, expression of site, surroundings, history, or simply happy people. Form follows no rules or precedents, and cannot be coaxed with clever tricks, sensational gimmicks, or verbal formulations. On the other hand, it rarely happens today by accident or through apathy. It takes work, imagination, and insight. Function follows form as often as form follows function. Form and content in their highest integration will transcend the designer, the program, and the locality and take on a life of their own. This enriches all three immeasurably.

Our open spaces must be useful, comfortable, and beautiful. They must integrate pedestrian (and bicycle and horse) patterns with use areas both flexible and rigid. These must facilitate sitting, lying, eating, socializing, organized games, free play, nature study, people study, and cultural activity. Surfacing must be adequate to traffic, or we have dust and mud. Enclosure must be adequate to direct traffic and to protect special uses both within the area and on the periphery. Shelter must be adequate to sun, wind, and weather protection. We have open spaces for intensive use—plazas, courts, squares, mostly paved; activity areas, as playgrounds and recreation spaces, game courts, and pool areas; and less intensive green spaces for free play and relaxation. But these are not mutually exclusive types with rigid boundaries, restricted to architects, recreation experts, and landscape architects. Each of these can influence the others; they may be hybridized or combined in various ways on larger projects. Always they are formed by structures, trees, ground forms, water; furnished with seats and other elements adequate to the proposed use or to promote use; and enriched with fountains, sculpture, fine planting, and other detail adequate to maintain concentrated interest for extended and/or repeated times.

Building–Open-space Design. It is not enough (even though obviously better than much of what we have today) to develop well-designed open spaces, even adjacent to well-designed buildings, with pedestrian access between. It is not enough because there is a further area of refinement in environmental design to be explored. This is the area in which building–open space is considered as one design problem, with more or less equal importance for both components, rather than as two problems, separated by the boundaries between technical and professional disciplines. This single problem has been attacked by some architects, some landscape architects, and some collaborative teams. Usually the structural or open-space preoccupations show through; occasionally a true and rich balance of disciplines emerges. No doubt these results are due as much to conditions of the problem and to client needs and attitudes as they are to professional attitudes.

We must always begin with theory, because that is the source of all ideas. Theory will end in practice or in oblivion depending on the accuracy and clarity of observation of reality which preceded its formulation. Open space was here first. The primeval landscape from which our ancestors emerged was all open, however cluttered with mountains and jungles. The first grass shack and branch stockade, almost indistinguishable from nature, represented the first enclosure and alienation of special space from general space. Now, after ten thousand years of expanding structural activities, special enclosed space has taken over dominant percentages of the urbanized metropolitan areas of the world.

Nevertheless, every building, no matter how large, must end and meet surrounding open space somewhere. The Pentagon, Willow Run, and the downtown Manhattan block all have exterior walls and roofs through which those within may move to view sky, street, parking lot, or surrounding landscape. The completely enclosed city of science fiction is still in the future. If and when it comes, it too will have exterior walls facing exterior open space, at least until the ultimate complete coverage of the land surface of the globe with continuous enclosed urban construction.

The problem of building–open-space relations begins with exclusion of one by the other through unilateral expansion. But it ends with these questions: How much of each do we need, and how should they be connected? How large is it desirable for single buildings to grow? Should complementary open space expand proportionately? Is a parking lot adequate complementary open space? If not, does open space of adequate size and character have to move farther away as the two grow in size (Manhattan and National Park)? What percentage of the population can spend what percentage of its time within buildings, without physical or visual access to outdoor space, without adverse effects on physical and mental health? Can indoor gardens (conservatories) equal outdoor space experience? Can roof gardens equal ground-level garden experience? Might the choice between vertical and horizontal expansion, normally based on location, land cost, structural economics, and functional demands, be influenced by these considerations if they were taken seriously? Finally, what is the effective relationship between paved-structural and green-planted open space?

There are no objective answers to these questions, because little or no objective research has been devoted to them. Very likely there are no universal answers, because of the multiple social, technological, and climatic variations around the world. Nevertheless, each of us has a subjective answer to them, and these subjectivities have objective importance. Most of us would prefer to live and work in rooms opening onto lovely gardens and plazas if we could afford the installation and the upkeep and if we could work out the organizational and management problems. Most of us achieve only fractions, or none, of these conditions, because of negative responses to these ifs. However, as our urban problems grow worse and as democratic pressures increase, we devote more and more resources to them. Adequate concepts of building–open-space relations will be fundamental to their solution. These concepts must be built into our decision-making procedures at the regional, city, land, and subdivision planning levels in order to achieve meaningful results. Otherwise we will be left to improvise expedients within the inadequate limits which planning sets, as we do now.

The prototype for all building–open-space relations is those between room and patio. In this sense there are four types of rooms: those with outside windows, those with outside doors, those with both, and those with neither. The last we can dismiss as not relevant to general situations. Each of the other three has a special type of outdoor relationship: windows establish a visual connection, stronger as they grow in size, making the outdoors part of the indoors; doors establish the possibility of physical circulation out and in, plus vision if they contain windows or are of glass; both together establish maximum integration of indoors and out. The room whose outside wall is one sliding glass panel has maximum outdoor connection; that with one small window has least. All of these connections establish outdoor design problems: What do we see through the windows? Where do we go through the doors? Usually this complex of problems is solved through three separate processes: building design, interior design, landscape design. What might happen if they became one coordinated process?

The exterior wall of the building, normally a boundary between two disciplines, two ways of thinking about the environment, two sets of economic and cultural values, would become the center of one unified design problem. Emphasis would shift from technical organization to space organization. The former would become the servant of the latter, instead of bullying it as it often does now. The integrated functional-aesthetic process which now determines the size and shape of the room could expand to the determination of the size and shape of exterior space which it needs. Outdoor design would cease to be a problem in rationalizing outdoor areas which are by-products of the relation between subdivision and building; it would become a process of giving form to the exterior demands of the building, as they meet those of neighboring buildings and open spaces. Site planning and land planning would cease to be processes of playing with isolated building blocks on an empty field; they would become processes of continual adjustment in a continuous network of indoor-outdoor relations.

The detailed relations between room and patio would be designed rather than accidental. Floor and grade or paving levels, transition between the two through openings, exact nature and extension of both sides of exterior wall sections, exact relations between structure, foundations, topsoil, subsoil, planting, moisture, paving, and outdoor construction—all could be explored and refined much more intimately and thoroughly than they usually are now. Close examination will reveal that our theories of these relations are incomplete and very one-sided. Continuity or change of floor, wall, and ceiling materials and of planting through glass walls (remember early modern architecture?), as conditioned by orientation, could be resolved more thoroughly.

The serious accumulation of such studied indoor-outdoor relations throughout complete buildings might have major impact upon their form and detail. It is one thing to design a building as a self-sufficient cube in a vacuum, another to design it as a concentrated nucleus in a continuous network of technical-functional-visual relationships. The glass cube, the masonry cube, the complex romantic-baroque sculpture, the system of interpenetrating solid and transparent planes, the post and-beam grid, neo-Renaissance symmetry or informal scatter, the pseudotraditional forms which persist in the architectural black market—all of these might change, in major or minor ways, if subjected to detailed indoor-outdoor analysis.

As buildings expand in size, if they expand horizontally, soon many of their rooms have no exterior walls. Then we must decide whether to accept that or introduce interior courts. If they expand vertically, in typical skyscraper form, then with each additional floor the radius of forces extruded outdoors expands. From ground to seventh or eighth floor we are within the scale of trees and may look out into them. Above that the neighborhood and community landscape gradually unfolds and becomes a part of the space beyond our window or balcony. The low-rise community may be one of limited vistas, private spaces, and small-scale concepts. The high-rise community is one world of vision; everything becomes visible and therefore one design problem as we go up twenty floors or more. The tall building is the greatest visual socializer of the landscape after the airplane. It brings out the singleness and continuity of the community landscape as no other experience can. The low-rise resident may remain isolated in a small and fragmentary world. The high-rise resident is at one with the community and the region. However, none of this means that the low-rise community cannot create a comparable sense of community and region by continuous and imaginative design. Nor does it mean that the high-rise resident may not, by wearing specially tinted glasses, ignore the squalor and ugliness below him and concentrate on the far horizons.

CHAPTER 10
Man and Auto

No industry in the country is as directly and immediately interesting to the average citizen as the auto industry. It is the miracle-worker, the pride and joy of the mass-production era, the living image of the triumph of the machine; also, it produces the cars without which the modern American cannot go to work, take a proper vacation, or in general get any fun out of life. Touch the auto industry sharply and the nation immediately becomes aroused. BRUCE CATTON[114]

TRAVEL, 1963

    82 percent of all trips by auto

    88 percent of all travelers by auto

TRANSPORTATION TO WORK, 1960

    64 percent by private auto or car pool[14]

Five million people saw the Futurama of the General Motors Highways and Horizons Exhibit at the New York World's Fair. . . . All of these thousands of people who stood in line ride in motor cars and therefore are harassed by the daily task of getting from one place to another, by the nuisances of intersectional jams, narrow, congested bottlenecks, dangerous night driving, annoying policemen's whistles, honking horns, blinking traffic lights, confusing highway signs, and irritating traffic regulations; they are appalled by the daily toll of highway accidents and deaths; and they are eager to find a sensible way out of this planless suicidal mess. The Futurama gave them a dramatic and graphic solution to a problem which they all faced. . . .

The real trouble with American high-

Within our basic rectangle of design relationships, those between building and open space can make possible the good life for man if the role of the automobile and of transit and transportation in general can be properly rationalized and adjusted. Automobile traffic is now the primary determinant of the form of urban and suburban development, and auto storage space is primary in the design of specific land use within such development. The tail has been wagging the dog for so long that it has grown large and strong with exercise. The assumption that we can drive everywhere is so common that it no longer occurs to us that we might walk anywhere. The idea of a pedestrian community appears either utopian or old-fashioned. Recreation within one hour's drive of home is less glamorous than that a day or more away. We chauffeur children, horses, boats, and mobile homes as well as ourselves.

This is a delicate situation. It can be interpreted in either (or both) of two ways: (1) The auto has freed us in space and time, has freed us to live where we please when we please, has freed us from home if it is cramped or dull, has freed us to go to work wherever it is available, has freed us to seek recreation where we can find it, and is in itself a recreation element (the song of the open road). (2) We have become slaves to autos, to gasoline and rubber and parts departments, to asphalt and concrete; we cannot get to work, to market, or to fun without them. We spend constantly more time in autos, and are constantly surrounded by more of them and by more of the surfaces they demand, their smells, and their noises.

Thus the motor vehicle becomes a substitute for bad housing and bad recreation and an element which makes possible, promotes, or justifies the decentralization verging on atomization of our industries and our communities. If tomorrow all our gasoline motors were to abruptly cease functioning, our production and distribution would collapse and we would find ourselves in a new wilderness. The motorcycle and the hot rod become major creative outlets for young America; whole generations have grown up with spark plugs and carburetors and bearings, clutches and transmissions, rear ends and brake bands as central elements in their vocabulary. The motor vehicle is the chief and most convincing expression of American independence, individualism, competitiveness, and democratic equality. Every driver is a king on the highway; that is one reason why we have so many accidents.

Most certainly this is a situation without precedent or equal in history or around the world—the most maximum mechanization of society that this globe has known, a population on wheels; a situation around which all concepts of planning from the most conservative to the most imaginative, from practical to crackpot, from centralized to decentralized, revolve faithfully and unavoidably, like moths around a bright light. Whether the corporate giants of the automotive world have grown through filling a major social need or the urge to get away on wheels as fast as possible (get away where?) is the result of sharp and high-powered promotion, we live today surrounded by, conditioned by, and dependent on motor vehicles and their paraphernalia. For most Americans the connection between adequate dwelling and adequate work or recreation or both depends upon automotive transport.

The "practical," or "curative," approach to the problems of circulation, particularly automotive, was given its most convincing and imaginative expression by Norman Bel Geddes at the New York World's Fair in 1939 and in his book *Magic Motorways*.

Motor car and motorway come to us from Messiah to bear us to utopia, away from all this urban squalor, out into the free country every night (but back again every morning), the most profitable, convincing, and generally accepted piece of escapism in our country. The farther out we can extend the commuter's range from the business-commercial-industrial core, the more customers and workers we shall have to draw into the same old congested, overvalued, investment-loaded cen-

ways is the simple fact that they are not designed for the traffic they bear. The automobile has advanced in much greater strides than have roads. It has attained a far greater point of perfection. Automobiles are in no way responsible for our traffic problem. The entire responsibility lies in the faulty roads which are behind the times. . . .

Almost every city has its Greenwich Village and its Dupont Circle. It is likely also to have its "Master Plan," by which an expanding scheme of rectangular blocks has supposedly been laid out to last for all time to come. And it also has its Traffic Problem. This adds up to one thing: the city and its traffic have become rival elements. When the tremendous concentration of motor cars first flooded the streets, it already seemed too late to rearrange the city to accord with the traffic. So instead of that an attempt was made to rearrange the traffic to accord with the city. The result was stalemate. . . .

By eliminating friction and the jams in social life today, planning makes for health—not alone the physical health that one may expect from decentralization and free movement, but for mental health as well. The sociologist Charles H. Cooley merely reiterated a widely felt suspicion when he stated, "The extreme concentration of population at centers has deplorable effects upon the health, intelligence and morals of people." When the time comes and transportation finally realizes its purpose— namely, to free men from bondage to their immediate surroundings—it is not only their bodies that will be restored by sun and air and contact with nature. It is their minds as well.

Motoring is one of the most popular recreations there is. It promotes the sense of freedom that comes from greater mobility. It introduces variety, change of scenery, a greater social diffusion, a widening of the horizon. . . .

An America in which people are free, not in a rhetorical sense, but in the very realistic sense of being freed from congestion, waste and blight—free to move out on good roads to decent abodes of life—free to travel over routes whose very sight and feel give a lift

LEFT: High style from Detroit.

132

to the heart—that is an America whose inner changes may far transcend the alterations on the surface. . . .
                    NORMAN BEL GEDDES[115]

Perhaps the most interesting single trend . . . during the week-long Society of Automative Engineers Congress in Detroit last week was a determination to fit the automobile into the upcoming planning of mass rapid transit. . . . because rapid transit and automobiles are mortal enemies, each one to the other . . . the automakers are looking with great question on all proposals for monorails, new subways or elevated systems which could put a giant crimp in auto sales.

The solution? Well, it turned up in Detroit in the form of a number of proposals for controlled "trains" made up of private cars and trucks, all under master command on new types of freeways. BILL DREDGE, Auto Editor of the Los Angeles *Times*[116]

In most large, traffic-plagued American cities today, a battle is raging between those who urge modern rapid transit . . . and those who favor more automobile freeways and expressways. Throughout the past decade or more, the freeway proponents have been victorious, for a number of reasons.

. . . Three reasons may be cited. One was the obvious, urgent need for some kind of transportation improvement. The second was the popularity of the automobile. . . .

But it was a third factor that turned the tide. . . . Pressing for the Interstate Highway System in 1956—and pooh-poohing "old-fashioned" plans to rebuild our rapid transit facilities—were the automobile manufacturers and their 64,000 local car dealers, the gasoline companies, the tire companies, and the influential motor clubs including the American Automobile Association. Their allies included the politically well-connected highway contractors and the highway department officials in city halls and state capitals; the trucking industry, which wanted faster roads for its trucks; the cement and asphalt companies; and the many industries that profit from cars and roads. . . . RUTH AND EDWARD BRECHER[103]

tral areas. The more we concentrate on commuting as a solution to urban problems, the more we accelerate the atomizing, community-destroying process of decentralization. This is not bad in itself, but only insofar as it attenuates the bonds between home, work, and recreation which are the essential framework of the community.

When Geddes projects the expansion of the average city's commuter range six times with "magic motorways," he projects good business for auto, oil, and rubber, but not good living for commuters. Thirty minutes each way, an hour a day over the same route, no matter how beautiful, is too long. A ten-minute walk is a more humane objective.

Whether one is cynical, idealistic, or realistic about its sponsorship, the Geddes book and the elaborate exhibit which it describes and expands were important, definitive, and conclusive at the time. They represented a popularization and glamorization of concepts of planning around a circulation skeleton which are still commonly and enthusiastically held by large sections of the planning professions, city fathers, and industrial interests directly concerned. The principles of "safety, comfort, speed, and economy," the principles of the separation of streams of traffic wherever friction may occur (those going in opposite directions, crossing, or going at different speeds; through traffic from local; stationary vehicles from those moving; pedestrians from vehicles; all other road-edge hazards from the stream of traffic), the principles of "intersectional friction, marginal friction, medial friction, internal-stream friction"—all of these are well established in the general theory of traffic engineering and city planning.

But means become confused with ends: we dwell, work, and play in order to experience the magnificent delights of the motorways between; workers in urban centers expand their forty-five-minute commuting range six times, widen the gap between heart and pocketbook six times (and lose that much more control over community administration at either end), in order to travel daily over all those miles of beautifully landscaped parkway. What about reducing the maximum commuting time to ten minutes? What about an objective of planning by which everyone would be able to walk to work? That is not so glamorous, but it is much more important.

Planning and design must be comprehensive at whatever level in scale they operate—home, workplace, or cultural-recreation center; neighborhood, community, metropolis, region, or nation. At all of these levels circulation is important, and its complexity increases with the complexity of the elements it relates. Complexity of relations increases as comprehensive planning decreases or fails to exist. Thus we have today a maximum complexity of circulation relations between elements whose relations have developed, and continue to develop, with very little planning or control. Circulation patterns and forms are always resultants, by-products, in fact graphic analyses, of the relations between the primary functional elements at whatever level. They tend to become dominants rather than resultants when those relations are not planned.

133

We seldom have a possibility of objective choice between single and mass transportation. The choice between good private cars, even on today's roads, and bad public conveyances, is no choice at all. The Los Angeles freeway system, now well developed, was planned with little reference to needs for rapid mass transit, on the apparent assumption that mass circulation by private car was a sound permanent principle. Considerable agitation was generated some years ago by a report from the local chamber of commerce stressing the need for a mass transit system, because it appeared that the freeways might have to be redesigned to incorporate it. Now a new mass transit system is being planned in about the same layout as the old Pacific Electric Railway, which was abandoned and destroyed to make way for the new freeway system.

It would seem that a sound theoretical analysis of the relations between private auto and mass transit facilities would give to the latter all travel that is regular in time and space, such as work, school, and shopping, leaving to the private car all irregular travel—recreational travel, business and professional travel, special trips, etc. It is when the public facilities are so inadequate that commuters take to their own cars that our major problems seem to develop. Fatal accidents are only the most startling aspect of driving cars, because death is so final. Apart from this we have accidents which cripple or maim or leave some mental block, the wear and tear, nervous strain, and personal and social waste of time and energy spent in cars merely to get somewhere; and we have the economic drain of initial purchase, regular running expense, and irregular repairs of a car in that economic jungle which is the happy hunting ground for used-car sharpers and phony mechanics, often exposed but never eliminated.

Man and auto live an ambivalent life. The auto is our friend and servant. It is to us as horse to cowboy or camel to Bedouin. It takes us where we want to go when we want to go most of the time. Our favorite recreation is sight-seeing by car. The auto is our symbol of participation in the triumph of industrial civilization. And yet view the world it has created. Where man the pedestrian once moved freely across the land, concerned only with the hazards of nature, he now lives precariously on a system of block islands, bounded by streets and highways which are the domain of the auto, singly or in torrents. The mere possibility of a passing car makes the street a zone of danger, forbidden to children and crossed with caution by adults. We kill more people on our streets and highways than in our wars. The essential elements of community and regional life—home, work, recreation, culture—have been disconnected and scattered, to be reconnected only by the auto. Almost the entire problem of mass transportation is now in the hands of the fundamentally irresponsible and irrational industrial-governmental complex which has grown up around it. It is so because it is not oriented toward the solution of mass transportation as an open problem, but toward the expanding use of the auto as a closed problem.

chairman of the technical committee on air pollution of the Western Oil and Gas Association.

The first hard pill that must be swallowed is this: there's still going to be air pollution of the type which can affect health adversely even after we have installed the auto exhaust devices which probably will rid the skies of smog, at least for awhile [emphasis supplied]. Los Angeles *Times* Smog Supplement, January 8, 1961[119]

The Poison Air around Us: . . . First of all, there is seldom a severe air pollution problem unless there is temperature inversion. *This means that the upper layer of air becomes hotter rather than, as is normally the case, cooler than the ground air. . . . Nobody knows what causes inversions. Some cities have them; other cities do* not. *They are not* caused *by cities. . . . inversions have come to communities that never knew them before. . . .*

Wind and especially rain can protect certain places. . . .

As to sources of pollution, world-wide there can be said to be only two really important ones. One is the burning of fuels containing sulphur. The other is the automobile. . . .

However, the most preposterous mistake in emphasis has been the lack of attention paid to the nitrogen oxides. . . .

Dr. Philip Leighton, the illustrious Stanford University photochemist, has predicted that if all the systems now planned for automotive smog prevention were completely successful (luckily a remote possibility) we would really start killing people rather quickly. . . .

What is the answer? It is my own considered conviction, and I know it is shared by many colleagues, that the only sure technical solution for the urban air pollution problem is the outlawing of the internal combustion engine in cities. . . .

What would we use in place of it? the best answer is the electric automobile. This solution is not as wild as it looks at first glance. . . . Nevertheless, I fear that it may be wishful thinking to imagine that the American public would amiably accept these fragrant little chariots as a substitute for the present glossy, gassy monsters. . . . DONALD E. CARR[121]

Victor Gruen has constructive proposals for the design of community transportation and circulation systems on the basis of length and purpose of trip. These incorporate pedestrian, auto, and various sizes and forms of buses and trains in harmoniously integrated systems designed to serve the residents of the community rather than perpetuate the total use of the auto.[120] Proposals of this type seem much more relevant to the circulation problems of urban metropolitan areas than our habitual clinging to oversimplified solutions, autos and/or mass transit.

All concentrations on traffic, transit, and transportation problems as though they were self-contained tend to forget that they have origins and destinations. In preindustrial times these had to be reasonably close together because of primitive means for movement. Industrial proliferation of rapid motorized vehicles has made this close connection technically unnecessary. The result has been scattering of development so that home, work, and play may be 50 miles or more apart. This scattering, beginning as freedom of movement and choice of origins and destinations, ends in total dependence on motorized vehicles, private or mass, and submission to the crises in traffic and smog which they produce. At some point we will recognize that these expanding crises require renewed attention to the relations between origins and destinations and perhaps to efforts to plan these relations so as to reduce or eliminate wheeled traffic between them.

There is a great deal of planning and design concerned with the movement and storage of automobiles and other motorized vehicles. There is also a great deal of planning and design concerned with the relations between these movement and storage patterns and the buildings and open spaces which they serve and connect. But there is almost no planning or design concerned with the safety, convenience, comfort, and visual experience of the pedestrian as he leaves the apparent security of the motorized vehicle and endeavors to find his way to the building or open space which is his objective. It is obvious that outside of specially designed buildings and open spaces, the pedestrian is unimportant, dispensable, and fair game for the operator of any motorized vehicle. Survival is for the fittest, that is, the most agile and quick-witted. Devices such as sidewalks, curbs, and pedestrian zones and protection laws are all admissions that the major open spaces of our cities—the streets and highways—belong to motorized vehicles and that pedestrians venture into them at their peril. There is something wrong with a supposedly civilized environment which is so dominated by motorized vehicles that pedestrians are sure of survival only in odd leftover strips and corners outside of the special buildings and occasional open spaces which are assigned to them. (See *Rhinoceros* again.[104])

What would we do if we began to redesign urban areas to favor pedestrians more than vehicles? First, we should perhaps recognize that our standard street-and-block system, a hangover from horse-and-buggy days rationalized by engineering and real estate practice, is out of scale and improperly related to present-day demands on street space. These

19.41 percent of recreation demand is to walk for pleasure. Downtown Fresno combines supplying some of this demand with convenient shopping.

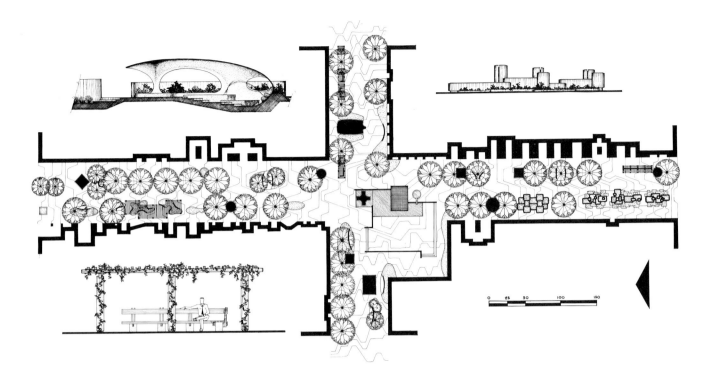

Legs and Wheels:

The street scene is bounded by sky, walls, and road. The sky, ever changing, the walls, old crumbling or sharp and new; variety of style and contour, texture, colour and character. The floor—a monotone—a monotone of tarmac.

Headed by the fire engine and ambulance the motor car has penetrated every crack and crevice of our cities, lanes, yards and courts. All the richness and variety of the floor has been submerged in the traffic flood and inhabitants of buildings venture out at their peril, making their way by means of islands, refuges, safety zones and beacons. Architectural Review[122]

demands include not only vehicular and pedestrian circulation but the scale and setback of the buildings fronting on the streets. In high-density downtown areas streets are often too narrow, in low-density suburban areas too wide. In high-density areas general vehicular circulation should be excluded. This would free the street space for pedestrian circulation, make possible detailed and delightful mall development, as in Fort Worth, Riverside, Burbank, and Fresno, and begin to recreate in such areas the classical Renaissance scale of building–open-space relations. Obviously such developments cannot proceed without careful and detailed preplanning of the entire related area. Vehicular traffic which formerly went through must be rerouted around it, parking space must be provided for all vehicles whose drivers want to enter the area, and adequate access for service and emergency vehicles must be planned. All of this activity will recognize the new areal scale of urban design demanded in these high-density centers.

The mall is not a standard formula to be applied indiscriminately to all such areas. Each must be examined specifically in terms of its own conditions, problems, and peripheral relations. Many varying relations between vehicular-pedestrian movement and building–open-space volume will be developed. But implicit in such possible variation is recognition of the new scale and complexity of demands on high-density urban space and of the need for unified overall design.

The cities of Europe, prototypes for some of our urban design concepts, are themselves in need of similar study. The centers of London, Paris, Rome, Florence, Bologna, Perugia, and many others need to be replanned to exclude general vehicular access to their most important segments. This might make possible a return to the classical serenity

137

of preindustrial days. (Or is Jane Jacobs's picture of the horsey streets of London more correct? Then we look forward to a serenity which hardly ever existed before. Only Venice, Split, Dubrovnik, and perhaps downtown Oslo remain as examples of the pedestrian paradises we might have.)

In lower-density areas the new scale is not so evident. In fact the absence of scale is their most common characteristic. Procedures and objectives for redesign are not obvious, but the need for design is. Streets and front yards must be considered as part of the open-space system of the city, along with parks, plazas, parking lots, and other miscellaneous spaces. Within this open-space system adjustments will be needed to establish better relations between pedestrians and vehicles, favoring the former. Furthermore the vertical-horizontal relations between abutting buildings and street spaces should receive design study to attempt repair for the results of so much careless, expedient, "practical" development. In low-density suburban and exurban areas the vast waste of space in largely undeveloped or useless front, side, and rear yards and unnecessary acres of street paving will require careful redesign study in the years to come, as the experience of town- and cluster-house living with common recreation facilities begins to sink in.

In parking lots and parking structures the qualitative experience of pedestrian movement from parked car to exit or objective and back will require increasing study. This factor is now almost totally ignored in the frantic and oversimplified utilitarian approach to such spaces. A glaring recent example is the appalling crudity of the parking structure which is an integral part of Los Angeles's glamorous new Music Pavilion. Architecture stops and engineering takes over as we pass, all dressed up, between pavilion and parking.

Certain simple and obvious objectives should be central to the design of parking lots and structures. It should be possible to step from one's car to a pedestrian walk, protected from cars and sheltered or enriched by planting or special construction. This walk should lead directly to exit or objective without crossing vehicular traffic. The obvious diagram is a star or gear system of interlocking fingers of parking and walkways. There should be enough shelter by trees or structure to protect cars and people from summer sun and winter storms. Parking structures should be designed as spaces for people, as well as warehouses for vehicles.

Such proposals face formidable obstacles. The design of parking facilities is now dominated by engineers and accountants. Each parking space in the suburban shopping center is valued at $10,000 per year. Thus every element which replaces a space is costing the owner money. These fancy design notions will add 20 to 30 percent to the area which now houses a certain number of cars most efficiently in an asphalt desert or concrete warehouse. Efficiently, let it be pointed out again, for cars, not for pedestrians. It will be said that we cannot afford the extra land, that we cannot give up any car spaces, that the center will fail, that such impractical meddling will destroy free enterprise, and so on. The arguments which can be developed against improving the comfort and convenience of the average citizen without producing an obvious profit are legion. No doubt the latrine diggers' guild developed similar arguments when the first plumbers proposed indoor toilets. But somehow time and progress march on.

CHAPTER 11
Planting Design

Plants combine art, science, and nature more equally and harmoniously than any other art material.

Planting design, including considerable though not all areas of ornamental horticulture, is a world which in the final analysis defies science, rationalization, order, and architectonic design. It is nature's last refuge from the ordering yet sterilizing hand of man. The architectonic designer, frustrated and unable to cope with its biologic mysteries, relegates it to interior and exterior decoration for his precise and predictable creations. Yet it is precisely the waywardness, the unpredictability, the factor X which is always present in planting design, that our overrationalized, overordered, overcontrolled, over-precised environment needs.

Pedestrian though the act of arranging growing plants on and in the ground may seem in relation to the abstruse aesthetics of painting, poetry, or composing, it is nevertheless design in form, texture, color, *and* time; it is our poetic lifeline back to Mother Nature in an increasingly denatured world. And being design in both time and space, it has symphonic and architectonic potentials which are very great precisely because they are so difficult to achieve. Every act of planting design, from potted geranium to major park, is an act of science, because the plant we select and maintain is a product of genetics, propagation, soil technology, plant nutrition, pruning, and plant pathology. It is an act of art, because it involves a choice among forms, colors, and textures which cannot be made upon technical or functional bases alone. And it is an act of nature, because when art and science have done all they can, the growth process which produces the effect envisioned by the designer is the same process which produced the original and continuing wilderness.

While those arts considered fine concern themselves with refined and subtle relations between man and nature, art and science, planting design embodies these relations most directly, most expressively, and most continuously. This may seem farfetched to the suburban lawn mower and the industrial grounds superintendent, but it is precisely this poetic potential which involved them in the situation in the first place.

The paternalism of practical men of affairs and technicians toward planting promotion carried on by ladies' garden-club auxiliaries is a recognition of the ultimate indispensability of planting in the environment. The fact that the best residential areas to which the practical men return each night from office or factory are those with the largest lawns and gardens (or indoor planters), with the most of the ultimate luxury of land and open space, is another recognition of this ultimate indispensability. The parallel persistence of the concept of the public park as a green oasis in the urban desert, in spite of neglect and open attack by politicians and commercial interests, is further evidence. Our technological society, focused on hard cash, commodity exchange, rationalization, and technology, is frustrated and uneasy with the space, time, and energy demands of planting designers whom it can neither eliminate nor fit into its value system. It cannot live with them or without them; the result is constant frustration for both parties. The ultimate rationalization of those architectural urbanists who say that cities do not need green space, thereby evading the problem of reciprocal architectural-planting design, merely abandons man to a technocratic science-fiction fate, the ultimate sanitary slum.

Planting design is the selection, arrangement, and maintenance of plants in and above the ground or in containers structurally divorced from the ground. The plants are selected from stock originating in the natural wilderness and processed from that wild state by horticultural techniques to the ultimate slim or full improved varieties in the nursery row. The plants are arranged first in plan or in the mind of the designer, then physically by setting out and planting in the ground, in relation to the demands of specific structural and land-use situations. The fact that the plants will grow and change as time and seasons pass means that there is no static or ultimate effect. There is only a series of changing relationships which are determined as much by the gardening techniques employed in maintenance as by the original selection and arrangement. The apparent maturity and stability of major tree and shrub plantings results from a delicate and easily disturbed balance of ecological factors and a rate of change so slow as to be imperceptible to our hasty eyes. Our increasing impatience with such slow development processes has led to great development of the technology of moving mature trees and shrubs and a high mortality rate for those left in the ground.

The selection and arrangement of plants is based on certain objective factors. First, the specific local and general cultural situation: soil, drainage, orientation to sun and wind, precipitation and temperature patterns, light, pathology. Second, the functional and visual demands of the plan for shade, screening, color, or space modulation. Third, the factors in specific plants which correspond to such requirements: size, rate of growth, longevity; form—structure and silhouette; texture—size, shape, and arrangement of foliage and structure; color of flowers, fruit, foliage at various seasons, twigs, stems, branches, bark; fragrance. In other

RIGHT: The American neighborhood, a major portion of the urbanized area of the country, has magnificent possibilities for coordinated symphonic relations between structures, topography, and trees.

142

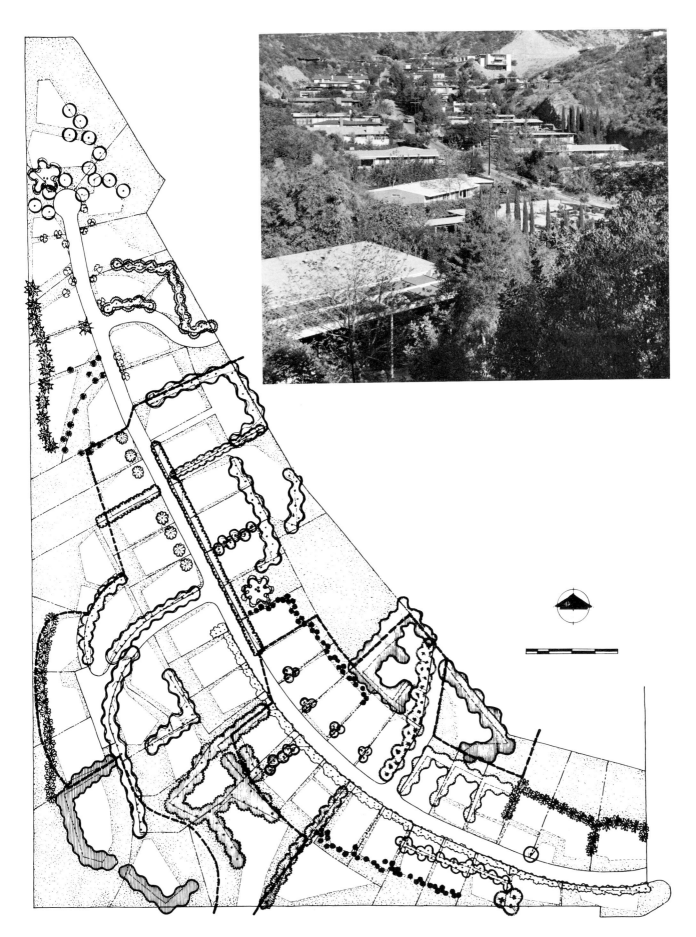

143

words, planting design must coordinate (1) cultural requirements for plants which will do well with expected maintenance in each specific location, (2) plan requirements for plants to perform certain specific functions or produce certain desired effects, and (3) design requirements based on the maximum potential in each species' physical properties and growth habits and in their possible combinations in groups.

Before we can begin to consider these basic requirements of planting design, we must be able to identify and classify our material. The science of plants and planting—which is basic to the art, design, and aesthetics of plants and planting—is a triangle, of which two corners are cultural: the relations between plants and the relations between plants and their habitats. The third corner is, of course, that central concern of botanical science, the detailed morphology and physiology of the individual plant plus the classification of the many kinds of plants on the basis of their physiological variations. Any good course or textbook of general botany covers this basic material, and it is a prerequisite to any serious activity in planting design. So also is basic acquaintance with horticulture, the technology of the propagation, installation, and maintenance of ornamental planting.

Botanical classifications by division, class, subclass, order, family, genus, and the exact species and variety are outlined in their most relevant arrangement in *Bailey's Standard Cyclopedia of Horticulture*.[123] In practice we deal with plants primarily by genus and species. Rarely is even the family relevant to us in day-to-day work. We are primarily concerned with the higher and more complex plant forms—the ferns; the gymnosperms, seed plants with no pods or other enclosures around the seeds; and the angiosperms, modern seed plants with enclosed seeds. Angiosperms include what we call flowering plants—herbs, shrubs, trees—the wind-pollinated inconspicuous kinds (grass, birch) and the insect-pollinated kinds with the showy flowers which are the *pièce de résistance* of our gardens. Gymnosperms include the conifers and also the cycads and the *ginkgo*.

The grouping of plants by genus, family, or habitat in landscape arrangements may have scientific value, as in the botanical garden, but it has no more relevance than literary associations to the establishment of generally sound relations between plants, people, and outdoor space.

Cultural requirements are a result of the complex and delicate reciprocal relations between plants, as living organisms, and their environment—everything around them including other plants. The science of these relations is plant ecology, and horticulture is its technology. In practice this technology is expressed in lists of plants which will thrive on, or adjust to, various categories of soil, moisture, light, and temperature conditions; which have specific ranges of susceptibility to pests and diseases; and which therefore have certain maintenance requirements, such as artificial irrigation, fertilizing, pruning, seasonal change, or regular spraying.

Plan requirements constitute a demand for certain sizes, forms, rates of growth, degrees of permanence, and sometimes more detailed effects. Here science and art begin to interlock. Scientific categories of plants and growing conditions are not totally predictable or reliable, because their content is not yet subject to total assembly-line control, even in the best nurseries. This element of unpredictability is a source of exasperation to technocrats but of delight to artists. Selection of the right plant for the right place is still as much a matter of intuition as of knowledge.

Design requirements are based on size, form, texture, and color in their various complications, ramifications, and interrelationships. Selection on the basis of size is based on land-use program, rate of growth, longevity, and maintenance potentials. (If it may get too large, we can trim or prune it regularly.) Selection on the basis of form is based somewhat on functional requirements, but much more on the search for meaningful space relations—geometric, naturalistic, poetic, romantic, sculptural, architectonic, or what have you. Selection on the basis of texture has little functional or horticultural relevance but is probably the greatest and most neglected area for refinement and coherence in planting design. We have learned to select carefully for relevant size and form and to inject color and fragrance at strategic times and places. But most planting tends to end as a hodgepodge of textures. Careful and sensitive control of texture relations through various sizes and forms in planting can be the principal determinant of success or failure. The variations in overall plant texture are so tremendous in the vegetative palette that the potentials for infinite subtlety are as great as in painting or music.

Color contributes to unity and variety more on the basis of seasonal effects—flower, fruit, foliage, exposed structure in winter—than continuously. All greens are not alike—there is a substantial range from light to dark, from clear to gray, and from dull to glossy textures in the leaves themselves. In addition to special nongreens in spring and fall, there are variations in gray, brown, red, purple, and multicolored forms. The bark and branches of some trees and shrubs are strong in color. Nevertheless, overall color relations in plants are more subtle than texture relations, with occasional exceptional accents in time or space. The possibility for making color relations stronger than those of texture could be realized in controlled areas with strong discipline in selection and maintenance.

Landscape classification, concerned with the establishment of relatively stable spatial relations of surfacing, enclosure, and shelter, will tend to concentrate on more permanent material rather than on the more transitory enriching elements. This concentration will vary from region to region as the proportions of quick and slow and short- and long-lived materials vary. In the north temperate regions we tend to think of the woody trees and shrubs, together with grasses and certain perennials and bulbs which are long-lived in the ground without change, as being most reliable. In the arid and semiarid regions these are joined or superseded by leaf and stem succulents and semishrubs. In the frostless tropics large, quick herbaceous material may be much more reliable, in combination with woody material. Wherever we work, we will tend to strive toward a durable spatial framework and to consider life expectancy, particularly in the trees and larger shrubs. A thirty-year tree is quick and temporary; a thirty-year perennial or bulb clump is a remarkable example of longevity. The annuals and biennials, unless conditions are such that they can reseed and naturalize, and bulbs and perennials requiring regular lifting from the ground are elements of decorative or horticultural interest, part of the legitimate furnishing of the garden and of the life which goes on within it.

Systems of landscape classification, by way of example, have been developed in various regions. Some have been neglected, some thoroughly elaborated, depending on the local level of organized landscape design. Typical of such published systems are that of Hamblin in the Northeast and that of Hoyt in the Southwest (first book; the second becomes confusing by endeavoring to include the humid Southeast). Others which may be mentioned for purposes of discussion are those of Taylor, Rose, and myself.

Hamblin classifies Northeastern material as follows:

TREES
  HEIGHT Tall—100 ft; large—60 ft; medium—40 ft; small—20 ft.
  HABIT Narrow, pyramidal; broad, spreading; irregular; horizontal; dense; open; roundheaded; spiry-topped; weeping; showy bark.
  LEAFAGE Late; early; compound; shade dense; shade light; large; small; laciniate or much lobed; colored; dark green; light green; colored in autumn; evergreen.
  GROWTH Quick; slow; hard-wooded; soft-wooded; easily moved; difficult to move; poor soil; wet soil; rich soil; insects and diseases; free from pests.
  USE . . .
SHRUBS
  HEIGHT Treelike (over 15 ft); 10 to 15 ft; 6 to 10 ft; 3 to 6 ft; dwarf erect; dwarf trailing.
  HABIT Drooping; narrow erect; horizontal.
  LEAFAGE large; small; compound; colored; cut-leaved; evergreen; fragrant; early; late; killed by frost; autumn coloration.

BARK Thorny; colored.
  FLOWERS By colors; very large and showy; fragrant; by month; erect spikes; flat clusters.
  FRUIT By season; eaten by birds; eaten by man.
  SOILS Very dry; very wet; full sun; shade-enduring.
  CULTURE No pruning; much pruning; thrive under neglect; winter-kill NE; insects and diseases; free from pests.
  USE . . .
Woody Vines
  HABIT Clinging; twining; tendril-coiling; scrambling; trailing flat on ground; vigorous; slender.[9]
  SIZE Tall; low.
  LEAFAGE Large; small; evergreen; autumn coloration.
  USE . . .
PERENNIALS
  By height; color; season; growth (long-lived, transient, weedy, spreaders, bulbous tender NE, deep-rooted, shallow-rooted, shrubby, need staking . . .); foliage; flower size and form; use. . . .[124]

146

Hoyt, in his first book, *Planting Lists for Southern California,* tends to mix botanical, ecological, and landscape classifications.[125] Thus his "General Lists," while referring to certain obvious physical characteristics, are nevertheless primarily botanical (palms, conifers, dwarf conifers, broad-leaved evergreens, deciduous trees, small trees or shrubs, evergreen shrubs, deciduous shrubs, shrubby vines, vines, evergreen vines, deciduous vines, herbaceous vines, herbaceous plants, annual flowers, biennials, perennials, ornamental grasses, ferns, bulbs, tuberous-rooted plants, subtropical fruits, succulents, native plants). His "Structural Form" lists are clearly landscape classifications (dense texture, texture open, erect trees, spreading trees, open-headed trees, roundheaded trees, pyramidal trees, umbrageous trees, weeping trees . . .). His "Cultural Aspects" are as clearly ecological (sun-loving plants, shade or half shade, smoke, dust, and drought resistance . . .). His "Purpose Adaptation" lists are partly landscape (certain forms), partly cultural (certain positions), and partly preconceptions as to landscape use which fail to recognize the design processes that should go on for each specific problem. Thus "Seaside Planting" is a culture list, but we determine trees for shade, for the highway or the street, by an examination of form and cultural relations. From the latter we can make up choice lists for specific problems and positions, but it is dangerous to repeat this secondary and more specific list for other problems which may be superficially similar. It is always better to go back to the primary relations between physical form and ecology for each new problem. Hoyt's "Ornamental Characters" are color lists; his "Distinctive Qualities" are form lists with a slightly romantic or sentimental twist; his "Garden Assemblage" lists are merely concessions to historical and horticultural sentiment.

It is my feeling that the system should eliminate its allusions to botanical or sentimental categories and to design preconceptions. By establishing a simpler and more orderly relation between ecological and landscape groupings, it would develop much greater flexibility and usability. Hoyt's newer book, *Ornamental Plants for Subtropical Regions,* follows the same outline in more expanded form. His remarks on soils and descriptions of plants and relations are in general very well written. He attempts to cover all areas south of Charleston (South Carolina), Gainesville (Alabama), Baton Rouge, San Antonio, El Paso, Phoenix, and San Francisco.[125]

Taylor has a much greater proportion of design preconceptions (street and avenue planting, plants for hedges, plants for border planting, accent and specimen trees and shrubs, plants for heavy formal effects, trees and shrubs for *allées,* plants for natural informal effects . . .), which tend to encourage mechanical stereotyped planning. He has very good cultural lists (congested city districts, various types of soil conditions, exposed lakefront and river conditions, seaside planting . . .) and landscape lists in our sense (different flowering effects, fruit characteristics, colored twigs, autumn coloration . . .) for the Northeast. Lists for Florida, Minnesota, the South Atlantic states, and the Oregon and Washington Coastal Plain, while doubtless useful as a beginning in regions unexplored professionally, are certainly no more than that. Regions as diverse in conditions as these must develop their own planting culture from within reaching out, rather than having it developed for them from without reaching in. Taylor indicates that this is his own attitude in these chapters. The lists show very little botanical preoccupation, and it is mainly subjective dicta, such as "The following groups comprise only plants which are most successful when used singly or in small groups," which tend to confuse the usability of the book.[126]

Bailey, in his "Class-articles" (alpine plants, annuals, ants, aquatics, arboretum, arboriculture . . .) gives us a complete survey of horticultural craft and preoccupations. This is basic humanized ecology, with occasional injections of sentiment.[123]

James C. Rose, in *Pencil Points* for April, 1939, gave us a "simplified form palette of plant materials" for the Northeast. It was an excellent projection of the kinds of relations a really thorough landscape classification will bring out.

Trees and shrubs are grouped by major forms—columnar, horizontal, pendulous, broad and spreading, round or oval, irregular and picturesque—and within those groups are separated into seven sizes, from 1 to over 50 feet, and into three values, light, medium, and dark.

> The forms are not necessarily the only ones which the particular plants assume, but they are sufficiently common as listed to render the classification useful. . . . The height is that of maturity or where it will serve a landscape purpose from ten to twenty years. . . . The values are those which are sufficiently common to be worth while listing, but individual selections must be made. These values are considered much as pigments in watercolors, which change when used in relation to light, distance, and other pigment. . . . No obscure plants are used, all of them can be moved, and tender plants are marked with asterisk.[127]

I have a rough and bulky collection of lists from various times and places. Much could be done to expand them, reorganize them, and establish cross-reference relations, but their general content is a good indicator of the kind of material which should be covered by a thorough landscape classification. They are subdivided into five groups: size, color, culture, form, and texture. The second includes listings by foliage, flower, fruit, and season. Bark colors should be added. Most of us are familiar with the general distribution of flower and fruit colors (blue being most scarce), but the distribution of foliage colors in this typical listing for one California region may be of interest: 190 gray, 36 silver- or gray-and-green, 211 gray-green, 167 light green, 43 yellow-and-green, 663 medium green, 31 red-and-green, 228 dark green, 68 purple-red. There are forty-four culture lists for various relations of soil, moisture, temperature, and cultivation.

Form lists include the following basic headings: bushy—clump form, drooping-recurved, erect—stiff or arching, spreading; columnar or fastigiate; deciduous and evergreen trees and shrubs; evergreen perennials; fast-growing; ferns; trailers or prostrate; mat-forming; irregularly ascending; short- and long-lived; loose, graceful, or straggling; pyramidal; rosette form, on stems over 20 feet; slow-growing; tree form—round or irregular, slender upright, spreading, weeping, small; climbing—by clambering, by clinging, by tendrils or roots, by twining. All of these, as well as the color and texture lists, are subdivided into size groups.

Texture lists are quite complex: leafless—branches rodlike, cactus form, leaves forming wings; leaves very small, scalelike; pinnate, leaflets very small or finely divided; linear—small, medium small, medium large, large, very large; sword- or strap-shaped—five sizes, plus pinnate and palmately divided; lanceolate—ditto; pinnatisect—ditto; Holly-like—ditto; ovate—ditto; cordate or obovate—ditto; lobed—ditto. Lists of fragrent plants complete the collection.

The most recommended general references are Donald Wyman's *Trees for American Gardens* and *Shrubs and Vines for American Gardens*.[128] These are excellent books and no doubt come closest to functioning as general references for most of the country. The subtropical areas, which Wyman admittedly does not cover very completely, are well covered by Roland Hoyt. Both Wyman and Hoyt minimize the difference between the humid East and the arid West, and this results in some confusion in their books.

Landscape problems are different east, west, north, and south, and we must recognize that they require different approaches for their solution. The Northeast is humid with cold winters; the Northwest is dry with cold winters. The Southeast is humid with mild winters; the Southwest is dry with mild winters. (The Pacific Coast is a special mild strip which is dry in summer and wet in winter.) The standard ten hardiness zones cross these regions in ribbons, creating a total of twenty landscape zones if we agree that humidity as well as temperature is important in landscape problems.

We should substitute "broad-leaved evergreen" for Wyman's "subtropical." (Subtropicals are only tender broad-leaved evergreens.) The three basic types of woody ornamental plants are deciduous, coniferous (narrow-leaved evergreen), and broad-leaved evergreen. The first two are typical of cold-winter regions, the third of mild-winter regions. Our map of natural landscape regions places the milder regions in a better relation to the colder regions than Wyman's description of "subtropicals" as "a special subject in itself, of interest to people living in a very small portion of this great country." Likewise his remark that "usually, in dry areas, the plants that must be continually watered are so burdensome that they are eventually discarded"[128] betrays an appalling ignorance of, or indifference to, the great tradition of garden design in mild dry countries around the world and the great area with a growing population which constitutes the dry half of our country.

Planting design is rarely pure. It is usually a by-product of other

149

This map illustrates the basis for determining the six typical regions in our country. The typical landscape problem within each region has distinctly different characteristics from that in any of the others. Note that each of the regions except the Southeast continues over the international boundaries into Canada on the north or Mexico on the south. (Each region should have its own basic handbooks of horticulture, construction, and design, which would bring general principles down to the specifics of local conditions. Such handbooks, more or less adequate, exist for the Northeast, Southeast, North Pacific, and South Pacific, but I know of none for the other regions.)

While actual regional boundaries can never be as sharp as lines drawn on a map, they are determined as follows: The heaviest lines mark the principal divisions. That which runs mainly east and west, except where it parallels the Pacific Coast, is the line along which annual minimum temperatures average 5 degrees above zero. North of this line is colder, south warmer. Wyman lists twelve broad-leaved evergreen trees as being hardy down to this average temperature and thirty-two broad-leaved evergreen shrubs as being hardy somewhat below it. It therefore seems reasonable to assume this line as a boundary between the Southern and Western broad-leaved-evergreen landscapes, on the one hand, and the North deciduous-conifer landscapes, on the other.

The heavy line running north and south through the center of the country is that along which annual precipitation averages 25 inches. East of this is wetter, west drier. Landscape and horticultural problems are as different between the humid East and the dry West as they are between the warm South and the cold North.

The lighter dashed lines indicate conditions which qualify the main boundaries and create transitional conditions around them. The principal transitional zone runs north and south across the center of the country. Its western boundary is the line to which 25 inches of precipitation extends in the ten wettest years in forty. Its eastern boundary is the line to which that amount recedes in the ten driest years in forty. Between these lines the climate may be humid some years, subhumid to semiarid others.

In the Northwest and North Pacific note another light dashed line which indicates that these sections also receive 25 inches of average annual precipitation. It is this condition which separates North and South Pacific. However, closer examination indicates that in the warm season from April to September only two small sections on the extreme North Pacific coast receive more than 20 inches of rainfall. (By contrast the dotted line across the center of the map indicates that practically all of the Eastern half of the country receives more than 2 inches of its rainfall during the warm season when plants grow.) It is this lack of rain during the growing season which includes the North Pacific in the dry-summer West Coast. Likewise the spots of high precipitation in the mountains of the Northwest (Idaho and Colorado) are also primarily cold-season deposits.

The boundary between South Pacific and Southwest is indicated as the narrow zone in which the average annual precipitation drops abruptly from over 10 to under 5 inches per year. This is a transition from a semiarid to a truly arid condition.

The final qualifying line is the dotted line across the Southeast and West which indicates the farthest south and west that zero temperatures have ever been recorded. While this may be a very occasional phenomenon, it does establish a questionable zone, quite broad in the Southeast, within which only the hardiest broad-leaved evergreens may hope to survive for very many years.

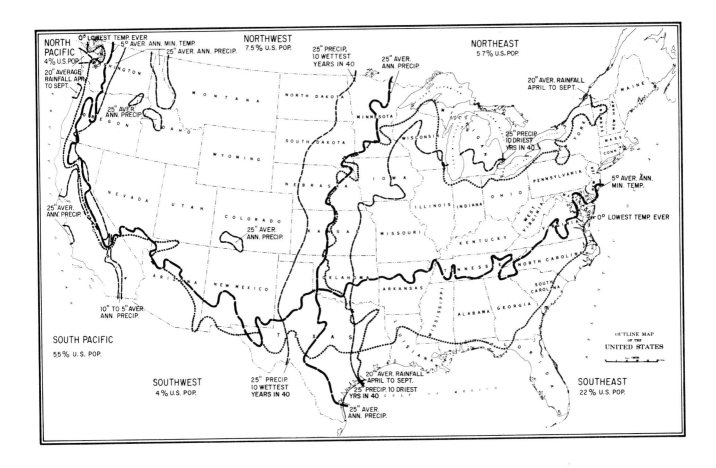

technical and functional demands upon the land. It is a by-product in the sense that most space-forming programs, under pressure from our lingering poetic conscience, recognize the necessity of leaving some (constantly shrinking) space for planting. This grudging acquiescence to a poetic pressure that is tolerated but not understood reduces planting to a minor decorative role, leaving the major space-forming function to structural elements. (Attempts to rationalize planting on technical and functional grounds—erosion control, windbreak, sun control, visual screening, noise reduction, atmospheric purification, climate improvement—are relevant yet incidental to the central question. We do not live by function and technique alone.) Thus we satisfy our economic conscience (the structural elements are more "valuable") and our poetic conscience (we still have some). From this develops the architectonic ego and the mystique of pure structural space formation. And yet the magnificent space-forming qualities of plants are apparent throughout wilderness and rural country areas, and indeed in every potted plant if we will but stoop to look. The still more magnificent space-forming potential of plants and structures working together has been demonstrated in great gardens and parks around the world and throughout history. Now, in the greatest age of affluence we have ever known, we say that we cannot afford the space or the resources which these demand.

In an age which worships technology and money the architectonic

151

ego is ubiquitous and insistent. The more successful the landscape architect, the less time he spends on planting design. Perhaps a quarter of his design time (which may be only a fraction of his total working time) goes to the details of planting. The rest goes to land planning and programming, site planning, abstract design, earthwork, rock, water, and structural design. All of these are important; all of them attest to the landscape architect's expanding importance in the world of environmental design. Yet somehow planting is persistently relegated to a decorative auxiliary role.

In the well-run larger office there will be a planting department, probably run by lady landscape architects, who take over the designs prepared by the gentlemen landscape architects and fill in the plant names. A kind of snobbery develops—great design is pure, abstract, with an inevitable tendency toward structural form, and planting design is secondary, a sentimental artsy-craftsy activity to which the great designers will not stoop. All of this may well be an efficient response to the demands of a society focused on success, technocracy, and minimum maintenance. However, the designer who aspires to art rather than hackwork must know when to lead as well as when to follow his clientele. He is its poetic conscience in the environment. If he abandons that role, he leaves it to horticulturists, garden clubs, conservationists, and park lovers, none of whom understand the problem as well as he should.

There are, of course, still many landscape architects and designers who have not relegated planting design to a minor role, who have not accepted the apparent efficiency of plans and specifications, who persist in arriving on the job with a truckload of plants and a crew of laborers and working out the design on the ground. These people, rarely the big names or the glamorous offices, are maintaining the impractical poetic conscience and the international brotherhood of those who love plants because of their innate fascination, not because of their supporting role in architectonic design or the money that can be made handling them. If we look to Japan, England, and the other great gardening nations of the world, we may find our way back to garden and park design in which plants and space are primary, not relegated to supporting roles for functional and technical programs. In such design the potential result is symbolic expression and experience comparable to that in great painting, sculpture, and music. We might perhaps begin to approach this result by requiring all physical development to leave enough land undeveloped by structure or vehicular surfacing to make possible adequate space-forming (not decorative) planting design.

In such gardens technology will be a tool, not a master. Every garden culture tends to develop rules of gardening which become rigid controls rather than flexible guides. It is in variable relations between the processes of nature and local gardening practice that the great potential of planting design lies. Remember that a weed is a plant in the wrong place. (Robbins, discussing alien plants growing without cultivation in

It's really the trees that tell the story. It's a love story of the kind the popular purveyors of romance don't seem to have heard about yet. It says that life has made a place in sterile barrenness, in which it can thrive long enough to renew itself. One morning I sat in Pearl Tucker's parlor and heard how gracefully the story unfolds.

The winds impart perpetual motion to the trees on the High Plains and to their shade. That morning the shadows of the leaves were flying into the windows of Pearl's parlor like a shower of birds. . . . Her new granddaughter was playing in the parlor . . . . She is amply supplied with toys, but the shadows of the leaves on the carpet attracted her. She kept reaching for them with chubby fingers, while the wind made them slip around like mercury. She'd put her hands down on them and they'd be on top of her hands. That was one fascination. But their most fascinating antic was to quick-slip and dart away whenever the wind stirred. That made her laugh with pure merriment.

If her grandfather had had no other aim in life, this would have been aim enough. In no previous generation had a man here been able to give a child such a rare, strange toy as tree shade. . . . That is progress, as individual human beings recognize it. IRA WOLFERT, discussing man's hundred years' war for survival on the High Plains[129]

In its inception the garden was a retreat. In other countries it might be a place for the cultivation of flowers, a background for pageantry, a setting for entertainment; in China it was essentially an aid to contemplation. The Chinese realized the benign effect of solitude, the exhilaration of far spaces. The garden was grandiose nature reduced to a scale model—not a crass bit of realism, an imperfect imitation, but the evocation of a memory, an emotion made visible. In the Occident, garden design progressed while uncharted nature was still considered menacing; in China the cult of gardens began with an appreciation of the wilds. DOROTHY GRAHAM[130]

California, speaks of naturalized, adventive, and waif aliens, describing degrees of adaptation to wild local conditions.)

One of the basic slogans which has spread the influence of modern garden design in California and elsewhere has been the idea of minimum maintenance. Beginning with efforts to reduce or eliminate the onerous routine of mowing the lawn, this idea has ended as the primary and often the only programmatic request of the owner, with or without professional help. Thus the modern design movement, spurred by the budget consciousness of owners and superintendents both public and private and reinforced by our general technological orientation, has firmly established the principle that gardening is a form of drudgery. Homeowners try to avoid it, either by design or by defaulting on development of their land. Superintendents of larger grounds operate on the principle that the least and most efficient maintenance is the best—which means the cheapest. Gone with the wind of such narrow-minded and lazy rationalization is most of the art and craft of real gardening as an activity which follows, implements, and brings to fruition planting design concepts.

Gardens and parks are areas in which people can have intimate continuous reciprocal relations with plants. Such relations have endlessly subtle and complex ramifications, exemplified by the great gardening cultures of Japan, England, and some other countries. The experience of living and working with plants of all sorts—propagating, planting, feeding, watering, spraying, pruning, cultivating, training—brings rewards which are well known to the worldwide brotherhood of plant lovers and horticulturists. Planting design which ignores this or minimizes it, using plants as abstract static design elements and maintenance as a necessary evil to be avoided, thereby ignores or minimizes one of the great potentials for outdoor experience and for countering the sterilizing and brutalizing pressures of urban life.

Gardeners have been converted to outdoor janitors whose job is to keep the grounds neat and clean for the least possible cost. They are on the lowest rung of the ladder, analogous to agricultural labor, insofar as economic returns are concerned. Little wonder that they know little or nothing of the real art and craft of gardening, that they become petty entrepreneurs intent on doing as little as possible for as much money as possible. Little wonder that gardening is considered maintenance labor rather than professional skill, that there are few schools and little dignity connected with it. Yet it is one of the most sensitive and demanding of human skills, ultimately impossible to completely rationalize, mechanize, or technicalize. In the best gardening thinking and feeling, manual skill and abstract imagination, go hand in hand, merged perhaps more closely than in any other activity. When we integrate high-level gardening culture with high-level landscape design processes, we make possible peaks of refinement such as we find in Japan and England. When we divorce gardening from design and downgrade it,

In our lifetime, all of us consume trees and the products that come from trees—wood, with which we build our homes, our furniture, some of our boats and wagons; paper, on which to write; syrup, which we use for food; flowers and leaves to cheer our spirits and decorate our lives; fruits and nuts, which sustain us. And there is, too, the simple living beauty of a tree which gladdens us and makes the earth a garden.

Yes, during our lives we take from the earth and it is right that we replace into the earth that which we have used. By planting trees that may one day serve generations unborn, we are functioning as God wants us to function.

This ground shall remember your being here. Tribes of trees shall descend with your children, to a day when the shade of the oak spreads wider than the shadow of war.

The roots are wise. Trust them. They know how to endure on the earth. Do you as well.

These younglings shall take profits from the sun and return them. They shall be at one with all around them: the mutest worm, the chattiest bird, the tallest biped; and they shall grandly fill their years. Do you as well.

When the tilt of the globe awakens them each spring they shall extol living: they shall put forth blossoms brighter than gold and scatter their riches with abandon, and be no poorer for it. Out of the clouds shall come their chemistry: and in the lash of the storm they will stand firm and grip the harder. Do you as well.

we get the kind of careless, thin, slovenly landscapes that are all too common in these United States, with or without professional plans. Garden and landscape development are part labor and part love. When we eliminate the latter, we sterilize the former. Public landscapes subject to routine, inadequate, and indifferent civil service maintenance and condominiums and retirement communities in which all landscape maintenance is provided by management (leaving the residents nothing to do but swim, play shuffleboard, or perform "arts and crafts") are the result of the general assumption that working with plants is all labor and no love. The ultimate alienation from nature and submission to mindlessness is exemplified by a population which can no longer take an interest in how lawns develop, flowers bloom, fruits form, or shrubs, vines, and trees achieve their most highly developed maturity.

From the point of view of the superintendent of any grounds larger than a private home, it would be difficult to organize a maintenance program in which the residents of the area could participate. But it would not be impossible, and it might be so worked out as to become an asset to the management. Participation in landscape maintenance can be recreational, educational, and therapeutic if properly organized and led. Residents of housing developments, students in educational institutions, and employees in enterprises with large grounds could all develop a sense of equity, of participation, of accomplishment, that might help to offset some of the normal management problems. The basic search for answers to social problems such as crime, delinquency, apathy, alienation, indifference, boredom, pessimism, and hostility might be helped by something as simple as participation in the maintenance of a well-designed and ongoing environment.

The trees shall remember your being here: the seed of its seed shall descend with your own to the day when the shade of the oak spreads wider than the shadow of war.

Here beyond the rumor and the clamour of the city unhurried roots will pry in clay and sunder rock: constellations of fruits will be planned in secret chambers silently, and every leaf and needle negotiate with the near star for growth and green. Here time is jewelled. What news there is, is of such making as the slow explosion of the seed; as wings released from chrysalis; items in the patient almanac of bud and cycle; rhythms of the zodiac; the sweet sensescence of autumn. Where better can you have made footprints than on this hill? How better than by planting, emulate the Lord? Each tree is trustee of the Mystery, and we the trustee of the tree. NORMAN CORWIN[131]

Plants supplement and expand structural space organization.

For two decades, the duration of *Rip Van Winkle's nap*, The American Forestry Association has been locating the largest living specimens of the various species of native American trees. The prime purposes of the campaign are to stimulate greater appreciation of trees, to establish a natural library of reference material and, through co-operation of the owners, to protect and preserve these monarchs to the end of their natural lives as cherished landmarks and as sources of seed to perpetuate the great size of their species.

. . . The list now comprises 355 National Champions. Seventy sovereigns have been dethroned by discovery of larger specimens. Thirty-three previously unreported species and varieties have been added. Nominators reported three trees destroyed. These were the Indiana American elder, a Plains poplar (cottonwood) in Wyoming, and the Missouri Palmer linden. These species have not been replaced in the list.

Forty-two states and the district of Columbia are growers of champion trees. Sharing the dubious distinction of fostering no trees of champion size are Iowa, Minnesota, New Hampshire, North Dakota, Rhode Island, West Virginia, and the two new states of Alaska and Hawaii. Perhaps some of their distinctive species have not been thoroughly explored.

The state of California leads with 41 monarchs. Maryland reports 38. Illinois claims 32 of the biggest trees, Michigan 31, Oregon 27, Missouri 24, Tennessee 19, Washington 14, Ohio 11, Pennsylvania and Indiana 10 each.

California's Giant Sequoia (the so-called General Sherman tree) remains the largest of all, with a girth of 101 feet 6 inches (base measurement). The smallest tree to wear the victory crown is a Highbush Blueberry, *Vaccinium corymbosum*. This little champ has a circumference of 3¾ inches at breast height, and is but 13 feet tall.

The tallest tree on record is a redwood in Humboldt County, California, extending skyward to 368 feet 7 inches. This towering specimen was discovered and measured by the forest engineering class of Humboldt State College, Arcata, California in 1956.

The bristlecone pine has replaced the redwood as the oldest living tree in the world. The oldest bristlecone sampled has been determined to be in excess of 4600 years, while the oldest known redwoods, including the giant General Sherman, have been "clocked" to be about 3500 years old. The bristlecone pine reported here is known as the "Patriarch," and is believed to be about 1500 years old. DOROTHY DIXON[132]

Total
Landscape

WESTERN REGIONAL MAP

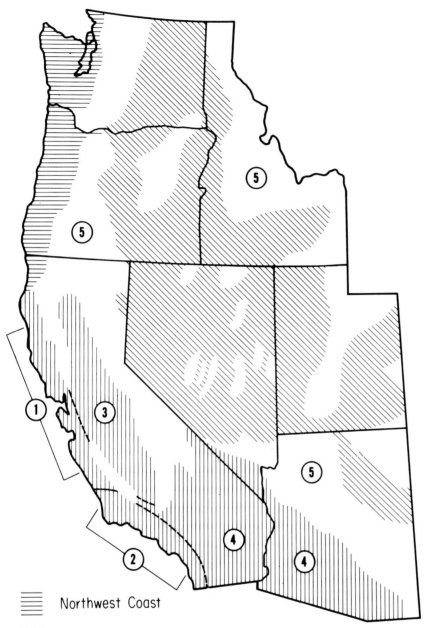

≡ Northwest Coast

||||| Southwest

⧄ Northwest Interior

① North Coast

② South Coast

③ Central Valley

④ Interior Desert

⑤ Mountains

A regional map of gardening conditions represents an ecological analysis in which climate is most important. People too could benefit from such careful analysis of their environments.

CHAPTER 12
Regionalism

The old-fashioned term "regionalism" is enjoying a new fling in the world of planning fashions. Popular during the New Deal thirties, it faded during the war forties and the Fair Deal fifties. The New Frontier and Great Society sixties seem to have brought it back. As architects and engineers have become planners, planners have become city, regional, county, state, and national planners. Landscape architects, endeavoring like all design professionals to expand the boundaries of theory and practice, are tending to deepen their concepts in terms of human experience and to broaden them to the scale of regional landscape. These two directions are not mutually exclusive. Rather they are complementary and mutually indispensable. The depth will keep the regional approach from becoming pompous and bureaucratic. The breadth will keep the human approach from becoming precious and self-conscious.

There are all sorts of regions for all sorts of purposes—political, economic, social, natural; geographic, geologic, anthropological, topographical, hydrologic, biologic; productive, distributive, communicative; work, education, recreation, culture; regions for daily living and for the exercise of power. One specialist's region is irrelevant to another. One man's region is too small for another and too large for a third. But there is a region for everyone. That, for the average citizen, is perhaps the area he is apt to experience in a year of ordinary weeks and weekends. For special purposes regions are a compound of centers and boundaries. Centers are foci of interest or importance for the purpose. Boundaries are apt to be fuzzy or arbitrary, measuring either the actual scope of the purpose or its ambition and reach for power. Physical boundaries are real, as coastline, river, mountain range, desert, or swamp. Political-social boundaries are abstractions, imposed on the physical structure for objective or subjective reasons. They may represent the expansive limits of a self-sufficient force, the confrontation of expanding competitive forces, or a division of a larger area for administrative efficiency, convenient control, rational planning, or creative design.

Landscape regions must combine physical-climatic structure and social scope, adjusted to existing political-economic patterns. Typically they will center on urban or metropolitan concentrations and will include their suburban, rural, or primeval hinterlands to an extent determined partly by the location and size of other centers, partly by topography and water features, and partly by the travel and communication potential from the center. The *regional landscape* is an integral part of the world we live in, as it is perceived and recorded by each individual human being and colored by his individual pattern of background and experience and his subsequent communication in a group.

The earth is a sphere, of rock and soil and water, surrounded by a blanket of air. The surface of this sphere is the total landscape. Every schoolchild now perceives and records this in geography classes in a highly academic and diagrammatic way. However, the connection between this total landscape of the geography lessons and the actual landscape in which he lives has to be learned over the years by a combination of direct physical experience and intellectual abstraction. The total landscape of geography is two-dimensional, compounded of colored maps and statistics. The actual landscape in which we live is, for every individual, a composite of everything he sees, feels, hears, or smells during his waking hours. Thus the landscape of a poor uneducated peasant in a backward country may be limited to a few farms and the nearest village, while the landscape of a successful citizen of a major developed country may in truth be the whole world in this age of the jet plane. On the other hand, the poor peasant may have an intimate integration with, and real sensitivity to, his surroundings, while the sophisticated globe-trotter may see all and understand or feel little or nothing.

The landscape is divided according to the patterns in which people move. There are two kinds of patterns: first, the daily or weekly routes from home to work, recreation, and services, which are repeated regularly in the lives of all of us; second, the special occasional routes of vacations, migrations, travel, going away to school or a job, etc., which

Our technology, cities and landscapes are now producing such negative conditions that the adequacy of our understanding of nature and man is becoming a critical daily question in planning offices. . . .

. . . the origin of some fundamental man-nature problems underlying present events [lies in] the emptying out and abstraction of our experience of nature and ourselves; the excessive transfer of physical science concepts into environmental and social studies; the fragmentation of our conceptual world; the vast estrangement between man and nature; and the loss of a sense of scale, form, and proportion which we are experiencing today. . . .

Our recent "Age of Analysis," however, has never focused upon form—this meaningful, symbolic aspect of reality. We have focused upon taking things apart, destroying the form and analyzing smaller and smaller parts of wholes. . . .

In our emphasis upon producing and consuming we have now acceded to viewing nature and ourselves almost entirely in terms of exchange value—as economic commodities. . . .

Such thought habits, even if metaphorical, have created the impression

Special features of the local scenes remain with the local residents.

that in relationship to technological change and urbanism we are somewhat helpless because we are dealing with something like the relentless, impersonal, and autonomous forces of nature. This is hardly the case. Human ideas create technologies, settlement patterns, and human problems—not forces of extra-human nature. . . .

There is the problem of scale of metropolitan or urban development in relationship to the natural environment. Every localized area or region has limited environmental capacities. . . .

. . . the problem of scale of urban development in relation to economics or costs. Many larger older metropolitan areas have already reached the point of diminishing return. . . .

. . . the problem of scale of metropolitan development in relation to human scale and what should be one of our primary conservation values—the conservation and development of human freedom. . . .

The first environmental planning programs had their origins in the city. This resulted in a deep preoccupation with urban planning and values. . . . Natural elements—land, water, space and the sustaining larger environment—have not come into full focus as important basic elements in our emerging landscapes. Consequently, functions such as regional water resources, stream pollution, land treatment needs, agricultural problems, open spaces, flood plain protection, regional landscape design, recreational facilities, forest preserves, sewerage disposal problems, ecological and biological needs receive inadequate consideration in most metropolitan programs. SANFORD S. FARNESS[133]

occur in the lives of many but not all of us. The regular routes are the most important, because they are the most constant in our lives and because they account for most of the area of our developed landscapes. The senses tend to become dulled or numbed by regular experiences, especially if they are bad, shoddy, or sterile as so many of our ordinary landscapes are. The special routes may rescue us from this dullness, brighten and refresh our lives, broaden and deepen our vision and insight. The eyes of the traveler may see the same scenes as those of the local resident, but the reactions and impressions recorded in the two brains are almost bound to differ.

The divisions in the landscape, in spite of the power of the airplane, are still primarily the major divisions of the natural world—first oceans, then inland seas, large lakes and rivers, deserts, swamps, mountains and hills, forests and jungles—in a constantly shrinking order of importance by scale or size. The normal living paths of people tend to be those of least physical resistance wherever possible. For most people, the primary impact of the airplane has been upon secondary, or special, travel patterns, rather than upon primary, or regular, patterns. Differences in life in narrow mountain valleys and great plains, on the shores of lakes and rivers, in deserts and forests, have been analyzed for us by anthropologists studying primitive isolated-community patterns. Although twentieth-century civilization has tended to break down such divisions and equalize all community living patterns, the special features of the local scenes remain with the local residents.

These natural divisions in the landscape are produced by two sets of interrelated forces. These are called by geologists the "constructive," those giant forces within the earth which cause its crust to shift, mountains to rise, plains to subside, oceans to roll in or out; and the "destructive," the weathering forces of the climate which are constantly at work upon all the surface of the earth, old or new, eroding it at higher levels, stabilizing it at lower levels, promoting or inhibiting vegetation and consequently animal and human life. The "constructive" forces move so slowly (except for an occasional earthquake or volcanic eruption) as to make little impact upon the landscape consciousness of the ordinary citizen. But the "destructive" forces of the climate are with us all of the time, forming perhaps the single most important topic of conversation for the human race. Weather happens every day; climate is a generalization of its annual pattern. The climatic patterns of the world, which are responsible for all the detail of topography, water features, rock forms, and vegetation, form landscape units or divisions with them.

The primary climatic division is, of course, the division between day and night which establishes the basic rhythm of our lives. It varies with season and latitude. The landscape by night is entirely different from that by day. Daily and annual spreads in heat and cold, wetness and dryness, brightness and dullness, and air movement and stillness are as responsible for landscape quality as any other natural features.

Following the landscape divisions created by climate, topography, water, and vegetation are those created by man. These are primarily (insofar as their physical results are concerned) divisions of density of occupancy of land by people and coverage by construction. Thus we have the *urban,* in which most of the natural landscape is obliterated by a coverage of buildings and streets; the *suburban,* in which this structural cover remains thin enough for a good deal of topography, vegetation, and/or water to remain in evidence; the *rural,* in which construction remains minimal but the natural landscape is more or less completely changed by agricultural operations; and the *primeval,* in which some works of man—a resort, a mine, a lumber camp—are placed in direct isolated contrast with the wild natural landscape. In the old days the distinctions between urban, rural, and primeval were sharp and clearly defined. The suburban (and exurban) is a product of twentieth-century technology in transportation, communication, and construction. It has become a means for destroying the boundaries between the other three and also for destroying those rural or primeval areas to which it spreads.

In addition to the natural and man-made divisions in the landscape—still primarily geographic divisions—we must consider those divisions most apparent to the average citizen in his daily life, social divisions. These again are based upon patterns of movement, daily, weekly, or less often, because the landscape is experienced while following those patterns. The average citizen is part of a community compounded of spaces and facilities for home life, work, recreation, services, and the transport connections between them. For children and young people school takes the place of work; for the housewife or servant work centers in the home. Within such communities there may be neighborhoods which provide all facilities but work. The neighborhood may in effect be a community for housewife and elementary school child, if they do not leave it more than once a week. On the other hand, lucky is the father who can walk to work in his own neighborhood. Neighborhood boundaries are indistinguishable in most communities, but the centers on which they focus—school, church, shopping—can be determined.

Several or many such communities may overlap and run together to form a city or metropolitan area. This, with its surrounding rural or primeval countryside and satellite communities, tends to become a region, with which the citizen has reasonable physical familiarity by virtue of regular or occasional travels through it. This is variable in size and amorphous in boundaries.

There are two additional types of landscape division which provide a conditioning context for regional thinking. These run consistently through the basic horizontal division into primeval, rural, and urban and the suburban scatteration process which is blending all three into one ragged patchwork quilt. They might be called private and public or detailed and general. The private landscape is that which is set aside for certain specific individuals, families, or groups by walls, fences, gates, guards, or the pure distances of private landholdings. Its basic characteristic is that the general public or casual passerby is denied both visual and physical access to it. It and the architecture which relates to it are then designed to suit the particular needs and desires of the particular people who control it. It becomes intimate, detailed, subjective, and special. By contrast the public landscape (including much privately owned land), to which the general public has visual if not physical access, is more impersonal, less carefully detailed, more objective and generalized. This contrast is usually exaggerated—each private landscape tries to be individually different from every other one; the public landscape is careless, slovenly, oversimplified, arbitrary, commercial, or regimented. The fact that this public landscape is a social environment in which we all live together and which expresses our community or region to visitors as well as ourselves seems to have little importance. Likewise the fact that the landscape of each individual is continuous throughout his waking hours, colored by his private background-conditioned glasses no matter where he is, is blurred over by the stress on the private sanctum. Close attention to the actualities of human experience of the world around would tend to reduce this contrast between private and public worlds.

Landscape Regions. By way of example, landscape architects in California work within a macroregion whose boundaries are geographic and climatic rather than political. From the north, it runs roughly from Eureka on the coast and Redding in the Central Valley through San Francisco and Sacramento, Paso Robles and Fresno, Los Angeles and Bakersfield, San Diego and Las Vegas, and Yuma and Phoenix, tapering out through Tucson to Douglas, Arizona. This includes four microregions: the subtropical coast of southern California from San Diego to San Luis Obispo; the interior desert covering most of southern California, the southern tip of Nevada, and the southwestern third of Arizona; the cooler and more humid coast of northern California, centering about San Francisco; and the great, hot, arid but heavily irrigated Central Valley of California. Geographically, but not climatically, it also includes considerable areas of mountains, in the Coast Ranges, the Sierra Nevada, the San Gabriel and San Bernardino ranges, and other mountain ranges.

This region is unified "ornamentally" by a floor on minimum temperatures—about 10 degrees—which permits the dominant planting to be broadleaved evergreens, and by a summer dryness which forces consistent and conscientious artificial watering of most ornamental planting. Of the four subregions, the two on the coast are unified by their exposure to the cooling and moisture-laden ocean breezes. The two in the interior are insulated from those breezes by hills and mountains. Thus the climate in the coastal zones is more uniform and more humid, and that in the interiors is drier and more extreme in both directions. Nevertheless, tender plants will freeze at somewhat higher temperatures on the coast than inland, because of their higher moisture content. The following table is indicative of the unified variety of this region:

163

	Temperature				Growing season, days	Annual precip., in.	Months with under av. 1 in.
	Jan. av.	*July av.*	*Max.*	*Min.*			
Eureka	47.3	56.1	85	20	328	37.58	4
Redding	45.3	82.0	113	17	278	37.54	4
San Francisco	49.8	58.9	101	27	356	20.23	6
Sacramento	45.6	73.9	114	17	307	15.88	6
Paso Robles	46.0	71.2	115	0	205	16.39	7
Fresno	45.5	81.3	115	17	295	9.43	8
Los Angeles	54.2	70.5	109	28	359	14.76	7
Bakersfield	47.0	83.5	118	13	277	6.12	9
San Diego	55.1	67.5	110	25	365	10.11	8
Las Vegas	44.6	86.1	118	8	239	4.84	12
Yuma	54.6	91.0	120	22	348	3.58	12
Phoenix	51.8	90.3	118	16	304	7.62	11
Tucson	49.6	85.1	111	6	245	11.16	8
Douglas	45.3	79.8	111	−7	212	12.78	9

By contrast, the Northwest coast averages 10 degrees colder in winter and from 30 to 60 inches of rain in winter, over 2 inches throughout the summer. The rest of the area of the Western states (see Western Regional Map on page 158) averages below-zero temperatures in winter, 90 to 105 degrees in summer, 10 to 20 inches of rain in the lower desert portions, more in the mountains. The mountains run through central Washington and Oregon to join those of California and through eastern Idaho, central Utah, and northeastern Arizona. The Northern cold-winter deserts and near deserts run through eastern Washington and Oregon, western Idaho, almost all Nevada, western and eastern Utah, and the northeast corner of Arizona. Thus, in addition to our Southwestern region, we might designate the Northwest coast and the interior mountain desert as the other two integral landscape design regions of the arid and coastal West. Similar regional analyses, in terms of climate and ornamental planting, could be made of the semiarid Great Plains, the subhumid Midwest, and the humid East.

Across the United States precipitation ranges from highs of 60 to 80 inches per year to lows of less than 5. Snowfall ranges up to 100 inches per year in the North, from zero in the South; humidity from over 9 percent to less than 20 percent, minimum temperatures from 60 below in the North to over 20 above in the South. Maximum temperatures are consistently high, in the 90s and 100s, except for a few favored spots in the Northwest. Percentages of possible sunshine vary from less than 30 in the North in winter to over 90 in the Southwestern summer. Growing seasons vary from 120 days in the North to 320 or more in the South. Topography varies from the small-scale broken rolling irregularity of the Eastern seaboard through the broad sweep of Midwestern prairies and the giant scale of the Rockies to the moderate scale of the rolling West Coast. Vegetation varies from the forest of the East through tall and short grass in the Midwest to the brush, sagebrush, and highland coniferous forests of the West. It also varies from a limited range of coniferous and deciduous forms in the North to a very wide range of broad-leaved-evergreen and special forms in the South.

Central Asia is arid and semiarid; the Middle East and the Mediterranean are semiarid and subhumid; France and Austria are humid and subhumid; England, Japan, and Korea are humid; China and Brazil are humid and subhumid. England lies between 50 and 60 degrees north latitude, south Brazil between 10 and 30 degrees south latitude; all the others lie between 30 and 50 north latitude. The reader will recall the origins of the Western preindustrial formal-landscape tradition as beginning in Central Asia, running through the Mediterranean (with isolated peaks in the subhumid regions of India, China, and Mexico), and culminating in France and Austria. The tradition spans from arid to humid climates. But it is subdivided. The Moorish version developed in arid and semiarid climates; the Renaissance-Baroque version in subhumid and humid climates. Likewise the peaks of the preindustrial informal landscape tradition were in Japan and England, both mild and humid climates.

In California San Francisco is the focal center of the north coast. Surrounded on three sides by water, it is practically centered on a great gap in the Coast Ranges, which opens up the Central Valley to the sea. In the summer, as the valley heats up and its air rises, cool moisture-laden air is sucked in from the ocean, lowering the temperature and raising the humidity of communities all along its route, far up into the western center of the great valley. All of the San Francisco Bay Region climates are determined by the summer winds and the local topography. There are roughly three temperature zones radiating around the Golden Gate: cool, moderate, and warm. In the first are San Francisco, Sausalito, and Berkeley; in the second are San Mateo, Oakland, Richmond, and Mill Valley; in the third are Palo Alto, Orinda–Walnut Creek, and San Rafael–San Anselmo.

In conjunction with temperature, wind, and humidity, topography shapes and governs the living space of the Bay Region. The communities of the east bay and the west bay string out around the central body of water on the plains and valleys that lie between it and the enclosing hills or are thrust up into them. Immediately around the Golden Gate the hills step down into the water, and the communities cling to their slopes. As we go north and south, valleys and plains open up—the warm and pastoral hollows of Marin County; the long plain of San Mateo and Santa Clara Counties, widening southward into the warm and fruitful Santa Clara Valley, with the peninsula commuter towns snuggled against the east toes of the Coast Range hills, out of the westerly winds. These sweep through a gap at South San Francisco, making it the least livable portion of the region, and cool the whole southerly portion of the east bay. One can trace on a map the long southeasterly line of these coast hills, formed by the San Andreas fault, along which the

west wind feathers out, to the abrupt break making the hollow which keeps Palo Alto warm. Farther south San Jose is a warm inner valley town. On the east bay side the plain between water and hills is wider and more exposed to west winds as one moves south from Oakland. Oakland is somewhat protected by the topography of San Francisco. Behind Oakland, in the Orinda–Walnut Creek area, are numerous small, sheltered, warm valleys among rounded hills—another "dormitory suburb." North of Oakland Richmond spreads over the northern extension of the shore plain, and beyond the north bay towns string out along the narrow shores of San Pablo and Suisun Bays toward the great valley, all in the main path of the wind.

The southern California area prides itself on being one of the fastest-growing in the country—even though a good deal of nostalgia for those smog-free good old days is expressed by those who were there then. The rapid growth in the population and in the construction necessary to house its activities has been met by largely horizontal development. This metropolitan area is the new city, the auto city, the city of tomorrow. The Los Angeles plain and the San Fernando and San Gabriel Valleys house some 7 million people in an area of about 1,500 square miles—an overall density of 4,600 per square mile, 7 persons or 2 families per acre. The United States Census lists densities of 5,451 to 7,498 per square mile for the central cities of Los Angeles and Long Beach,

San Francisco is the heart of one of the richest and most identifiable natural and cultural regions of the world.

with 4,217 for the urban fringes. By contrast, New York–New Jersey ranges from 7,016 to 24,697, with 3,542; Philadelphia has 15,743, with 3,800; Chicago ranges from 4,287 to 15,836, with 3,128; San Francisco–Oakland ranges from 6,935 to 15,553, with 2,809; and Boston has 14,586, with 3,667. The evenness of spread and absence of concentrated nuclei in the Los Angeles–Long Beach area have resulted from single-minded concentration on detached one-family housing, exclusive reliance on private automobiles and massive freeway construction for mass transportation, and widespread decentralization of commercial, industrial, governmental, cultural, and recreational facilities. This thin and even spread has resulted in a massive destruction of meaningful open space (continuous pieces of 100 acres or more). Today Los Angeles–Long Beach has 130 acres of permanent publicly controlled open space per 1,000 persons, compared with highs of 2,850 acres for Ventura and 5,470 for Santa Barbara. The net visual result of the new auto-city concept spread over 1,500 square miles has been a near-total loss of diversity and variety in scale and character of building–open-space relationships, a monotony of aspect that becomes as deadly as smog in such vast continuity. In fact smog, the result of exclusive reliance on gasoline-powered motor vehicles, is only the final touch, eliminating the saving grace of color, in the complete visual sterilization of the landscape. All of this has occurred in one of the most magnificient settings of mountains, plains, hills, valleys, and shorelines in the world.

However, the period of maximum differentiation between Los Angeles and other American cities came to an official end with the termination of the thirteen-story height limitation some years ago. This act recognized that a city can only spread horizontally so far before it must begin to grow vertically as well. Since that day Los Angeles has inexorably moved toward becoming more like other American cities, in spite of continuing emphasis on suburban tract housing and freeway construction. Now buildings of twenty to forty stories are noticeable additions to the skyline, changing the entire scale and aspect of the city. Multifamily-housing-unit starts exceed single-family starts. The pressure for development of a mass transit system continues to grow, in spite of open or passive resistance by industry, government, press, and the Southern California Automobile Club.

Southern California, led by Los Angeles, is rapidly, persistently, and aggressively destroying its only really reliable asset—the physical environment. It is producing the ugliest, most monotonous, most sterile and boring urban complex, but one of vast capacity for absorbing incoming population and generating profit for investors. In order to continue to grow, it must continue to attract both. If present trends continue, they will eventually destroy the image of southern California which is its best attraction for immigrants and investors. It has no other basic assets—no minerals save oil, no export industry because of transportation costs. Urbanization is driving out the agriculture which originally developed southern California. Everything else there has been promoted, developed, and improvised on the basis of environment. Postwar prosperity is based on Federal spending for defense and space programs. These are based on brains, which are attracted by environment. This environment is being destroyed by a persistent refusal to do anything about its quality. There is no agency, public or private, which is concerned in any real way with environment quality. The leaders in local government, business, industry, and press are vastly interested in quantity but rarely in visual quality.

This area is expected to become one of the four major continuous metropolitan belts in the country (the other three being the Atlantic from Boston to Washington, D.C., the Gulf from New Orleans to Houston, and the Great Lakes from Buffalo to Chicago). It extends along the coast from Santa Barbara to San Diego and inland to Bakersfield and Palm Springs. Topographically it is a region of coastal plains backed up by mountain ranges paralleling the coast at varying distances from it. Santa Barbara, Ventura–Oxnard, Los Angeles–Long Beach–Santa Ana, and Oceanside–San Diego are essentially coastal complexes. Mingled with the mountain ranges are various intermediate valleys, with variations between coastal and inland conditions. Ojai, Santa Paula–Fillmore, Moorpark–Simi, the San Fernando Valley, the San Gabriel Valley, and Escondido are typical of these. Completely separated from the coast by mountains and distance are the south side of the Antelope Valley, the Pomona–San Bernardino–Riverside Valley, and the Coachella Valley.

The vision of the continuous southern California metropolis, greeted with joy by some commercial interests and with gloom by urban designers, is not yet a reality. Santa Barbara, Ventura, Bakersfield, San Bernardino, and San Diego are all clearly separated by mountains, farmlands, and military reservations. However, the first is susceptible to bulldozer and carryall, the second to speculation and high taxes, and the third to obsolescence and economy drives. Therefore the vision remains a distinct possibility. The influx of some 1,000 persons per week into the southern regions provides the population pressure which may bring it to fruition if continued.

Urbanization in California has been among the most frantic and careless in the nation. Control efforts by public administrative and planning officials have been able to accomplish little more than a rationalization into a moderately utilitarian pattern. Considerations of scale, community structure, visual experience, urban and landscape quality, and the optimum requirements of good relations between people and their social and physical environment have gone with the wind of hasty and profitable development. Around each urban center, conditioned only by topography and land ownership, the same fragmentary crazy quilt of suburban and exurban development has spread. Open country has been devoured and destroyed at a staggering rate. Tremendous areas of this destruction are not so much by coverage as by contamination. A scattering of houses at one per 1 to 5 acres across tremendous areas of land destroys the landscape visually and functionally, whether it be agricultural, wilder-

LETTER FROM LOS ANGELES

The town is inland from the coast 25 miles. There is no landing for steamers. You are taken off in boats, or in a small steamer when she can get over the breakers, and thence by swift stages, over level roads and through a vast expanse of flat country, unrelieved by a tree or a bush, till you arrive in the suburbs of the town. The town consists principally of two nearly parallel broad streets, with one story squat buildings, relieved at far intervals by a second story. It has many shops and generally an air of business. There are three hotels, of which the Bella Union is the best. . . . The soil is sandy loam, which dries quickly after rain. The town has some charming features. It is snuggled among undulant hills, with a broad opening towards the seaward plain. In winter, the hills wear the richest verdure.

The gardens and the outside lots for two miles around are forever green, by reason of summer water supplied by the Town Council to every cultivator. Vineyards cover a very extended area, all on flat land. The peculiar features are the graceful pepper-tree, giving evergreen shade and picturesque beauty to the highways, and the rich groves of lemon and orange trees. . . .

Los Angeles will soon extend its buildings over the undulant hills that wave in green beauty close by: then, dotted with cottages and ever flowing gardens, and adorned with groves of lemon and orange, with vineyards and stately palms, we cannot imagine a city of more fairy-like enchantment. . . .

The springtime is now here. On February 8, 1869, the almond tree is all in flower; oranges and lemons, still full of rich fruitage, are sending out new leaves and new flowers and fragrance for another rich harvest. . . . The air is all melody with the music of innumer-

ness, or desert. The land parcels are too large to garden and too small to farm, either on the desert or the more salubrious coast. Nature, in southern California, does little to heal the scars of neglect after hasty and careless development. The result is and will be many square miles of exurban wasteland, not urban, not rural, not wild, not open, not desert. These might be called the gray areas of the urban fringe, analogous to the gray areas around older urban centers in their ambivalence, mediocrity, actual or potential blight, and social and landscape destructiveness. They constitute a new and special area for study. Suburban areas can be urbanized (in the good sense), nonurban areas can become open-space reserves and surrounds, but these exurban sprawls are neither. Perhaps careful and specific redesign could develop regrouping and meaningful structure–open-space relations. Ultimately these will be problems in exurban renewal and redevelopment. They may, of course, by resubdividing and zone changes, move up (or down) the ladder of suburban and urban development.[105]

San Francisco and Los Angeles are not comparable entities. The former is a city of some 800,000 on a 45-square-mile peninsula between bay, Golden Gate, and ocean. The latter is a metropolis of some 2,500,000 in 450 square miles spread across the Santa Monica Mountains and the plains around them. However, each dominates a region of approximately comparable size and population. The populations are in the neighborhood of 5 to 6 million and growing fast. (Los Angeles is growing faster.) San Francisco is the clearly defined physical core of a collection of nine separate counties fringing the bay and housing some unruly and aggressive satellites—Oakland, Richmond, San Jose. The Los Angeles basin is split between two counties, and the fragments of the city which form the true core might be considered as the downtown and Westlake areas and the strip development along Wilshire Boulevard. San Francisco is surrounded by satellites; Los Angeles surrounds its satellites like an amoeba.

The Los Angeles urban area occupies a plain about 35 miles square, sloping gently from north to south, bounded by mountains to the north, hills to the east, and ocean south and west, dotted with a few isolated blocks of hills. Through a gap in the center of the north boundary, above the downtown area, it extends into the San Fernando Valley northwest and the San Gabriel Valley northeast, both in turn rimmed by hills and mountains. Urban development covers the greater portion of the plains and valley floors and begins to invade the hills and mountains.

The San Francisco urban area centers on a large bay surrounded by hills and low mountains which are separated from the water by sloping plains and tidal flats. These are narrow to the north and west and wide to the south and east. Urban development has covered the plains and more rounded hills in the center, and is spreading to rougher hills and level areas farther away. The bay opens to the ocean west through the famed Golden Gate and to the Central Valley through

Carquinez Strait northeast; to the south the bay merges imperceptibly through tidal marshes into the broad Santa Clara Valley.

Los Angeles is a land city although rimmed by beaches and small harbors. The Bay Region is oriented toward and around the water which covers most of its center, even though its beaches are few, bracing, and lacking in the balmy qualities of the south. The Bay Region landscape is intimate, detailed, and picturesque and refreshing wherever (as in San Francisco, Marin County, and Berkeley) topography and water have resisted suburban sprawl. Wherever the land levels out between hills and water or the hills are gentle enough not to resist rape by developer, sprawl has taken over. It is comparable in spirit and aspect, but not in overall scale, to that which covers the south. The question of scale is critical. One can perhaps tolerate sprawl when it is broken up into comprehensible units by hills and water. When it expands to cover without relief an area 35 miles square, such as the Los Angeles basin, it becomes monstrous, frustrating, sterilizing, and exhausting.

The Los Angeles area was a magnificent site for a potentially great city. Inadequate discipline by either nature or man has caused failure to achieve this opportunity and the resultant mess. The topography is large and simple, and there are no internal water bodies. The San Francisco area topography is smaller-scale, less spectacular though more picturesque. Water and topography combine to force more discipline on development, so that the results are not yet too bad. However, it is remarkable how little access most residents of this water-oriented region have to the water. By contrast Los Angeles, a land-oriented city, has ample access to beaches west and south.

Climate north and south, even though within the highly touted mild California limits, is nevertheless sufficiently different to create different living patterns and different approaches to design. The climate in both regions is conditioned by wind and topography. Offshore breezes bring coolness and humidity except where blocked by hills and mountains. Thus to be warm one moves to the leeward side of the hills; to be cool one moves windward. But warm is warmer longer in the south, and cool is cooler longer in the north. The north is humid, and the south is semiarid. Locations comparable in relationship to ocean, wind, and topography will average 10 degrees higher temperature and 10 inches less precipitation in the south. Humidity is often well below 50 percent in the south, usually well above that figure in the north. One cannot sit outdoors without heat after sunset on the ocean side of hills anywhere south or north. But a much larger percentage of the Los Angeles Region is sheltered by substantial hills and mountains—for instance, all of the San Fernando and San Gabriel Valleys. In the south, at the beach as well as inland, there is a surplus of light, heat, and glare for a large part of the year. Every building needs complete surrounding by a belt of filtering, shading, and diffusing elements—trees or structures. Few have them—such is the nature of cosmopolitan design. In the north the surplus elements are wind and fog. The climate is more moderate, more temperate, less extreme. Problems in the south have to do with heat and drought; those in the north have to do with coolness and humidity.

Of course the unity of California is emphasized by the fact that heat and drought are problems at some seasons in some parts of the north, and vice versa in the south. The total range of climate is about the same, but the north is never as hot and dry as the south, nor is the south ever as cool and humid as the north—in their more extreme portions.

The same forces of exploitation and speculation are at work in both regions and tend increasingly to make them alike. Around San Francisco Bay almost every community views its offshore tidelands as areas for possible fill and development. Alameda has already taken a major ugly step in this direction, destroying the beaches on which I spent my boyhood. If the bay could be filled with soil, the region would be indistinguishable from Los Angeles in ten years.

It is the topography of nature, rather than the hand of man, that has given the Bay Region its peculiar charm. This fortunate and delightful small-scale irregularity, set off against the broad sweep of water, is most hospitable to human habitation and most difficult to destroy, although an excellent and energetic start has been made. San Francisco, the only city of Eastern or European density on the West Coast, has a picturesque and dramatic fascination which seems to result from the completely irrational application of a gridiron street pattern to its rugged hills. It is a moot point whether a city designed rationally to fit the contours would have developed comparable character. The justly famed charm of San Francisco is largely concentrated in its northern half; the south side is as dreary and ugly a row-house city as one can find. New commercial row housing in San Francisco has a peculiarly determined and competent ugliness that is hard to beat.

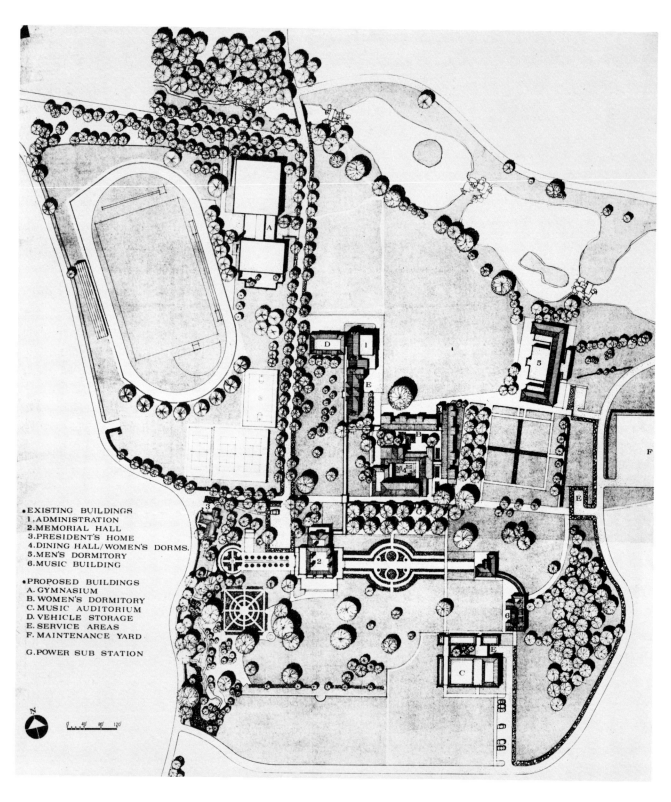

● EXISTING BUILDINGS
1. ADMINISTRATION
2. MEMORIAL HALL
3. PRESIDENT'S HOME
4. DINING HALL / WOMEN'S DORMS.
5. MEN'S DORMITORY
6. MUSIC BUILDING

● PROPOSED BUILDINGS
A. GYMNASIUM
B. WOMEN'S DORMITORY
C. MUSIC AUDITORIUM
D. VEHICLE STORAGE
E. SERVICE AREAS
F. MAINTENANCE YARD

G. POWER SUB STATION

N

0   40'   80'   120'

In the long-cultivated landscape of England, plans for new campus development must reflect the new demands of the program and the subtle legacy of history and nature.

CHAPTER 13
Total Landscape

The landscape is an endless *continuity* of experience, a continuous network of reciprocal relations between structures, open space, and nature. This is no doubt true for geographers, travel agents, policemen, bus drivers, and who else? Is it true for architects, landscape architects, engineers, city planners, doctors, lawyers, Indian chiefs, and the average citizen?

By objective physical survey the landscape is no doubt such a continuous network of relations, a lifelong experience limited only by vision and motion. Quantitatively the landscape is total; it includes everything we see wherever we are. Qualitatively, however, is a different matter. We see? Who sees? Quality does not reside in the scene, nor does it reside in the observer. It resides precisely in the relationship which exists at a given time between the two. This is the design problem for all who are concerned with the quality of the landscape.

The physical landscape is objectively the same at one time and place whether it is being viewed by one person, four thousand persons, or three iguanas. But subjectively it is different for each observer—a little different for each member of a homogeneous group, as each middle-class American, quite different for members of different groups, as middle-class Americans and African Bushmen. These subjective differences stem from the fact that people are all different (even though they are all alike). They are born of different parents with different sets of genes, in different places, and they grow up and live in different environments. They tend to be similar or different as their heritage and environment are similar or different. In the brave new world heritage, environment, and reaction will be controlled and predictable. Until then we will have to stumble along with the present exasperating unpredictability. One man's meat is another's poison; one man's beautiful modern house is another's chicken coop.

Professional discipline introduces a new dimension to the variability of human reaction to the landscape. Specially focused points of view develop and are consistently refined. The architect is focused on the aesthetics of structure, the engineer on practical technology, the land-

The better landscapes of England are products of continuous cooperation between man and nature.

scape architect on open space and nature, the city planner on land use, circulation, and economics. Each sees the landscape in a somewhat distorted mirror. He who could combine all four points of view in objective balance would be a superman. And yet somehow we must combine all of these viewpoints, and many more, if we are to save our landscape from total automated ruin.

The vehicle for this combination is the mind and body and faculties and perceptions of the average citizen, our client who is the majority inhabitant of this landscape. Since the landscape must be designed area by area, *in toto* for each area, the majority of the citizens of each area at the time of its design will be our clients. This can be good or bad; we have only to shift focus to convert a majority to a minority, or vice versa. Design too can be gerrymandered.

The landscape must be designed *in toto,* area by area, precisely because its quality is a direct result of the total combination of all elements seen from a given point or circulation pattern. The good building, garden, auto, sign, or lamppost is lost when surrounded by mediocrity and confusion. But we have no designers who are adequately prepared for this total responsibility. We have some individuals who can give it a good try, and we have some groups who can approximate the need by teamwork. But this is not the same thing as having an organized and conscious approach to the development of designers able to cope with the environment as a whole whatever the nature of its component elements may be. The architect's focus on structure renders him unable to evaluate open space properly; the engineer's focus on technology renders him unable to evaluate human needs properly; the landscape architect's focus on open space renders him unable to evaluate buildings properly; the city planner's focus on quantitative generalities renders him unable to evaluate qualitative particulars properly. Well-known ex-

174

ceptions exist in all fields, but general experience confirms the truth of these generalities.[81]

The average citizen is the appropriate vehicle for the development of a theory and practice of complete environmental design. By putting ourselves in his or her skin, seeing the world as he or she sees it, or *might* see it if properly informed and guided, we may be able to escape from our private world of professional preconceptions into the broad real world of free inspiration and conception. This does not mean that we must abandon our private aesthetic, our private inspiration, or "stoop to the common level." It does mean that by establishing reciprocal relations between our private sources and the real (continuous) problems of the environment, we set in motion processes which will bring out the greatest potential in both.

When we design in continuity, we do not view a piece of land as a base for a building which is an *objet d'art*, with landscaping as a decorative frill around it. Rather, we view that piece of land as a center for the development of a nucleus of indoor-outdoor space and material relations. Nor do these relations stop at the property lines, except in the rare case where the site is larger than the demands of the problem. Each such nucleus is unavoidably involved with other nuclei next door, to the rear, and across the street. Together, willy-nilly, with or without conscious consideration, they grow into cellular and molecular structures or accumulate in blocks, neighborhoods, communities, and regions.

We do not view engineering technology as an institution to which individual problems and society as a whole must adjust. Rather, we view it as the means, for which man has searched for thousands of years, for release from poverty, drudgery, isolation, and bigotry. We did not invent the machine in order to become its slave or the servant of those who own and control it.

We do not view open-space and landscape development as competing with structures or as being the only salvation for the automatic ugliness of construction. Rather, we view them as the essential supplement and complement of all buildings, something demanded by each structure itself through the technical, functional, and visual forces which it extrudes. This is not to say that all such relations become one-to-one or that we cease to understand and appreciate great buildings or urban complexes, great gardens or parks, or great rural or natural scenes. It does mean that we integrate all of them in an environmental complex which maximizes their quality, which does not lose them in a sea of confusion, mediocrity, and blight.

We do not view the master planning of land use and circulation or the study of local or national economics as automatically leading to the good environment. Rather, we view them as essential prerequisites which may make it possible to find the good environment. Planning which does not have this objective clearly in mind can quite easily become an obstacle to this search, and may even render it impossible. Traffic planning for its own sake (the tail wagging the dog), obtuse and rigid zoning by type of building and category of use, adjustments in plan and zoning related to the amount of political pressure applied— all tend to divert planning from the pursuit of quality in the environment to the rationalization of its exploitation. What we need, then, is to consider traffic and transportation as having origins and destinations which are subject to planning; to make zoning into a tool for area-wide design control via density and coverage limitations and flexible design-approval procedures oriented toward quality rather than expediency; and to see to it that the implementation and administration of master plans and zoning ordinances are based on professional competence and community decency rather than political expediency and mutual backscratching. This is easier to say than to do, but the possibilities are improving constantly.

What will we do if and when it becomes possible to attack the problems of the environment on the basis of balance, integration, and continuity? We shall not know until that day. But we can hope for certain things: for continuous consistent design concentration all the way from the regional plan to the precise detail of every building and open space physically or visually accessible to the general public; for a concept of the building–open-space relationship as the heart of one design problem rather than the by-product of the conflict between two; for an approach to the auto-pedestrian relationship in which the environment of the latter receives at least as much emphasis as that of the former and in which the transition between the two becomes a recognized design problem; and for a focus on pedestrian access between building and building and between building and open space which works toward minimum intervention by the auto—or even by mass transit systems.

Collaboration. Design solutions today are complicated and frustrated by the multiplicity of design fields and their lack of adjustment to the true areas and boundaries of the problems which they purport to solve. Spaces within buildings are single design problems which are attacked by a multitude of decorators, artists, furniture designers, lighting consultants, weavers, ceramicists, kitchen and bathroom consultants, and so on. Parcels of real estate are single design problems which are attacked by architects, engineers, and landscape architects or by their commercial or amateur equivalents. Neighborhoods, communities, regions, and other geographic or topographical units are single design problems which are attacked by the entire complex of social forces and processes that use the land on a competitive basis, within the framework of master plans, zoning ordinances, and subdivision controls.

This brings us back to the coordination of the professions. Teamwork on small jobs today is training for teamwork on big jobs tomorrow. Problems of relations between professions are parallel to those of relations between groups of people on a national scale and between nations on a world scale with which we are preoccupied today. The parallelism lies in the choice between pursuing narrow self-interest in blind competition and pursuing broad self-interest in enlightened cooperation. It is not so much a question of collaboration or competition as of how to have both together, and what kind of each. Collaboration between architecture and landscape architecture is inherent in every land development problem in which buildings do not cover 100 percent of the site. Collaboration between architecture and interior design is inherent in every building problem. Yet how often does it take place? How often is the building left with loose technical, functional, and even aesthetic ends trailing, left for the owner to patch up? What are the limitations on collaboration?

1. Owner's option: This is subject to his economic resources, desires, prejudices, social pressures, quirks, and whims.

2. Proximity: It is easier to collaborate with a designer whose office is next door than with one in the next block, city, or state.

3. Compatibility: Collaborators must like and respect each other, and there must be a spirit of mutual give-and-take. A prima-donna approach on the part of either will make collaboration difficult or impossible, as will the assumption by one designer that he knows as much about the other's area as his collaborator, or more. This is complicated by the fact that on most jobs the building is the most important part of the project. This makes the architect the principal designer, and it is natural for him to assume that he must coordinate all design in the interest of unity. From here it is only a small step to the unconscious arrogance which assumes that the principal designer is really the only designer on the job. The boundary between coordination and coercion may be difficult to recognize. Sometimes this is complicated by a fear that the landscape or the interior may be overdesigned and may compete with the building or be out of harmony with it. The definition of over-design is, of course, the prerogative of the principal designer. If architect, landscape architect, and interior designer view the building with entirely different eyes, compatibility may be impossible and collaboration a waste of time. On the other hand, unanimity may sterilize compatibility. It will certainly bring boredom to design. Collaborators must bring fresh thoughts and new visions to the job. Vitality and richness in design result from the effort to resolve contradictory ideas and approaches. There are no simple answers to such questions from either side. The only final criterion is the final quality of the entire site development. If each designer concentrates on this with sufficient mutual consideration and tact, the detailed problems can be worked out.

4. Competition: This must have an objective and a reason for existence. Competition on an equal, friendly basis for quality in design concepts and their detailed development on paper and in reality is healthy, constructive, and essential to cultural growth. Competition on an unequal or unfriendly basis, conditioned by social or professional position and prestige, economic rewards and resources, personal vanity, prejudice, charm, or contacts, is unhealthy and destructive of the processes of individual development and group work which are essential to cultural growth. Competition is a game which is played within rules or customs

which are written or developed by people. This game may be constructive or destructive—witness the relations between amateur and professional sports—but the choice is ours. We establish the rules and we can change them. Competition is not a law of nature.

At this point a letter which I wrote in September, 1964, to the editor of *Arts & Architecture* may help to expand the discussion:

Your quotations from Messrs. Damaz and Orsini on the relations between architecture and "the arts" (painting, sculpture, mosaic, murals) represent a constructive contribution to a pregnant discussion. Mr. Damaz says artists and architects "should" get together and collaborate. This is a righteous and praiseworthy principle which has been accepted in theory for some time now. Mr. Orsini says it is not so easy—that collaboration is apt to mean the loss of the artist's identity, fundamental expressive power, his conversion to a decorator status. He says further that "successful integration of these arts can only come from their being considered as one totality. . . . painting, sculpture, and architecture as we know them, become transformed in unity and become a new art-form, a new unity of expression." This is a much more realistic and subtle statement of the situation than Mr. Damaz' over-simplified and idealistic notion that their separate compositions can become integrated if artist and architect come to understand and respect one another.

Landscape architects are very familiar with the problems and potentialities of collaboration with architects. We have had a great deal of experience, and much excellent work has been done. Nevertheless, we have not progressed much beyond the stage of mutual respect and understanding between various individuals. As a counterforce to these modest efforts we have recent pronouncements by leaders of the architectural profession to the effect that architecture covers total environmental design, that all other design efforts are subsidiary to it and should be coordinated or controlled by it. Recent proliferation of signs saying "Planning, Architecture, Engineering" (with landscape, graphics, and other arts in the back room) are the practical expression of this policy. We seem to be getting back to architecture as the mother of the arts—or, perhaps, the shrewish and determined stepmother. How much of this policy derives from practical problems of practice, how much from economics, esthetics, ambition or the search for status or power, would be difficult to determine.

There are two ways to consider this situation. One, most common and normal, is from the points of view of the various arts as they exist, each as a vested interest with a special point of view, a special concept of expression, encased within a more or less rigid and legally buttressed set of boundaries. This seems to be industrial society's development from the free and flexible interaction among the arts common to handicraft cultures. Here we are forced to take a tour through a series of established preconceived points of view, each with its own set of blinders and specially tinted spectacles. We become involved in the power structure of the design world, in which architecture and engineering compete for top honors (they deal with central problems, spend the most money), planning remains an aloof Big Brother, and the other arts scramble for lower positions. We must also recognize that within each art there is a strong creative core carrying forward the powerful expressive and constructive desires of human culture. Important work is being done by a strong minority within each field. We must further recognize that the need for collaboration among the arts is widely recognized among them, and that there is a widespread willingness to work together. This runs head on into the determination of each art to maintain its own identity and integrity, derived from its history, education, organization and legal status, and security problems. Painting and sculpture, in Mr. Orsini's words, "search for significant form." Architecture, based on "function and social responsibility," works with the central structural shelter problems of society, and derives from that experience theories of total environmental design that become more credible as urbanization increases. Engineering, based on technological necessity, remains secure in an increasingly technological environment. Planning, concerned with large questions of land use and circulation, becomes a theoretically coordinating umbrella over the turmoil of the lesser arts. Landscape architecture, concerned with land planning, site planning, open space design and the use and arrangement of natural materials—earth, rock, water, plants—and minor structures, finds itself increasingly overlapping, and at times competing with architecture and engineering. Open space, in our times, is not the great central spine or core of urban design as it was in the Renaissance tradition. Rather, it is a more or less accidental byproduct of the relations between land subdivision and construction of all types. Organized park and school programs, and the efforts of dedicated conservationists, planners, architects, and other designers to preserve or develop open space, run counter to this general social attitude. The fate of landscape architecture as a meaningful design profession is tied to the growth or shrinkage of open space. Without that, it becomes mere exterior decoration.

The alternate way to view the relations between the various fields of art and design is from outside them all, from society at large, in terms of what their activities mean to the citizen, whether "average" or "enlightened" in cultural matters. Here we have a problem. The citizen who does not participate in art or design production rarely knows enough about them to comment intelligently—although he very likely knows what he "likes." The artist or designer, on the other hand, finds it difficult to escape from the special position we have described. Nevertheless, we must try.

The citizen—all citizens—lives within a landscape which is a result of continuous interaction between the processes of nature and a constant stream of physical development decisions made by other citizens. This landscape is one experience in space at any given time for each citizen, regardless of its components. It is also continuous in time throughout his life, regardless of the extent of his or her movements in space. Thus, the landscape (environment) is a composite of all processes and decisions, regardless of source.

Natural ecology, dry or wet, hot or cold; engineer and subdivider; architect and/or builder; farmer or horticulturalists; landscape architect, contractor, gardener; artist and interior decorator; mechanical engineer and industrial designer; do-it-yourselfer at home or in commerce and industry, all participate in the continuous development and modification of the landscape in which we all live.

It would follow then, that this one total landscape is one total and continuous design problem, to be solved by one total and continuous design process. From this point of view the fragmentations of control over the landscape among many political jurisdictions and private owners, and the fragmentation of design processes among many specialized fields, represent obstacles impeding comprehensive solutions. Architecture's official attempt to pre-empt total environmental design has elements of credibility, because of its central and dominant position, its great history of creative production, and the need for total design. However, architecture's pre-occupation with structure renders it a questionable candidate in an over-structured environment, from which the balancing elements of open space and natural materials have been largely eliminated. Landscape architecture, although weaker numerically and economically, could perhaps be a more convincing candidate for total environmental designer, precisely because of its pre-occupation with open space and natural materials, and its continuous experience in building harmonious connections between buildings, sites, neighborhoods and miscellaneous landscape elements. However, the quality of the urbanized (humanized) environment begins with the relations which are established between structure (buildings, streets, utilities), open space, and natural materials. This returns us full circle to the central and primary relationship between architecture and landscape

179

architecture (building and landscaping) in determining the quality of the environment. Engineering has long been a candidate for total environment controller on the grounds of practical technological necessity. However, even an age as practical as ours has recognized that we do not live by technology alone. Planning, essential to the establishment of a rational and functional framework within which all of the other arts can make maximum contributions to the landscape, is too abstract, too generalized, too disconnected from visual specifics to attempt environmental design. The various other fields of art and design, all essential to the furnishing, enrichment and refinement of the landscape, are too limited in scope to attempt overall design—with some individual exceptions.

So we begin to approach an expansion of Mr. Orsini's suggestion, that true environmental design might begin with the central relation between architecture and landscape architecture and grow to something greater than, and unlike, either as they are practiced today. How much each might contribute to, or survive in, this hypothetical new expanded field is interesting, but irrelevant to the basic idea. This would have to develop as a result of sincere concerted efforts by schools, organizations and individuals. Suggestions have appeared in many places—Renaissance Italy and France, traditional Japan, Soleri, Frank Lloyd Wright, Friedman in Arts & Architecture, Karp and Kiesler in Landscape magazine.

Such a field of environmental (or landscape) design would tend to expand in scale (urban renewal), close the gap, and merge with planning. Engineering would remain the technological component of the field, perhaps increasingly integrated.

Finally, we must return to an expanded version of the question discussed by Damaz and Orsini. Could the arts (several or many) be "integrated" with a new art of environmental design which was already a product of the organic merging of architecture and landscape architecture? The same question would, of course, remain—could the arts retain the integrity of their search for significant form, or would the new art of continuous space organization (indoor and outdoor) force them to play merely decorative roles? The same possibility would exist for organic merging, producing new and more refined forms and concepts in special locations within the continuity of landscape spaces. Painting: structure, sculpture: open space or garden, and multiple variations can be imagined, and have been attempted by artists like Noguchi. The writer has long felt that, next to relations with architecture, relations between landscape architecture and sculpture had greatest potential for rich integrated development if we could get beyond pedestal-sculpture concepts.

There remains the question of expression (significant form) as it relates to function and social responsibility. Design begins with problems—of shelter, of gardening, of communication or magical symbolism, of work songs and play dances. What we call fine art or cultured expressions develop from these as civilization becomes richer and more complex. Such expression is not confined to the fine arts of painting, sculpture, and music. Architecture has produced Greek temple, Gothic cathedral, Renaissance palace; landscape architecture Moorish, Italian, French and Japanese gardens. All of these went beyond simple function and social responsibility to become high and enduring expressions, significant forms preserved for their own sake. Although the drives of commerce and industry and the population explosion have reduced us to a scramble for functional solutions, the potential for expressive form is always there. Witness the FDR Memorial and the Harper Humanities Garden at the University of Denver.

However, to paraphrase Mr. Orsini, the contemporary (artist-designer) finds himself existing in a void. . . . values are vague, and there is no common purpose. . . . This situation leaves the individual artist with the necessity of creating his own values and purpose. Many of the functional problems presented to architects and landscape architects contain the potential for high expression, if clients' concepts, programs and budgets were less restricted. Recent years have seen a substantial widening of horizons and enriching of perspectives on the part of design clientele.[134]

At about the same time the following open letter went out to the professional press and schools:

During recent years there have been four important design competitions that because of their content, programming and results have served to exemplify the attitudes and capabilities of our design professions toward the general landscape. It is important to consider this because of the growing expansion in scale of design projects in our environment, and the growing recognition of the interconnection of all such projects in the totality of the general landscape.

Reading backward in time, these competitions were for Allegheny Square, the Seattle Civic Center Fountain, the Franklin Delano Roosevelt Memorial and the Toronto City Hall and Square.

The results of these four competitions suggest a professional disinterest in the continuous quality of the general landscape. The attitude seems rather that the landscape is a negative receptacle, stage or setting for the work of genius sought by the competition. Parallel to the general American concept of the landscape as a playground for speculators, the professional concept seems to be that it is a gymnasium for genius.

The Toronto competition was for a new city hall and square. Although the building was obviously primary, the square was given considerable importance in the program. It was clear that the two were considered complementary to one another, that they were intended to combine as a unit of architecture and open space in the great Renaissance tradition. Prime competitors had to be architects, but they could of course include other designers on the team. The jury was composed of highly respected architects.

One submission was based on the idea that, since downtown Toronto was already heavily over-built, the solution should minimize the building and maximize the open space. It was felt that this would constitute a truly responsible contribution to the downtown area. In order to accomplish this the scheme depressed the bulk of the building two stories below grade, surrounding it with a romantically designed continuous sunken garden 35 to 80 feet wide. This left only three structures above grade—library, council chambers and mayor's office, and a sculptured tower. These were given a special jewel-like richness. The site became almost total open space, including the roof of the main building. This was precisely the kind of relief the surrounding congestion needed. However, the scheme, perhaps considered anti-architectural, received no recognition from the jury and its central idea was not even mentioned (perhaps not understood) in their summary of the various approaches sent in. The winner was a somewhat sensational building with a completely undistinguished square. None of the entries selected for award gave more than negative importance to the square.

The Franklin Delano Roosevelt Memorial is the most famous or notorious of these competitions, brought forth the greatest effort, and created the greatest controversy. It was an exciting problem, a good site, and a well-written program. Although it stated very carefully that the solution was not necessarily structural, by some peculiar quirk of professional politics the prime competitor had to be an architect, again with the option of setting up a design team. The jury was composed of three architects, one art museum director and one landscape architect. The winner was a sculptural-structural solution of uncompromising verticality. Two of the other first stage winners were structures of bold and demanding form, two were horizontal landscape schemes. Thomas Creighton has given an excellent survey of the competition in his book "The Architecture of Monuments" (again a revealing title for a book about a competition which did not demand structure).

181

The site for the Franklin Delano Roosevelt Memorial lies between the Jefferson and Lincoln Memorials, on a diagonal axis off the central Washington Monument. A vertical or demanding structure in this location will set up a competition with the existing structures and disrupt the basic axial structure of the central composition. This exists whether we approve of it or not. Therefore the memorial should be of a horizontal landscape nature, rather than a vertical or demanding structure. Creighton's summary includes 120 structures, 62 sculptures, 38 shafts, and 70 landscape solutions. The winner was a brilliant design in the wrong place. In general the competitors and jurors appeared to pay insufficient attention to the environment of the memorial.

The Seattle Civic Center Fountain competition again had a two-part program, fountain and surrounding plaza. Both were stressed in the program, although it was clear that a great hydrostatic display was primary. The competition was open to all designers, and the jury consisted of one architect, one planner, one sculptor and one landscape architect. The jury was disappointed in the submissions. Few seemed to grasp the potential for exciting water display, or for powerful combinations of water, sculpture and open space. The fountains of Rome are still unequalled. Of the five first-stage winners four had excellent landscape-sculptural concepts but only one had a potentially brilliant water concept. Unfortunately the latter had the weakest open space design. This led to some dissension in the jury, but it finally agreed that the water concept was primary. The results of the competition were summarized in an excellent booklet published by the City.

Allegheny Square loser

Latest and perhaps most controversial is the Allegheny Square competition, sponsored by the Urban Redevelopment Authority of Pittsburgh. An exciting

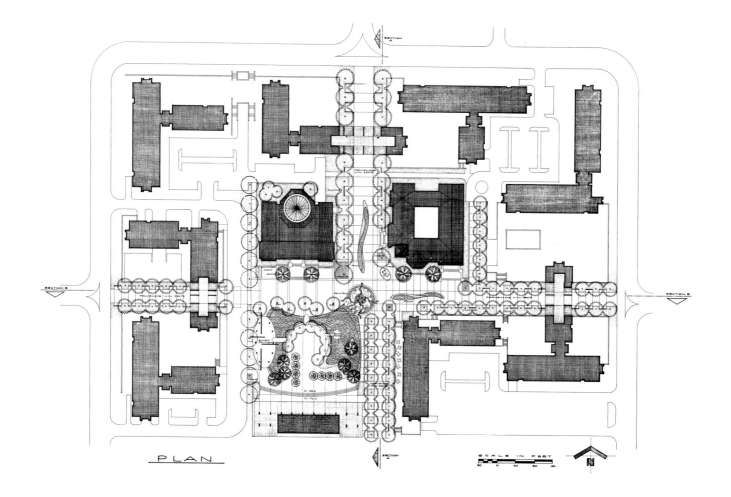

PLAN

SCALE IN FEET

182

SECTION A
SCALE 1" = 40'

SECTION B
SCALE 1" = 40'

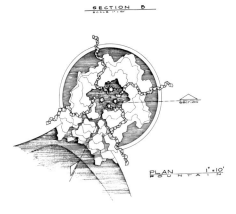

PLAN
FOUNTAIN
1" = 10'

SECTION 1" = 10'
FOUNTAIN

EXHIBIT PAVILION
SCALE 1" = 10'-0"

SECTION

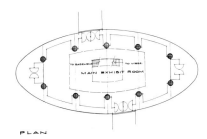

MAIN EXHIBIT ROOM

PLAN

ELEVATION

and classical problem involving a substantial open space, two historical buildings (one classical, one romantic) and a surrounding of distinguished modern apartments; a good program open to all designers; a jury of highly respected names—four architects, one landscape architect, two lay members, all led to a resoundingly disappointing and exasperating conclusion. Although it was a two-stage competition the jury selected only one entry out of 305, as the immediate winner. Only that one has been published to date, and we do not know whether any of the others will be.

There were special, exciting and subtle possibilities in this problem. From that point of view, the winning solution is a step backward to a mechanical, over-simplified, neo-Beaux Arts approach to open space.

The modern revolt of fifty years ago seems to have made the full circle back to the academic, bureaucratic approach from which it started. Certainly the design is simple, so simple that it ignores substantial elements of the problem. Within the continuous enclosure of apartment structures three buildings demand recognition—a romantic library with a tower, a planetarium which is a symmetrical, window-less cube, and a new office building, likewise symmetrical, a typical three-dimensional grid on pilotis. The fact that the two symmetrical buildings face each other across the main open space makes it easy to produce such an over-simplified design. The library, representing precisely the touch of fantasy, wonder, and intimacy that is needed to save the square from death by boredom, is ignored. The exclusion of its difficult picturesqueness is typical of the conformity to arbitrary preconception, the refusal to recognize complex potentials, that leads to the sterilization of design. The four substantial promenade spaces which connect the square radially with its surroundings receive minimal recognition. Trees are treated as decorative elements rather than structural components. Likewise barely recognized are the program requirements that the square accommodate substantial crowds, and provide for important exhibits.

To re-capitulate—The Toronto competition demonstrated a determination to maintain the dominance of structure over open space, regardless of the amount of structure in the environment.

The Franklin Delano Roosevelt Memorial competition demonstrated a determination to produce a forceful and impressive monument, regardless of its effect on the environment.

The Seattle Civic Center Fountain competition demonstrated an inability to solve plastic, irrational, non-functional open space hydrostatic display problems in integrated, imaginative and meaningful forms. In this case the square was the environment for the fountain.

The Allegheny Square competition demonstrated, just when opportunities for great and challenging civic design are expanding, a return to the security of the Beaux Arts womb and the arbitrary regimentation of axial symmetry, a retreat from the exciting potentialities of uninhibited design which have as yet had little impact on our landscape. The Establishment appears to be taking over. Design will no longer represent a threat to the status quo in the environment.

More recently the San Francisco Civic Center Plaza competition has demonstrated the final congealing of the contemporary academic approach. Although surrounded by pure neo-Renaissance architecture, the plaza had to be "modern." The winning plan was the standard Mondrian grid that is one of the chief clichés of "modern" design. (But still better than the final design recently approved by the city.)

Total Landscape Design? The questions which emerge from this discussion are these: Have we yet advanced in social organization to a point at which we can project the conscious, objective, detailed, controlled design of the entire landscape within natural zones and regions rather than within political boundaries and legal property lines? If so, do we really want to, and how would we go about it? What series of increasingly larger unit stages might lie between the present multiple fragmentation and the ultimate inclusive overall concept?[81]

Such total design is not unprecedented. It has been proposed and has achieved physical results at various times throughout history. Autocratic regimes—Egyptian, Roman, Chinese, French—have projected and produced giant authoritarian projects which included only interstitial space for the average citizen. Versailles and Paris were perhaps the culmination of such projects. Our age of industrial democracy has produced projects broader in scale and richer in human detail. TVA, Kitimat, Chandigarh, the Greenbelt and New Towns, Vallingby and Farsta and Baldwin Village have achieved physical reality. There are many paper projects of larger scope, the dreams of architects and planners from Wright to Le Corbusier. The scale of our designs for actual construction has increased tremendously in the last decade. Urban redevelopment and renewal legislation and programs have established the social basis for total cityscape design. We hear of vast developments in the Soviet Union and China which represent to some a monstrous plot against civilized progress and to others the wave of the future.

Man will shortly be charged with designing his habitat entirely, for nature will have become most unnatural. Under these conditions THERE IS ONLY ONE KIND OF ARCHITECTURE; TOTAL, *which embraces at every scale, and in every medium the task of shaping our environment.*

The classification of activity grown out of the tentative steps of the last decades are no longer useful for the purposes I have in mind: that of defining a field. Where does urban design or city planning, landscape architecture, industrial design, graphic design, sculpture and painting separate themselves from architecture?—philosophically and artistically?

Such separation can be useful only at a sophisticated technical level on points of performance. The differences are not to be identified at the conceptual level.

It is the subconscious recognition of this widened spectrum of creative action which is producing today a new breed of functionaries who can operate with many media and on many scales; as scientist, city-planner, engineer, architect, painter, film-producer, graphic artist, sometimes in a single personality.

. . . [We need] The creation of a SINGLE FIELD OF ENVIRONMENTAL DESIGN WHICH WILL ACCOMMODATE THE GENIUS OF SCIENCE, TECHNOLOGY AND ART ON AN EQUAL FOOTING, AND WITH EQUAL OPPORTUNITIES. SERGE CHERMAYEFF[83]

At any rate it is clear that the physical and social potentiality for such total design exists today and will probably expand tomorrow.

Whether we want to propose such design is a more devious and delicate question. The writing of this book is an affirmative answer, of course, and embodies a statement of faith that a democratic process can expand to the control of design at any scale. We as a nation are not interested in authoritarian redevelopment of the landscape. That is design for power, not for people. Those who fear that large-scale design will mean regimentation of the landscape are not without grounds. These are apparent all around us, in many large and hasty residential, commercial, industrial, and governmental projects. They include the implications of blind destruction of community patterns contained within the new Federal highway program. These implications are not clearly written in. They exist in the attitudes of those who will carry the program out and in the absence of controls over such attitudes.

The potential of the democratic apparatus for control still exists for those who will use it. They need—and often have—those essential elements of political action: information, leadership, and organization. The United States is full of political and community spirit and organizations available for the protection and improvement of community patterns, if only they can be mobilized and clarified. Perhaps they are right who say that if democracy dies, it will be of atrophy and apathy from within more than of subversion and war from without. Basically it must be said that life today is not static. If we do not move forward, we will slide backward. The conservative dream of standing still in *status quo* is no longer possible. Every push in the right direction is a blow for freedom, and every failure to push is an aid to reaction.

If we increase the scale of landscape design projects, will we increase the stultifying pressure of authority and squeeze creativity out? Is Parkinson's law anticreative? An examination of urban redevelopment projects, our largest effort to date, would seem to answer this in the affirmative. As Vernon DeMars has said:

I admit that harmony is the term—and the thing to achieve. But I do feel that there is a premise on many architects' parts that whatever the size project you have (and this is paticularly true of housing and has been for a long time—the word "project" has gotten to be almost a nasty word because of this point), you must have unity. But you also have this unfortunate corollary: not merely monotony but a kind of deadly monotony. Something more subtle needs to be done. . . .[135]

See also Vernon DeMars in *The People's Architects,* published by The University of Chicago Press in 1964.

In *Planning and Community Appearance*[90] governmental influences on community appearance are studied exhaustively. The AIA-AIP committee reviewed much that had been written about community aesthetics; gathered texts of as many statutes, ordinances, and court decisions related to aesthetic regulation as could be unearthed; analyzed the various existing kinds of regulations and through discussion arrived at a common attitude toward them; and finally, reached agreement on a basic philosophy about the regulation of community appearance, consonant both with the valid political traditions of our culture and with sound aesthetic principles. From this philosophy the committee developed the concept of a *community design plan and program.* From other sources, an advanced effort to introduce freedom and flexibility into urban design is the "planned area" zone in which normal controls are taken off if the new design is approved by the planning authorities.

The effort and need to produce a renaissance of civic development can be one of the forces helping to taper off the cold war drives. The possibility of worldwide peace and disarmament seems greater and more realistic now than ever before in history, in spite of brush-fire wars and summit collapses. It is impelled by the unprecedented technological demand to choose between coexistence and destruction, which is understood today by the simplest peasants throughout the world. This has produced a mass pressure for peace which is felt in every policy-making office around the globe. Current businesslike efforts to maintain "normal" war with napalm and pellet bombs will not survive this pressure.

Implicit in the problem of converting 40 to 50 billion dollars and 6 million people to constructive peacetime production is a vast expansion in the clearance of slums, the redevelopment of blighted areas, and the construction of good housing, schools, colleges, universities, hospitals and other health facilities, park and recreation developments, and all of the other multitudinous community facilities needed to bring the American dream to physical fruition. We must all live together in towns, cities, and suburbs which may be the most sanitary but are certainly the most ugly and nerve-racking in the world. Ugliness seems to be a built-in by-product of our total official structure of land and building development. Exceptions in rare spots are carry-overs from the larger vision of the nineteenth century or the result of herculean efforts by enlightened individuals. The agonizing reappraisal and reconstruction implicit in the present state of the American landscape can take up much of the slack of the change from war to peace and can bulk large in the vigorous cultural competition between the divergent social systems of the world.

True complete landscape design will constitute a new area of design which will fall between the normal practices of city and regional planning and of architecture, engineering, and landscape architecture. This will involve new principles, new methods of approach, less reliance on rules and precedent, more concentration on the actual nature of the relations between people and their surroundings. It will necessitate a gradual expansion in perspective from normal public space- and site-planning programs through larger and larger elements of street and neighborhood to community and regional patterns. Brenda Colvin (*Land and Landscape*) and Kevin Lynch (*Image of the City*) give us thought-

The U.S. is embarked on the most exciting and ambitious project that it has ever undertaken: the creation of a more agreeable and attractive society, which is to say, the creation of a new civilization. This lofty enterprise, neglected during the last century of booming, freewheeling industrial growth in America, will entail a prodigious amount of civic and community building and planning. . . . The question arises: can a democratic, middle-class, capitalist country like the U.S. hope to create a great civilization? Can it exercise the necessary wisdom and cultivate the necessary taste? Will it accept the implicit restraint and inevitable infringements of property rights that such a civilization implies? The Architectural Forum[136]

The United States was once a standout performer as a vigorous, productive society. Exceptionally strong in design and production methods, American basic industries and mass-producing consumer industries set world standards.

Yet, today a process of technical, industrial and human deterioration has been set in motion within American society. The competence of the industrial system is being eroded at its base, and entire industries are falling into technical disrepair.

. . . This deterioration is the result of an unprecedented concentration of America's technical talent and fresh capital on military production. The price of building military power and adding to it has been the depletion of American society, a depletion process that is now well advanced.

. . . At present . . . the bulk of military production is concentrated in industries, firms, and plants that have always been specialized in this work, and rarely have a prior history of civilian work.

. . . In the United States, sustained growth in military work has been achieved at the cost of gross depletion of education, medical care, housing, and every other sort of human care of human beings. Guns and butter cannot be had together over an extended period—not even in the U.S. This is the real issue.

The U.S. is armed with 3,400 strategic delivery vehicles, but there are

186

only 140 *places with populations of over*
100,000 in the entire USSR. . . .
SEYMOUR MELMAN, Professor of Industrial Engineering, Columbia University,
addressing Town Hall, Los Angeles,
California, January 19, 1965[137]

ful and sensitive projections of the attitudes and procedures that will
be needed.

The Typical Ordinary Landscape. Design of the landscape will determine the exact form and arrangement of everything to be seen or experienced by a given individual or group of individuals within a given area
or movement zone. The typical paths followed by average citizens on
ordinary days (home to work, shopping, or school and back) and on
special days (home to recreation, health, service, or culture, an hour
or a day away) lead them through a landscape which is a composite
of multitudinous decisions by persons mostly unknown to them. Whether
or not they own their own homes, they probably had little or no direct
voice in their design. (The voice of the consumer has definite influence
in mass house design, but the producer sets the frame for the discussion.)
Very likely they were not done by an architect, but rather by a builder-
draftsman combination. They are set in a pattern of lots, blocks, and
streets established by engineers in conformity with demands by accountants and entrepreneurs and within a loose and generalized framework
of zoning and planning regulations established by various government
agencies.

In suburban areas the landscape pattern within the citizen's yard
and those of his neighbors is a composite of his own efforts and those
of previous residents, as guided by experience and the house-and-garden
press, plus the efforts of the various nurserymen, gardeners, and fence
and patio salesmen who may have been able to sell some of their commodities and services. In the front yard these individualized efforts meet
the organized community's effort to improve its appearance, as expressed
in street trees, sidewalk, curb, gutter, driveway-apron and street-paving
design, and control of power and telephone lines and poles and other
utilities. This effort varies from a maximum in the best residential districts to little or nothing in slum areas.

In urban areas, where building coverage eliminates practically all
ground-level open space except streets, parking lots, and occasional parks,
the citizen lives in a structural landscape—regular street canyons whose
architectural walls are a composite of the decisions of dozens or hundreds
of builders, engineers, architects, draftsmen, bankers, and owners. In
these areas the citizen may very likely walk, at least to the nearest public
transportation—subway, elevated, bus. He walks through streets crowded
with people, all sorts of people in all sorts of clothes, and all sorts of
vehicles. These streets are cluttered with odd miscellaneous furnishings
and equipment—show windows, signs, lights, traffic signals, hydrants,
power lines, benches, railings, trash cans, etc. All of these oddments
are designed somewhere at some time by industrial designers, mechanical
and electrical engineers, draftsmen, artists, or others.

In suburban areas the citizen probably travels in his own car or in
a car pool, perhaps to some mass transit stopping point. He travels
through streets where buildings are separated by more or less planted
open space, and fewer people, furnishings, and vehicles are to be seen.

The vehicles become a good deal more important in the landscape, because of their constant size and motion and the increasingly self-conscious ostentation of their form and color. The wholehearted application of the well-established merchandising design principles of styling and obsolescence to a landscape element as important as the automobile can produce terrifying results. The recent attempt by the automobile industry to marry Buck Rogers produced only one offspring; Frankenstein. In the interaction between foreign and domestic cars it is as yet difficult to predict whether the former will be corrupted or the latter purified.

The citizen's route to work, whether by public vehicle or private car, runs through urbania, suburbia, or a hopeless scramble of streets, highways, and tracks; residential, commercial, and industrial structures; occasional trees, spots of vacant land, or fragments of agriculture or nature. He travels to a workplace—field, mine, construction site, factory, shop, or office—which is usually strictly functional, designed for production, not for comfort or relaxation, although occasionally and increasingly including some employee amenities and some front for good public relations.

Evenings, weekends, or holidays the pursuit of recreation or relaxation will lead to movies, bowling alleys, skating rinks, parks and playgrounds, churches, beaches, mountains, forests, and so on. Lucky is the citizen who lives near such facilities. Usually he must travel considerable, often arduous, distances to them.

This landscape which surrounds the ordinary lives of average citizens is seldom pretty and almost never beautiful. It is dull, disorderly, squalid, monotonous, tawdry, thin, sterile, drab, dirty, gaudy, noisy, confused, chaotic, anarchic, regimented, exhausting, nerve-racking, stultifying, frustrating—a great place to be from. It is sanitary and functional some of the time in some parts, and it is profitable to someone most of the time in most parts. It is rarely, if ever, exhilarating, inspiring, cheerful, restful, relaxing, uplifting; it rarely, if ever, gives the citizen any sense of great accomplishment, a great future, or a great potential within himself and his community. The occasional cultural flower or natural breathing pore produced by the arduous, unrewarded, and anonymous efforts of whole-souled do-gooders is hard to find in the general welter of barren purposeless development. The great mystified outcry about the growth of juvenile delinquency can easily be answered by an open-eyed examination of the ugly, brutal, and cynical environment which surrounds most juveniles.

Where is this spatial poverty of the American scene, this failure to capitalize on our cultural and technical opportunities and potentials, relieved? Where are those lovely scenes and fine surroundings that we find pictured in books and periodicals and on the movie screen? We find them where the pressure of population grows less, and the pressure of financial resources grows greater, in:

Well-to-do homes and neighborhoods (approximately 14 percent of American nonfarm homes).

Well-to-do rural areas.
Some public buildings: Museums, city halls, universities.
Some public parks.
Some commercial developments done by good modern architects.
Some parts of the natural landscape.

Most of the people do not live in these portions of the environment or see them except occasionally. What about the portions where most people live and work? Need they be described further? We know we have tremendous sordid slum areas in both town and country, blighted areas that are still larger and nearly as sordid, and that even our acceptable "standard" residential sections are vulnerable to any critical analysis in terms of planning, design, community facilities, open space, etc. Both the programming and the design of the general American physical (spatial) environment are poverty-striken, penurious, economy-of-scarcity–minded. Indeed it is the programming which determines our basic space standards; good design can do no more than dress these up in their best clothes. The poverty of our general spatial experiences is a poverty of too much to a minority and too little to the majority, and this is the central problem of all our concern with housing and planning and the general health of the country.

So what is beauty in the landscape? A relationship between observation, participation, background, and scene. The satisfaction of needs developed in the past—and the suggestion of a better future. Motion almost in balance. Equilibrium about to be achieved. The suggestion of the consummation of the citizen's lifelong search and effort: security, peace, quiet, green pastures, fun, life, sociability, community, friendliness, food for body and mind, shelter from a hard world, relief from noise and confusion, spaciousness and freedom for expansion and growth—*what our world lacks*. As Louis Kahn has said, the effort to achieve beauty, once it begins to produce results, is more important than the final achievement.

CHAPTER 14
Design for People

All design problems originate with clients who have development programs of some sort. Most art production, even the purest, is for sale, if only because artists too must live. Clients and art purchasers are people. The client as enemy is one who interferes with his designer's aspirations toward art production. But the designer without art aspirations is a superficial and feeble practitioner. The artist-designer must know when to follow his client's desires and when to lead him to experiences he could not have imagined were available. Clients, on the other hand, must know when to tell their designers what they want and how they feel and when to give free rein to the designer's imagination. Every designer knows that his production is greatest when he has sympathetic, reciprocal, understanding relations with his client.

Clients may be single individuals or groups comprising families or organizations. These clients may be private types who will use the development themselves; private types, such as the commercial developer, who represent unknown and voiceless users (with apologies to motivation and market research); or public types representing a community or other political subdivision, through election or appointment. Some users of the landscape are able to speak directly for themselves through ownership, but most can speak only through indirect and devious channels.

The effect of consumer pressure on commercial developers and absentee landlords is directly conditioned by the amount of competition existing at the specific time and place and by the efficiency of communications between owners, producers, and consumers. It is still further conditioned by the efficiency of communication between designers and consumers: the consumer can only choose between alternatives which are known and understood by him. The effect of citizen pressure on public development is directly conditioned by the health of the specific political structure involved and by the efficiency of communication between government and people.

Our relations with the people who constitute our private domestic clientele are direct and simple: we meet with them, talk and work with

LEFT ABOVE: House in New Mexico. Designed as a sculpture for living. Complete integration of art and function.

LEFT BELOW: In this public housing development in Los Angeles the designers created maximum art quality within the bureaucratic limitations of the Federal policy.

191

them, and do our best to produce the best specific solutions for their specific problems. While even here attitudes of commercial exploitation and artistic impatience appear in our work, this is a relatively clear and open relationship. But our relations with the people who constitute the customers of commercial developments stop with the owners of those enterprises, who become the self-appointed representatives of those customers insofar as we are concerned; and our relations with the people who constitute the users of public spaces and facilities stop with the administrators of the agencies which operate them, who become the appointed representatives of the public insofar as we are concerned. A fourth kind of client organization has appeared in recent years, the cooperative or mutual ownership association, in which a specific number of individuals or families pool their resources in a democratic organization (one member, one vote) for some specific development such as a small community. In such cases we find ourselves dealing, not with certain individuals who represent a blank and faceless public, but with machinery, such as committees and membership meetings, which makes possible a maximum contact between professional and group clientele.

What do people need? They need a sense of security and of creativity. The sense of security requires adequate food, shelter, clothing, health protection, education and information, the feeling of group membership, love, comfort, luxury, reciprocity in production and consumption, dignity, equality of opportunity. The sense of creativity requires a feeling of accomplishment, of adding something to the world, improving it, receiving group approbation for accomplishment, understanding the world better, helping others to do so (so they can help you to do so), participation in group, community, or social creation, being wanted for special talents, being part of the stream of human progress, the immortality of the human race.

What do citizens need around them physically? Pleasant views and vistas, well composed in three dimensions and in relation to their movements. A sense of adequate comfortable enclosure at human scale in the spaces they occupy—houses, gardens, streets. A sense of graceful continuity and transition from themselves and these occupied spaces to the larger landscape around. A sense of articulated relation to community— from home to work to recreation, from house to neighborhood to community to metropolis to region to nation and on to continent and hemisphere and world.

Citizens need also a sense of relation to history, to the stream of tradition from past through present to future; a sense of building the future in the present on the past, not embalming the past in static reproductions, for history cannot repeat itself; a sense of resolution of the contradiction between the need for change and new forms and the respect for history. Each day the world is as good as it can be—but tomorrow it can be better. But even in our brave new world of America we cling to the past—in the East to colonial Williamsburg, in the South to the plantation, in the West to the Western story and the mission.

How can the landscape help supply such needs? As a result of constructive social programs: housing, health, recreation, culture, education, raising our real standard of living, rebuilding our decaying cities and towns and controlling our tumorous suburbs. There is enough profitable and creative work here to occupy our entire nation for generations to come, a better way to win the cold war than any amount of brinkmanship.

Building, street, and open-space patterns are shaped by habit, preconception, precedent, and occasional flashes of new thought. The new thoughts break through more readily in single isolated buildings and their landscape contexts than in the continuity of streets and open spaces which is conditioned and guided by the entire institutionalized superstructure of financial, building, and land management habits and attitudes. The quality of landscape experience produced by these patterns is primary in actual life; if recognized and elevated to conscious equality with the other primary considerations of land and building development, it would have major impact upon our communities.

The landscape is organized, reorganized, developed, and redeveloped in terms of function, profit, sentiment, changing use patterns, and changing technology. The exterior spaces created by this process are largely by-products, unconsidered results of the pursuit of primary objectives. Much effort is then expended to beautify these accidental spaces with foundation plantings, street trees, flower beds, and *objets d'art*. Proper selection, arrangement, and maintenance of the primary space-forming elements—buildings, trees, street patterns, ground forms, pedestrian surfaces—would render unnecessary and irrelevant much "beautifying" activity. Two parallel traditions of open-space design, the architectural square symbolized by Sitté, and the park meadow symbolized by Olmsted, lie dammed up and waiting to merge their inspirations in a great new renaissance of landscape spaces. This is apparent in limited preview in the townscape studies of Gordon Cullen and *Architectural Review*, the urban plazas of the Seagram Building and the Mile-High Center, and many similar efforts.

In talking about visual quality in and of the landscape we may well be completing a historical circle. In the days of the Beaux Arts and the City Beautiful movements there was much talk of beauty while ugliness grew like a grass fire. Came the modern revolt, in part against such hypocrisy, and attention to beauty became passé. Form followed function (or structure) like a shadow, it was said. Except in a few stubbornly skilled hands all of the time-honored means for qualitative improvement—proportion, scale, refinement, detail—began to be forgotten. "If it functions it must be beautiful" became a pragmatic slogan parallel to that older Americanism, "If it works it's right" (or "good"). The engineer who designed the swaybacked Richmond–San Rafael Bridge in northern California (derisively called "Leaping Lena" or "Galloping Gertie" by outraged citizens) can say with great self-righteousness that it must be beautiful because it is the most economical form. But

193

we are learning that beauty does not come automatically, and rarely by accident in these high-pressure days. In spite of the victory of modernism over eclecticism and traditionalism we are still ruining the landscape with ugly urbanism and suburbanism faster than any other country on earth. Surely it is time to return to the conception of beauty, visual quality, and spatial experience as positive goals equal in importance to bathrooms and swimming-pool filters. Only by this path can we establish the direct responsibility of every designer, every developer, and every landowner to the quality of the general landscape.

We must understand just how people live in relation to the landscape and just how it affects their lives—the totality and continuity of their experience in time and space. What does the citizen of our landscape do every hour, every day, every weekend, every vacation and on other special occasions, and what kind of landscape surrounds this activity? Design for people must recognize their variations in size and form, their perception of the world through five senses, the nature of their consciousness, comprehension, intellection, memory, attitudes, needs, desires. This recognition must be sympathetic as well as rational if it is to produce successful design.

Why does the same house produce different reactions in different people? This is a result of differences in their heredity and backgrounds. As Dr. George A. Kelly said to the 1959 Institute in Psychotherapy in Los Angeles:

> Man has been represented as an incorrigible interpreter, one who must interpret at all levels of awareness in order to live, even in order to be credited with being alive. The round of interpretation, prediction and validation is the basic cycle of human experience and the succession of such rounds constitutes a measure of personality growth. This is growth that goes on all the time . . . it is this inherent growth process, based on spiraling experience, that psychotherapy must seek to exploit.

If the notion of science is taken seriously as a refinement of the psychology of man, Kelly continued, something like the psychology of "personal constructs" is a natural consequence. Moreover, he thinks, such a notion extends from the experimental laboratory to that special kind of laboratory called the therapy room:

> It makes the therapist and his client teammates in a scientific venture, just as a graduate student and his dissertation directors are teammates. It turns interpretations into testable hypotheses, rather than letting them remain as authoritative dicta.[138]

In other words, reasonable discussion of reactions to the landscape around us may lead to reexamination and reinterpretation of those reactions.

People are all alike and yet all different; unable to change and yet constantly changing; grubbing in the garbage heaps of prejudice, discrimination, and segregation, crawling through the sewers of war, picking each other's pockets, living on each other's backs—yet with their heads

Harvard's Bruner

... first decided that a man's values and needs strongly determine his perceptions. ... Bruner's second conclusion embraced the idea that "man has an enormous capacity to restrict surprise at his environment." The factors determining perception give each person a coherent view of the universe. Of all the patterns one might perceive in reality, one's motivations, fears, and needs together select the pattern he will perceive. And whatever the pattern is, it will be consistent, so that when man encounters something he has never seen before, he can fit it into his scheme and make sense of it. According to Bruner, these "models of the universe" we all carry about in our minds help us to reduce mental strain when we deal with things we know nothing about. We "restrict surprise" at our environment by preparing in advance for everything it can confront us with.

"Cognition" is defined as "the process of knowing." Cognitive psychology deals with man's ability to build conceptual models of his world, to go beyond available information, and to predict the nature of things he has not previously experienced. ... he concentrated on man's "brutal selectivity" in perceiving the world; he tried to understand cognitive processes through language.

Roger Brown ... has been investigating the effects on perception of the ways different languages "encode" reality. In particular, he has been comparing the color names available in English and in Yoruba, a Nigerian language. Speakers of English divide the visible spectrum into six colors. ... But speakers of Yoruba use only two names. ... Do users of English per-

ceive different relationships among colors than users of Yoruba? ... Brown got just this result. ... Clearly, the language we use helps make us "brutally selective in perceiving."[139]

The late John Knox Shear, in a rare examination by an architect of the general human client, showed penetrating sensitivity in 1956 when he said:

The complete man asks of architecture many things; asks, of course, that his buildings provide him with the means of carrying on his activities ... asks, too, for the sensations of space and form and their modulation through color in light which were significant to him even as a child: the sensation of caves, of coming into or out of tunnels, of islands, of open glades in the trees, of craters, of high smooth mounds in flat pastures, of bridges, of the space and texture in the floor of a tall pine woods and the light there, and the light and space under a great tent or in old barns; and the sensation he used to get in crouching under tables or on top of roofs; and even the invigorating spatial sensations of peering through knotholes.

The complete man has known and knows all these and he asks that his architecture afford him something akin to them; not all of them at once, of course, nor all in a short sequence; but enough in any architectural environment that his senses be rewarded as he performs his activities. For he is a creature of senses and demands a rich diet of sensation. And he demands still more, for he is a creature of intellect as well; and because he is he asks his architecture for more than usefulness and for more than sensation.

The complete man asks also that his

architecture have meaning; that all its parts speak to him and to others. He asks that his buildings say where they are—in space and in time and he asks that they speak of their purpose and abilities and the means of their forming. ...

The complete man, then, asks for a rich assortment of utility, of sensation, and of meaning in his architecture. He is aware, of course, that they are interdependent and as such each has the power of strengthening the effect of the others, and that taken together they constitute the whole architecture which he needs but which he does not have. The architecture which has the ability to speak to his spirit. In its stead he has today some brilliant and beautiful parts with a necessarily partial ability to satisfy the whole man. ...

And in our vain preoccupation [we are] neglecting the man for whom we are building; neglecting that thoughtful and thorough study of his needs and his attitudes which reveals the proper point of departure and the proper goals of architecture.

That study will reveal at the outset that man is a creature of opposites; that he is attracted to many apparently disparate phenomena; that he doesn't feel he has to be against yesterday in order to be for today—doesn't have to turn his back on history in order to look forward; that the genius of a particular place and its people is still a desirable source of influence on form even in a day when he readily acknowledges the interdependence and cross influence of all places and all people; that function has a more inclusive meaning than we have been ascribing to it. ...[140]

in the stars of great science, great art, human imagination, freedom, and brotherhood. These stars will light the way out from the garbage heaps and sewers.

How do people relate to the landscape? Lying down, sitting, standing, walking, running, climbing, swimming, riding, flying, working, relaxing. Life equals work plus recreation for more work for most of us—eight hours work and sixteen hours free for recreative activities. Whether we work in order to play or play in order to work, this is the daily round of life—home to street to work to street to home to street to movie to street to home. The sixteen hours free time are eaten away: six to eight hours sleep, one to two hours commuting, three hours for meals, one or more for chores and errands. Weekends and vacations are the great breaks, bundles of extra free time which can be used constructively or destructively. As workweeks shorten and the shadow of automation lengthens over the land, sociologists and recreation leaders worry more and more over what people will do with the new leisure. Of course, if paychecks shorten with workweeks, leisure will become mere unemployed time spent looking for more work. But it is clear that leisure time is expanding for many and that this carries with it potentials for a major cultural renaissance or depths of decadence and degradation such as we have never known. The recreation profession, expanding from the programming of playground and playfield activities, can help us to avoid the latter and find the former.

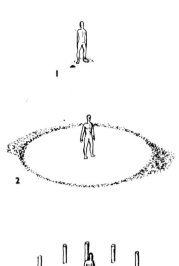

Life, of course, is more than a simple relation between home, work, and recreation. It might rather be called a relation between necessary, or compulsory, time and free time, between the things we have to do and those we do because we want to. This is a subtle and variable relationship. For most of us the pressures are such that we feel that we have to work, we have to eat, sleep, bathe, etc. The rest is free time, insofar as it is not eaten up by problems of transportation, communication, and distribution of the necessities of life. But the cultured life transforms eating, sleeping, and bathing into refined pleasures, and some areas of work are so rewarding as to remove the sense of compulsion. Perhaps when all work becomes free and voluntary, the millenium will be here.

The landscape for each citizen must become an organic part of the landscape for all citizens. Each person sees what he looks at, senses what is around, hears sounds, smells smells, touches surfaces, remembers previous associations with similar elements, or fails to react because of conditioning by a sterile environment. People relate physically to the spaces around them in patterns which can be reduced to prototype diagrams, as the English architect Erno Goldfinger did many years ago.[141] Such diagrams can be connected with the landscape which exists around us by a kind of psychological topology. That is where design begins.

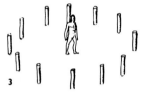

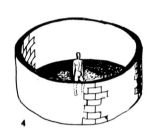

PICTORIAL	PLASTIC	SPATIAL
2-dimensional (flat)	3-dimensional (convex)	3-dimensional (concave)
Static	Stereoscopic	Kinetic
Apprehended consciously from without	Apprehended consciously from without	Apprehended sub-consciously from within

196

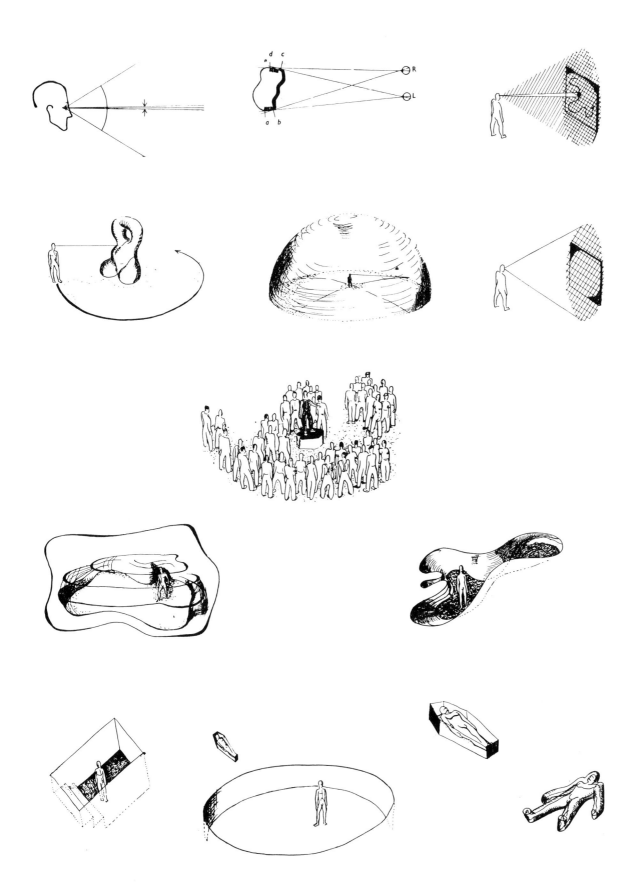

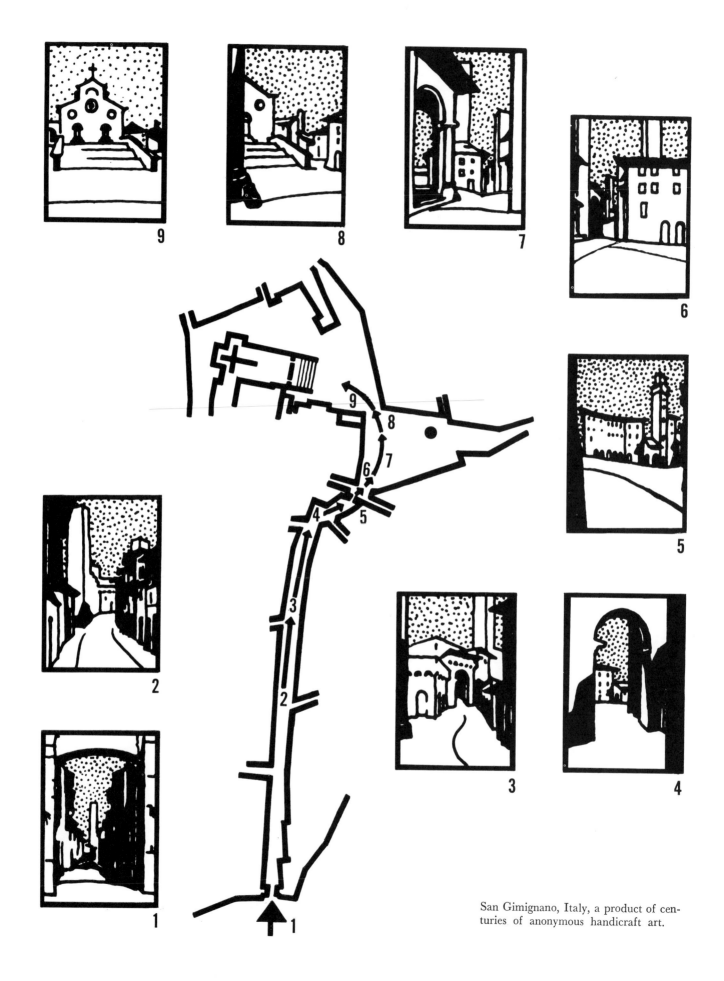

San Gimignano, Italy, a product of centuries of anonymous handicraft art.

CHAPTER 15
Principles

The principles of art must interlock with the real world in order to succeed.

In school design begins with principles. The art elements—line, shape, color, texture, mass, space—are organized through rhythm, balance, emphasis, and proportion into a harmony of unity and variety which may be beautiful. The fact that the following of this principled path does not guarantee the production of beauty indicates that the large unknown in the equation is the human factor, the designer and the client. It is their talent, imagination, skill, understanding, sensitivity, and sympathy which determine whether the design process produces a more or less successful solution to a problem and/or a work of art which brings forth a growing response from an expanding audience.

How do these art elements and principles relate to the general landscape? A line in the real physical world may be a sharp junction of two materials, as the edge of a concrete walk, a body of quiet water, or the edges of the members in a structure. This is a fixed and positive line which does not change when we move, although the changed angle of vision may give it a changing aspect to us. Such lines are as important in landscape design as in painting, giving direction, movement, continuity, and guidance to eye and foot in following through a composition. The construction and relative weights of a linear pattern can determine whether the observer is held within the picture plane or garden space or escapes to the no-man's-land beyond and is lost. This is true whether the garden space is enclosed and self-contained or is merely a stage from which to view a broad panorama. When we move from simple controlled spaces to the continuity of the general landscape, linear patterns and their control take on an enormous complexity.

The importance of linear patterns can be grossly exaggerated, and this has occurred many times in conscious landscape design, particularly in the formal schools. Two-dimensional patterns on the ground can easily become so insistent as to bypass the primary objective of creating an inspiring sense of volume and movement in space. This is accomplished in the main by the arrangement of three-dimensional forms in relationships which create a sense of structure, tension, and volume, comparable to that in great painting. In such an effort a flat, highly patterned ground plane may be very important in relation to other vertical elements. But in general (though not always) the arrangement of elements above ground should dominate its treatment.

The other type of line, the silhouette of topography, rocks, vegetation, structures, or other objects, is of equal or greater importance in landscape design. This silhouette line, which changes with every movement of the observer, is more dynamic, more variable, and more expressive of spatial relations than the fixed line.

Shapes or forms are complete or nearly complete areas of material bounded by perimeter lines which may be either fixed or silhouette. A concrete terrace has a fixed shape, a tree has a silhouetted shape which changes as we move. A hill has a variable form which we differentiate intellectually from the general ground plane from which it rises. A partially buried boulder has a silhouetted form and, as with the proverbial iceberg, we tend to construct the buried shape in our minds. A building is a composite of fixed shapes—wall planes, door and window openings—and silhouetted forms which result from the varying three-dimensional combinations of these as we move about. Formed art objects—sculpture, pottery—and the shell forms of industrial design—cars, refrigerators, utensils—are also variable silhouetted forms, although if they are radially symmetrical the silhouette may remain constant. Although these shapes and forms bounded by lines are of importance in drawing, diagramming, and patterning, their primary function is to give us a sense of three-dimensional form in space. They do this by the changes in silhouetted forms as we move, and by the changed relations between forms with fixed outlines as we move. In the final complexity of the real world fixed and silhouetted forms are played against each other in highly variable patterns. It is by learning to orient ourselves within these patterns that we are able to move through the world with pleasure, comfort, or at least fortitude.

Color brings the world to life for us, makes it real and positive, lively or quiet, exhilarating or depressing. In among the generally quiet weathered greens, browns, blues, and grays of the world of nature, with the occasional splash of brightness from minerals, vegetation, or animals, man has brought the entire controlled range of synthetic-coloring techniques. Such freedom brings commensurate responsibility, and this grows as the coloring materials become more durable and resistant to weathering. Billboards, cars, and buildings can take on any color of the rainbow (plus a few we seem to have added), and sometimes they seem to take them on all at once. The productivity of horticulture, which seems generally to concentrate on expanding the nongreen area of plant color, adds considerably to this palette. Add to this our pattern of free, independent, disconnected decisions within each piece of real estate and each production enterprise (sometimes called the American system of organized irresponsibility), and you have one of the principal contributors to the visual indigestibility of our landscape. In desperation (and perhaps to affirm our puritanical heritage), we escape from the excesses

The Iceland poppy is one of nature's freshest voices.

Jan Peter Stern captures some of the waywardness of nature in this sculptured wall.

200

Patterns and textures of aluminum, wood, and plants complement each other when properly combined.

of commercialized technology to "decorator colors," pastel shades, and the rigid browns, grays, and natural materials of "pure" architecture. But the creative insight into the great potential for the controlled use of color to bring harmony and balance into a chaotic landscape is always available.

Tone is the relationship between color, light, and texture. The same color will have a different quality in strong light than in full shade, on a dull or rough surface than on a smooth or shiny surface. The forces of nature are among the elements of landscape design; visual qualities change with variations in obscurity or clarity of atmosphere, temperature, humidity, sun, fog, and clouds. The hard clarity of the Southern desert has the mystery of unlimited distance; the richly variable density of Northern humid atmospheres has the mystery of variable distances and perceptions of form. Line, form, and color are approached and handled with different emphases in different climates. The knowledge of, and sensitivity to, these variations is not picked up easily by the casual visitor. Rather, it is part of the adjustment of continuous day-to-day living, for artist and designer as well as ordinary citizen.

Texture is variation in surface within a form or area or around a mass. It is closely related to scale. At intimate scale it is detailed surface, as the relations between glossy paper, sandpaper, and corrugated board. At medium, or human, scale it is the variations in size, form, and arrangement of leaves in vegetation, the pattern of brick or boards in a building, the size of particles in rock or soil, the effect of wind- or gravity-induced movement in water. Each of these elements has within it again the variations in intimate texture which can be seen or felt close up, and which condition the medium textures. At large community or general landscape scale texture is the patterning of buildings and streets in a town, the patterning of vegetation at grass, shrub, or tree scale, the arrangement of water in streams, ponds, or lakes, the group movements of animals, people, or vehicles. Writers and sociologists speak of the texture of society as the kind of impression it gives those who experience it.

Mass is solid three-dimensional form. Boulders and hills or mountains are solid masses of material which we perceive as forms but know by experience and association to be solid. Vegetation may appear as a visual mass at a distance, although we know and can verify by close inspection that it is really a delicate and continuous structure of trunks, branches, stems, twigs, and foliage enclosing considerable volumes of space. The arrangement of structure and foliage in plants determines whether they appear as masses or open space definers. Buildings in the landscape usually read as geometric masses, with glass adding translucency and reflections. In recent years the new building which has more glass than solid walls has added a new dimension in translucent volume and multiple reflection to the landscape. Engineering structures in the bridge and power-line category are great linear space definers, while dams and highways are sculptural masses and linear sculptures.

Space is volume defined by physical elements. We live in atmospheric space as fish live in water, looking out now beyond the surface of our global ocean of air into the black immensity of interplanetary space. This air space in which we live achieves form, volume, comprehensibility, and scale only when it is defined by tangible visible elements and only to the extent that it is so defined. Topography and trees are the great space definers in nature, and to these we have added human construction at every scale from fence to skyscraper. Every physical element above or below the horizontal ground plane on which we are standing defines space, qualifies it, gives it height, depth, simple order, complex structure, or indefinite continuity, within the range between agoraphobia and claustrophobia.

Rhythm is produced by a repetition of equal or similar elements. This is not necessarily a simple or regular pattern. Even as musical rhythms can vary from the simple beat of rock 'n' roll to the highly developed and complex patterns of the Watusi drums and the magnificent organization of great symphonies, so landscape rhythms can vary from the simple symmetrical *allée* of one kind of tree to the freely spaced grove of several in subtle but recognizable patterns. Nature's rhythms are seldom simple, at least to the naked eye. The elements repeated—the rise and fall of a range of hills, pebbles on a beach, flowers in a glade, animals in a herd—are similar but never identical, and the patterns of repetition are rarely regular. The classical symmetrical formal garden or park has been the darling of those who love authority and the static life for thousands of years. But absolute symmetry and mechanical regularity are too complete, too finished, and too dull. They leave the observer nothing to contribute, no participation in completing a potential pattern, as free creative citizens should.

In contrast with such rigidity, we might think of the fine free balance of a mature natural forest and its analogy in the free-associational patterns of a Jackson Pollock or Mark Tobey painting.

Balance is the arrangement of physical elements in patterns or structures which give the observer a sense of equilibrium and stability. Abstract compositions must be developed in relation to the real existing landscape context and to the willful mobility of the human observer. Academic formal design seeks to trap the observer in a completely controlled system of circulation and vision in which nothing is left to chance. Here we struggle to escape from the fixed station point on major or minor axis to the casual diagonal view. Informal design, both naturalistic and romantic, recognizes and concentrates on the irrational human search for freedom of movement, unexpected, accidental, and variable experiences, a sense of the relationship between time and space which is lost in fixed formal compositions.

In the real, fluid, moving world of life compositions change with every step or turn of the head. Far hills may be balanced by near trees, tall buildings by panoramic views, heavy rock outcrops by broad placid water bodies. Balance becomes a live structure in which we must live

John Bracken speaks of:

Empathy—the Motor Response in Perception: . . . Of all other forms of composition, the urge actually to move into the scene and become part of what one sees is significant to landscape design. . . . Through the principle of empathy we have an explanation of that continual suggestion of movement in visual space which is fundamental to an understanding of landscape effects, and especially of plant scenery; we see that the mind, through the eye, possesses the means by which various impressions cause the individual peculiarly to associate himself with the scene.[142] As William H. Whyte, Jr., says:

The city grandiose: Most urban redevelopment projects, give or take a few malls, promise scenes like this: pompous, formalistic patterns that look fine from the top of a tower or in an architect's perspective, but will be oppressive voids to the poor pedestrian.[143]

A small pool can become a focus for a cluster of professional offices, a center for relaxation and introspection.

Play elements must facilitate creative interpretation and variable use if they are to succeed.

and move in order to complete it rather than a fixed composition which we stand here to look at. Both the formal and informal schools have suffered from the mechanical accumulation of precedent, academic concentration on similarities to the exclusion of variables, literal interpretations of oversimplified objectives, and the failure to recognize man's basic need for orderly flexibility in relation to his environment. Formal design becomes too tight and enclosed, informal too loose and open; the former becomes too disciplined, the latter too free; both become essentially irresponsible in relation to people. Great prototypes, however they may be cataloged, usually contain elements of both approaches: balance and movement, rhythm and irregularity, harmony and contrast, order and accident, control and unpredictability.

Emphasis is the means for articulating the parts of a controlled composition or arrangement. It makes it possible to contain variety within a unified, rhythmic, balanced structure. It marks changes in the continuity or direction of circulation or vision, changes in the character of use, site, or surroundings, changes in the quality of spatial experience, important connections or parts within a general design. Emphasis balances rhythm and repetition by accenting a change before monotony sets in. It can only occur at intervals which give us relief from the continuity of similar experience. The church or school in the suburban community, the open grassy glade in the forest, the pool in the running stream, the clump of birch in the pine grove—all of these provide emphasis to revive our interest in a repetitive environment. On the other hand, the skyscrapers in an urban center, the billboards along a highway, or the marginal enterprises along a peripheral commercial street, by the monotonous and anarchic repetition of emphasis, bludgeon us into a callous disregard of our surroundings.

Proportion is the means by which all of the parts are unified as well as articulated within the whole. It creates a sense of scale by the proper sizing of all of the parts in relation to the size of the whole. It is basic to rhythm, balance, and emphasis because it determines the individual dimensions and dimensioned relations of all parts within the whole. It is the primary tool for refinement and control of all design concepts, whether classical, romantic, or both. By determining the quantitative relationships of lines, shapes, tones, colors, textures, masses, and spaces, it determines our sense of fitness, of repose or liveliness, of all parts being of the right size, of the entire arrangement having good scale, i.e., creating a sense of empathy in the people who experience it. It is proportion in design that determines the complete success of the relations which are established between people, buildings, sites, and surrounding landscapes.

Primary is the question of scale, that is, the relations between horizontal and vertical dimensions, of areas bounded or marked, and physical elements above ground. Here we get back to Goldfinger's elementary principles: the man alone in the flat desert, with no third dimension; the man in a well 10 feet in diameter and 60 feet deep, where claustrophobia becomes imminent. There are abstract relations without dimension, as 1 vertical to 2 horizontal, but these are meaningless until related back to human dimensions. Is it 5 feet vertical to 10 horizontal (a little garden), or is it 5 miles vertical to 10 horizontal (Yosemite Valley)? Proportion, the relations between the sizes of the various parts of the design, is the tool by which scale is developed. Unity, whether subtle or obvious, is essential. Variety within that unity will humanize it and save it from sterility. Rhythm and repetition are tools for the achievement of unity, strength, clarity, and coherence in the overall spatial concept.

Scale is that relation between the dimensions of the parts and the whole in any portion of our environment which gives us sensations of bigness or smallness, complexity or simplicity, unity or disorder, as we pass through or stay in it. Le Corbusier's Modulor and Ghyka's Golden Rectangle are tools for the establishment of proper scale relations. The term occurs frequently in professional talk: "You're out of scale," "Bad scale," "That's more in scale." The sensation of scale, produced by a relation of proportions is basic to the sensation of space.

There are various sources of scale: the human form; animal forms; structural elements; inanimate objects such as plants and rocks; the elements of the site itself—ground forms, water forms, etc.; and the surrounding landscape—prairie, valley, hills, mountains, desert, lake, ocean. It seems obvious that, in general, the scale of the human environment should be that of the human form. If too big in scale, our surroundings tend to dwarf and isolate us; if too small, they cramp and crowd us. The scale of the ant or the elephant is not for man, although the scale of the human environment must recognize the scale of the baby and the child and the scale of man as a collective social force producing monuments and great public spaces. The sensation of scale is also partly a matter of personal psychology: claustrophobia and agoraphobia are its most extreme expressions.

If the monument has died, it is because the collective consciousness of man has died; monuments are not for individuals, unless they are leaders great enough to symbolize that collective consciousness. The effect of monumental scale is a function of the control of its development. It is used by authoritarians and fascists to intimidate and terrorize the population; monuments in a democracy give confidence to the common man. But the general scale in the general environment must have a close relation to the adult form; the monumental scale is occasional and climactic; the child's scale is reserved for his portions of the community. We also need variation in scale from boudoir to mountains. Indoor scale is determined by the human form and structural necessities. Outdoor scale is determined by these two plus the scale and character of the site and its views.

The question of scale is basic to the harmony, repose, and stability of our physical environment. The fact that no effort is made to coordinate the scale of site, buildings, roads, and miscellaneous elements is one of the primary sources of the cacophony in which most

Principles of design must produce environments which are in repose but not static, variable yet harmonious, reflecting the unsteady equilibrium which is life at its best.

of us live. Everything, from pincushions to mountains, has a relation to human scale insofar as we human beings are concerned. Within this human scale there are variations from baby to average adult and from occasional midget to occasional giant.

As we plan and design, our concentration on general and more detailed relations of form, color, and texture and on the relations between form and space is determined entirely by the scale of the elements with which we are dealing, in relation to human scale. A small garden is like a room: every detail, precise shape, and arrangement is important, because all can be comprehended almost at once, in general and in particular, from one station point, by one pair of human eyes. On the other hand, in great parks covering hundreds of acres precise relations and details are unimportant except in special corners and sections. The big form relations of parks and community spaces are a matter of relative proportions—relative to each other and to people passing through them—of the elements and the spaces between them, as much as of any careful precision in their planning.

Precision and attention to detail are always a function of the exact manner in which people will be brought into relation to the elements being planned and designed. The relation of general size, color, and texture of collective forms—as buildings, or trees in blocks, groups, or planes—and their placement in space determines their effect on that space. However, there must always be some sort of constant progression in scale elements between the person and all the things smaller or larger than himself which surround him. A landscape has no scale until elements of recognizable scale, and intermediate between the landscape and human scale, are interposed in some way between scene and observer. Vehicles, trees of ordinary size singly or in small groups, or structures with details of recognizable scale all have this function of relating landscapes to the scale of man. We have all experienced the kind of shrinkage in apparent size which one building or tree gives to any piece of raw land as soon as it is introduced.

Harmony is a product of the proper proportioning of the various functional and art elements through rhythm, balance, and emphasis, to produce a sense of unity, coherence, continuity, strength, clarity, order, and stability. It means that all of the parts fit together, through similarity or contrast, that they are all of the proper sizes and quantities and in the proper position in relation to one another. It means that the composition is sufficiently unified by an overriding concept, idea, or quality to have an identity greater than the accumulation of its parts. It also means that the composition is sufficiently varied by changes in material, art elements, rhythm, balance, emphasis, and proportion to avoid being monotonous, boring, static, or mechanical. Harmony results from the inclusion of neither too few nor too many parts, ideas, qualities, or materials. This proportioning of the parts is based on the size of the whole; i.e., a city can contain more of everything than a private home.

The choice between clarity and clutter is not a choice between styles. We can find equal amounts of clear form and of confusion in Chinese, Japanese, Renaissance, romantic, and modern gardens. The choice is simply and only a choice between good and bad arrangements of space and form.

Nor is it a choice between simplicity and complication, order and disorder, or regimentation and accident or anarchy. These are all phases of the either-or complex, an attitude which is much too common in our discussions. Simplicity is only the easiest way to achieve clarity; a complicated clarity is also possible, that is, a complication in detail within an overall compelling unity. Witness Gothic cathedrals, the architecture of Frank Lloyd Wright, paintings such as Picasso's "Three Musicians." Excessive order is regimentation and formalism; excessive disorder is anarchy and romanticism. Only the excesses are mutually exclusive. People need the opportunity for detailed physical disorder—the hat on the chair, the chair seldom twice in the same position—within the framework of a larger order, accepted and developed by them. Likewise the operation and recognition of accidental forces and elements is not foreign to sound planning but rather tends to give it life and vitality. In other words, the need for flexible living arrangements, within a controlled shell or framework, is primary in landscape design as it is in architecture.

"Beauty" is a word which has been much discussed but seldom defined. It is a product of experience, usually of high-level occasional experience which involves a relationship between one or more human beings and an arrangement of physical and/or social elements. To experience beauty is to bring order, repose, inspiration, relaxation, wonder, delight, freedom, and self-discipline into our lives. Beauty is a rare and occasional experience in our world, but in other times and places it has been more consistently and continuously part of the lives of some people. It is not an important element in the American scale of values; in fact we tend to view the word with some suspicion, as being probably expensive and impractical. To Hollywood it may mean cheesecake and glamour; to Detroit, tail fins and chrome grilles; to Wall Street, a chorus of cash registers; to the East, Williamsburg; to the South, the broad verandas on the old plantation; to the West, the rattle of six-guns in the wide-open spaces. And yet a beautiful woman will turn all heads on any street; we drive thousands of miles to view the wonders of the national parks; and every American home and garden contains at least some objects of art which, regardless of their success, have no other purpose than to bring beauty into our lives. No matter how eggheaded the word may seem, the crassest soap salesman among us cannot avoid an occasional effort to bring it into his life.

Some would say that aesthetic and social quality are synonymous, and some would say that they are completely irrelevant to each other. The former insist that art is for the people, the latter that art is for art's sake and that only the initiates can really understand and appreciate it.

These oversimplified antitheses may be theoretically possible in the smaller-scale arts such as painting and poetry, but they are irrelevant to the spatial arts. Landscape design is always done for people, and as long as the wealth produced by society is funneled through certain channels for land development, work in those channels will be aesthetically relevant to serious designers. It is the relation between area, program, development budget, and maintenance guarantee which determines the aesthetic potential of the landscape job. And it is the relation between client and designer which determines the degree of realization of that potential. The work of the spatial arts, including landscape architecture, is permanent in intent if not in actuality. As such it is a permanent addition to the humanized landscape, to the general community, and it is the quality of its planning and design which determines whether it raises or lowers the existing level of conception. In the spatial arts form has more continuity than content; spatial uses embodied in the original program may be entirely changed in the course of history without major alteration in the form of the space. Consider the changing uses to which old buildings in Europe have been put since the Renaissance.

Social quality does exist by implication in the immediate programs for landscape work, as it does in the programs for all kinds of work. It will be apparent to those who are conscious of social responsibility, and there is considerable variation in the degree of that consciousness among designers. Other things being equal, work which improves the environment of that very considerable section of the population which lives below the "American standard of living" is more important socially

John Ely Burchard, former dean of the School of Humanities and Social Studies at Massachusetts Institute of Technology, said to the AIA in 1956:

So I am asserting here as flagrantly as I can that the good life is not a matter of good gimmicks or of physical ease; it is a matter of things that uplift the spirit. High averages will not define it. The Arch of the Etoile and the tree lined streets that come to it and depart are more important to the good life of the poorest Parisian than a tenth of one percent improvement in his standard dwelling. I mean this rejection of the high average to apply to all elements of the good life—to the poetic life, to the political life, to the visual life, to the spiritual life. It is a life which occasionally though not too often must reach to ecstasy. Not too often because ecstasy cannot be prolonged, as the readers of Dante's Paradise can discover. But a life without these high points is not the good life. . . .[144]

One may, of course, ask what happens between ecstasies? Is this not a good rationalization for maintaining the slums of Paris? Can we not have both ecstasy and high average? Nevertheless, the good dean's point is well taken.

than work which improves the environment of those who are already living better than that. That is to say that it is better or more useful to work for those who need you more than for those who need you less. But in actual practice we find that those who need us more cannot afford us, even with cooperative organization. The public work which serves them, while it is most certainly socially useful within its generally inadequate limitations (it is good as far as it goes), tends to suffer from severe aesthetic restriction.

Thus there are three kinds of opportunity—aesthetic, economic, and socially useful. As serious artists we want to produce the maximum aesthetic quality, which means that we must have freedom of imagination comparable to those freedoms of speech, thought, and association which are guaranteed us by our Constitution. While of course no one expects to get rich in the spatial arts (some seem to by accident), we do think it is reasonable to expect adequate economic incentives for the risks we take. And the idea of social usefulness, that is, of working for more and more people in wider and wider sections of our environment, persists in growing in spite of setbacks and snobbery.

There is an interesting relationship between design, principles, and standards. Principles are guides for design. They are recognized and used at the discretion of the designer. The ultimate quality of the design depends as much upon his imagination, skill, and sensitivity as upon its content of principle. Standards, in theory derived from principles when they are established and proved, become rules for design. It must follow them. A host of mandatory codified architectural, building, and engineering standards are examples. As designers know well from sad experience, such standards develop quickly from rules into substitutes for design, complex and frustrating straitjackets which make it impossible for the designer to make his maximum contribution to the problem. Often they render impossible the only rational and creative solutions. If we spent more time selecting and training designers and educating the general public in sound principles for understanding design processes and judging the results of design and spent less time on rules for design, we would make possible maximum social benefits from design processes. In any society the fundamental responsibility for design quality lies in the area of programming. If the programmers and controllers of landscape design projects of any scale think only in terms of public relations, business, and technology, they offer little inspiration to the serious designer and may place stifling frustrations in his path. But if they think in truly humane terms of community improvement, civic design, and great landscape beauty, they will transmit to their designer inspiration and opportunity as well as responsibility.

The Human Denominator. We can hope that the common denominator for more and more design at every scale will be the individual human being—his needs, desires, dimensions, physiology, and psychology; his sense of space, a composite of all senses and all surrounding elements;

Jacques Maritain, a leading Catholic philosopher . . . in "The Responsibility of the Artist" . . . has addressed himself to both esthetic and moral problems. . . . He begins with the autonomy of art: "The first responsibility of the artist is toward his work." Therefore there is no direct relationship between art and morality: "A man can be a great artist and be a bad man." But the artist is a man as well as an artist, and as a man he is concerned with morality. Thus a conflict arises, and Maritain does not minimize its seriousness, nor will he ask the artist to subordinate his artistic conscience to his moral conscience. Yet he thinks a reconciliation is possible through love. . . .

Maritain goes on to discuss a related problem. "The motto Art for art's sake," he writes, "simply disregards the world of morality, and the values and rights of human life. . . ." Art, he insists, is "basically dependent upon everything which the human community, spiritual tradition, and history transmit to the body and mind of man."

There is also a danger on the other side in the slogan Art for the people, for this denies the autonomy of art. The evils to which it leads have been made obvious in the totalitarian countries, but the problem exists in every land. . . .

The artist, as Maritain sees it, has a social responsibility, but it should never lead him to violate his artistic conscience. ("Let him incur damnation, if only his work enriches the spiritual treasure of the world.") On the other hand, society has responsibilities to the artist: "In actual fact what the artist, the poet, the composer, the playwright expects from his fellow men, as a normal condition of development for his own effort, is to be listened to, I mean intelligently, to get a response, I mean an active and generous one, to have them cooperate with him in this way, and to feel himself in a certain communion with them, instead of being confined, as happens so often nowadays, in an intellectual ghetto." GRANVILLE HICKS[145]

The recapture of pedestrian space must also provide the possibility of riding through it at ease.

his sense of fitness, which he has learned through life; and his senses of history, society, nature, and culture.

The effort to build better relations between individuals and groups and the world around them will require understanding of the fact that this one world is a composite of many, even within the United States. In addition to the world of nature and the man-made physical world which competes with it, there are many social worlds. The world of Madison Avenue public relations—white, Aryan, Christian, suburban, blonde with an occasional brunette, middle class, prosperous, comfortable—is really a synthetic umbrella over the tense and complex heterogeneity of our country. The world of individualism, by capitalist democracy and Freud out of the Reformation, is a crowded universe.

Each of us first shrinks the real world to a size comprehensible within his personal experience, then expands that private world back to the size and importance of the real. The result is the vast and exciting traffic jam in which we live. Out of it coalesce various coordinate nuclear social worlds: big business, or Wall Street, vast and serene in its minority control of two-thirds of the country's production and its major influence in Washington; small business, or Main Street, struggling free enterprise around the borders of the big, hoping to get in, rising and falling like storm-tossed waters; labor, organized and unorganized, blue shirt and white collar, concentrated on wages, hours, and working conditions, still indispensable to production even with automation; agriculture, dreaming of the 60-acre family farm while big-time industrialization takes over, paralleling collectivization beyond the Iron Curtain; men of affairs, hard, brown, hairy-chested, pipe-smoking, stag-partying, running the world surrounded by guns, fishing tackle, and art photos; women, beautiful, fashionable, glamorous, elegant, exotic or wholesome, worshipped and insulted, trapped between kitchen, nursery, and career; minorities—foreign-born, Negro, Jew, Mexican, Oriental—each with rich cultural background and the gentleness and understanding or the belligerence of the underdog; children, coming into the world every day with open eyes, open minds, and vast potentialities; teen-agers, facing the hard realities their parents have bequeathed them as they leave the wonderworld of childhood; the fluid class structure of the United States—upper-upper, lower-upper, upper-middle, lower-middle, upper-lower, lower-lower—in which anyone can rise to the top but there is most room in the lower levels; the world of personal aggrandizement and self-satisfaction, in which every man is for himself, dogs eat dogs, and the devil takes the hindmost, and the world of public service, a sprinkling of sympathetic do-gooders struggling to save society from its own narrow insanity; the world of competition, our *raison d'être*, and the world of cooperation, which makes it possible; the world of status, where no one is on the same level, and the world of democracy, where everyone is on the same level; the world of war, hard-nosed, hard-bitten, hardheaded, bulging with surplus military hardware and ambition, convinced that might makes right, and the world of peace—dear hearts, gentle people, true Christians, good Samaritans, nonviolent pacifists, reformers, redeemers. These and others are the social worlds which react on nature to produce the American landscape.

Most people are bored, and as civilization becomes more and more mechanized they will become more and more bored. Nature is the only thing that is not boring—a cat, a tree, for example. ALBERTO MORAVIA[146]

Where everything is possible nothing is possible, so what choices can men make? Man is extended technically and man is at the same time deprived. The beautiful landscape is vanishing and man is imprisoned in his own devices; a victim of vicariousness, living in a plush second-hand world. SERGE CHERMAYEFF[83]

I believe that we are lost here in America, but I believe we shall be found. And this belief, which mounts now to the catharsis of knowledge and conviction, is for me—and I think for all of us—not only our own hope, but America's everlasting, living dream. I think the life which we have fashioned

in America, and which has fashioned us—the forms we made, the cells that grew, the honeycomb that was created—was self-destructive in its nature and must be destroyed. I think these forms are dying, and must die, just as I know that America and the people in it are deathless, undiscovered, and immortal, and must live.

I think the true discovery of America is before us. I think the true fulfillment of our spirit, of our people, of our mighty and immortal land, is yet to come. I think the true discovery of our own democracy is still before us. And I think that all these things are certain as the morning, as inevitable as noon. THOMAS WOLFE[147]

Dr. Boas considers the discrepancies between the sphere of order and uniformity reported by reason and the world of flux and diversity in which we live. Soon, however, the reader finds himself perceiving novel relationships; he sees the temporal world presented

as the source and crucible of man's aspirations to order and clarity; he sees the realm of reason as a projection out of man's urgent needs.

Professor Boas begins by saying that "eternal" statements, whether in the form of scientific laws or ethical norms, violate, disfigure, and simplify nature as we experience it in time. "Logic," he writes, "has nothing to do with history." This is because Logic cannot encompass variety, ambiguity, or the particularity of love and pain. And reason cannot come to terms with memory, with duration—or with hope, whose very essence is "to be unreasonable." If the world were reasonable and uniform, if it were like a laboratory, there would be no justification for hope; we would only predict. But the world we know is wayward; we hope for fulfillments and moreover, work to realize our dreams. Clearly, this would never occur if traditions could not be overturned, if we lived in a stable, uniform, rational realm.[148]

EPILOGUE

This book is a fragmentary exposition of a complex subject—the quality of the total landscape. Its *raison d'être* is the conviction that this quality is dependent upon the balanced relations which are achieved between the structural developments of man and the rock, earth, water, and plant forms of nature. While most city fathers and officials, owners, planners, architects, designers, developers, bankers, and builders will accept this thesis in general, few will fight for it in specific practice. All too easily, with polite regrets, they eliminate the saving, natural, "landscaping" elements—2 to 20 percent of the budget—in the interests of "economy," "functionalism," "practicality," "maintenance," "higher and better use of the land," and at times even "urbanism" or "architecture." They forget, or never learn, that this small fraction of the total budget, properly spent, may well account for 50 percent of the ultimate visual aspect ten years hence.

Their excuses are all easy rationalizations for opportunist surrender before those dominant forces which, in the name of "progress," "development," "expansion," and "growth," destroy landscape amenities for many generations yet unborn. In our elaborate American structure of divided responsibility (organized irresponsibility), it is all too easy for those majority elements that equate construction with progress to forget the elimination of a minor frivolity like "landscaping." Left to mourn are those with obvious axes to grind—landscape architects and contractors, garden clubs, conservationists, nature lovers, horticulturists, nurserymen. And yet some day we will realize that with this minor frivolity, this 2 to 20 percent of the budget, this useless waste of valuable land area, went all the potentiality for a balanced, harmonious, livable, humane, truly functional and practical landscape for sound and cultivated community, regional, and national development.

REFERENCES AND ACKNOWLEDGMENTS

1. Anthony Wayne Smith, "The Divine Right of Technology," *National Parks Magazine,* Washington, D.C., December, 1961.

2. Henry Miller, *Nexus,* George Weidenfeld & Nicolson, Ltd., London, 1964, p. 308.

3. H. G. Wells, *The World Set Free,* W. Collins Sons & Co., Ltd., London, 1914, pp. 220, 228. Copyright, 1914, by E. P. Dutton & Co., Inc. Renewal, 1942, by H. G. Wells. Reprinted by permission of the publishers.

4. Ralph Barton Perry, "A Definition of the Humanities," in Theodore Meyer Greene (ed.), *The Meaning of the Humanities,* Princeton University Press, Princeton, N.J., 1938.

5. W. L. Thomas, Jr. (ed.), *Man's Role in Changing the Face of the Earth,* The University of Chicago Press, Chicago, 1956. Copyright University of Chicago, 1956. See also Phillip Wagner, *The Human Use of the Earth,* The Free Press of Glencoe, Crowell-Collier Publishing Co., New York, 1960; and Ron M. Linton, Chairman, et al., *A Strategy for a Livable Environment,* U.S. Department of Health, Education and Welfare, 1967.

6. C. Wright Mills, *The Power Elite,* Oxford University Press, Fair Lawn, N.J., 1956.

7. W. H. Whyte, Jr., et al., *The Exploding Metropolis,* Anchor Books, Doubleday & Company, Inc., Garden City, N.Y., 1958; Christopher Tunnard and Henry Hope Reed, *American Skyline,* Mentor Books, The New American Library of World Literature, Inc., New York, 1956.

8. John Kenneth Galbraith, *The Affluent Society,* Houghton Mifflin Company, Boston, 1958.

9. Edmund R. Leach, "Culture and Social Cohesion: An Anthropologist's View," *Daedalus,* American Academy of Arts and Sciences, Cambridge, Mass., Winter, 1965.

10. Agnes Meyer, "Voluntary Action in a Democracy," *American Association of University Professors Bulletin,* Washington, D.C., Spring, 1955.

11. See Charles Abrams, *Man's Struggle for Shelter,* The M.I.T. Press, Cambridge, Mass., 1964.

12. Daniel Seligman, Lawrence A. Mayer, Francis Bello, et al., The Editors of *Fortune, Markets of the Sixties,* Harper & Row, Publishers, Incorporated, New York, 1958.

13. See Peter Blake, *God's Own Junkyard,* Holt, Rinehart and Winston, Inc., New York; 1964; William Bronson, *How to Kill a Golden State,* Doubleday & Company, Inc., Garden City, N.Y., 1968; and Peter Nairn, *The American Landscape,* Random House, Inc., New York, 1965.

14. U.S. Bureau of Census, *Statistical Abstract of the United States 1964.*

15. William Appleman Williams, *The Contours of American History,* The World Publishing Co., Cleveland, 1959.

16. Lawrence S. Kubie, M.D., *Neurotic Distortion of the Creative Process,* University of Kansas Press, Lawrence, Kans. 1958; The Noonday Press, Farrer, Straus and Giroux, Inc., New York, 1966.

17. G. Scott Wright, Jr., "The Ignorant Silence," *Saturday Review,* New York, Mar. 18, 1961.

18. George Geiger, "Preface to a Consistent Philosophy of Education," *Saturday Review,* New York, Nov. 21, 1959.

213

19. Catherine Bauer Wurster, "Toward a Plan for the College of Environmental Design," unpublished memo, University of California, Berkeley, Calif., 1964.

20. Hyman Rickover, "American Cherishes Education Myths," Los Angeles *Times,* Jan. 31, 1965. The author's use of this quotation does not in any way signify Admiral Rickover's approval or disapproval of any of the concepts or theories expressed in this book.

21. Kevin Lynch, *The Image of the City,* The M.I.T. Press and Harvard University Press, Cambridge, Mass., 1960.

22. Based on U.S. Bureau of the Census, *U.S. Census Population: 1960, Number of Inhabitants,* United States Summary, Final Report PC(1)-1A, 1961.

23. John Kenneth Galbraith, "Age of Wordfact," *The Atlantic Monthly,* Boston, September, 1960.

24. Anatol Rapoport, "Language Hygiene and Mass Communication," Sixth International Design Conference, Aspen, Colo., 1956.

25. Charles Maurice de Talleyrand-Perigord (1754–1838), famous French statesman, leading political figure next to Napoleon I.

26. Dwight MacDonald, "A Critique of the Warren Report," *Esquire,* New York, March, 1965.

27. *The Practical Standard Dictionary of the English Language,* Funk & Wagnalls Company, New York, 1936.

28. Sir J. Arthur Thomson, in Norman Foerster, *The Humanities and the Common Man,* The University of North Carolina Press, Chapel Hill, N.C., 1946.

29. Allen Wheelis, *The Quest for Identity,* W. W. Norton & Company, Inc., New York, 1958.

30. Albert Einstein, *Essays in Science,* Philosophical Library, New York, 1934; orig. *Mein Weltbild,* Querido Verlag, Amsterdam, 1933.

31. Don K. Price, "The Established Dissenters," *Daedalus,* Cambridge, Mass., Winter, 1965.

32. Sean O'Casey, *Inishfallen Fare Thee Well,* The Macmillan Company, New York, 1949.

33. See Constantinos Doxiadis, *Between Dystopia and Utopia,* Trinity College Press, Hartford, Conn., 1966.

34. Alan Watts, *Nature, Man and Woman,* Pantheon Books, Division of Random House, Inc., New York, 1958.

35. Sigmund Freud, *Civilization and Its Discontents,* The Hogarth Press, Ltd., London, 1930.

36. Jens Bjerre, *Kalahari,* Hill and Wang, Inc., New York, 1960.

37. Gyorgy Kepes, *The New Landscape,* Paul Theobald & Co., Chicago, 1956.

38. Andreas Feininger, *The Anatomy of Nature,* Crown Publishers, Inc., New York, 1956.

39. Barrows Dunham, *The Artist in Society,* Marzani and Munsell, New York, 1960.

40. Ananda K. Coomaraswamy, *The Transformation of Nature in Art,* Harvard University Press, Cambridge, Mass., 1934.

41. Frank Avray Wilson, *Art into Life,* Centaur Press, London, 1958. See also Kenneth Clark, *Landscape into Art,* John Murray (Publishers) Ltd., London, 1949.

42. Louis Kahn, from announcement of lecture, sponsored by The Architectural Panel, Los Angeles.

43. Adolph Gottlieb, in *The New York School,* Los Angeles County Museum of Art, 1965.

44. *Oxford Universal Dictionary,* 3d ed., revised with addenda, Oxford University Press, Fair Lawn, N.J., 1955.

45. Suzanne K. Langer, *Problems of Art,* Charles Scribner's Sons, New York, 1957.

46. See also R. G. Collingwood, *Principles of Art,* Oxford University Press, Fair Lawn, N.J., 1938.

47. E. B. Tylor, *Primitive Culture* (1871). Quoted in Edmond R. Leach, "Culture and Social Cohesion: An Anthropologist's View," *Daedalus,* Cambridge, Mass., Winter, 1965.

48. B. Malinowski, "Culture," *Encyclopedia of the Social Sciences,* vol. 4, p. 621, New York, 1931. Quoted in *ibid.*

49. R. Bain, "A Definition of Culture," *Sociology and Social Research,* vol. 27, pp. 87–94, 1942. Quoted in *ibid.*

50. Daniel Bell, "The Disjunction of Culture and Social Stucture," *Daedalus,* Cambridge, Mass., Winter, 1965.

51. Herbert Marcuse, "Remarks on a Redefinition of Culture," *ibid.*

51a. Amaury de Riencourt, *The Soul of India*, Harper & Row, Publishers, Incorporated, New York, 1960.

52. Reprinted by permission of Schocken Books Inc. from *To Hell with Culture* by Sir Herbert Read, Copyright © Herbert Read 1963.

53. Jean Paul Sartre, address at Moscow World Congress, published by *National Guardian*, New York, Nov. 8, 1962.

54. Dr. Norman Bethune, quoted in Ted Allan and Ralph Sydney Gordon, *The Scalpel, the Sword*. Copyright 1952 by Allan and Gordon. Published by Little, Brown and Company, Boston.

55. Harry Levin, "Semantics of Culture," *Daedalus*, Cambridge, Mass., Winter, 1965.

56. Richard Lippold, as quoted by Calvin Tomkins in "Profiles: A Thing among Things," *The New Yorker*, New York, Mar. 30, 1963.

57. Edgar Wind, *Art and Anarchy*, Alfred A. Knopf, Inc., New York, 1962. Originally included in one of the Reith lecture series over BBC; published in *The Listener*, London, Nov. 24, 1960.

58. S. I. Hayakawa, "The Creative Process: Some Recent Theories," lecture at Hollywood High School Auditorium, Los Angeles, 1960.

59. Stuart Hampshire, BBC lecture reprint, *The Listener*, London, Oct. 13, 1960.

60. Le Corbusier, *Towards a New Architecture*, Frederick A. Praeger, Inc., New York. Originally published by Payson & Clarke Ltd., New York, n.d.

61. Eliel Saarinen, *Search for Form*, Reinhold Book Corporation, New York, 1948.

62. Laszlo Moholy-Nagy, *Vision in Motion*, Paul Theobald & Co., Chicago, 1947.

63. Elie Faure, *Spirit of the Forms*, Harper & Row, Publishers, Incorporated, New York, 1930.

64. Fred W. Emerson, *Basic Botany*, 2d ed., McGraw-Hill Book Company, New York, 1954 (Blakiston Co., 1954); used by permission of McGraw-Hill Book Company.

65. A. K. Lobeck, *Geomorphology*, McGraw-Hill Book Company, New York, 1939.

66. Joseph Needham, *The Skeptical Biologist*, W. W. Norton, New York, 1930.

67. Bertrand Russell, *Our Knowledge of the External World*, Mentor Books, New American Library of World Literature, Inc., New York, 1960.

68. Christopher Caudwell, *Illusion and Reality*, International Publishers Company, Inc., New York, 1947; by permission of International Publishers Co., Inc.

69. Joseph Schillinger, *The Mathematical Basis of the Arts*, Philosophical Library, Inc., New York. Copyright 1948 by Frances Schillinger.

70. David E. Lilienthal, "A Skeptical Look at Scientific Experts," New York *Times*, Western ed., Oct. 25, 1963; also in Lilienthal, *Change, Hope, and the Bomb*, Princeton University Press, Princeton, N.J., p. 61, 1963.

71. James Feron, "C. P. Snow Sees Third Culture," New York *Times*, Western ed., Oct. 25, 1963.

72. Eric Weil, "Science in Modern Culture," *Daedalus*, Cambridge, Mass., Winter, 1965.

73. Rene Dubos, "Science and Man's Nature," *ibid*.

74. Robert S. Morison, "Toward a Common Scale," *ibid*. See also Scott Buchanan on the fine arts, in *World Order*, Center for the Study of Democratic Institutions, Santa Barbara, Calif., Center Diary 15.

75. James S. Ackerman, "On Scientia," *Daedalus*, Cambridge, Mass., Winter, 1965.

76. See "A Statement by Louis I. Kahn," *Arts & Architecture*, Los Angeles, February, 1961.

77. Le Corbusier, *Creation is a Patient Search*, Frederick A. Praeger, Inc., New York, 1960.

78. John Ciardi, "On Form as a Language," *Saturday Review*, New York, Oct. 31, 1964.

79. Reginald Howard Wilenski, *The Meaning of Modern Sculpture*, Faber & Faber, Ltd., London, 1932.

80. See report on public and private decision making, by Okamoto & Lisskam and Robert Alexander, for California State Development Plan, Department of Finance, Sacramento, Calif, 1966.

81. See Garrett Eckbo, "The Decision-making Totem Pole," AIA *Journal*, Washington, D.C., July, 1966. See also Joseph Esherick, Jr., in "Architects' Bibliography," *Image*, Student Publication, School of Architecture, The University of Texas, Austin, Tex., 1965:

Society for General Systems Research Yearbook; Charles Churchman et al., *Introduction to Operations Research;* Martin K. Starr, *Production Management;* William R. Ashby, *An Introduction to Cybernetics;* Morris Asimow, *Introduction to Design;* M. K. Starr, *Product Design and Decision Theory;* Kenneth Boulding, *The Image: Knowledge in Life and Society;* Minnie L. J. Abercrombie, *The Anatomy of Judgement.*

82. William Zeckendorf, address delivered at Sixteenth Annual Convention, California Council AIA, San Diego, 1961. Courtesy *Daily Pacific Builder,* San Francisco, Oct. 27, 1961.

83. Serge Chermayeff, "From the Other End of the Spectrum," *IMAGE,* Student Publication, School of Architecture, The University of Texas, Austin, Tex., 1964.

84. Garrett Eckbo, "The Personalized/Anonymous Landscape," AIA *Journal,* Washington, D.C., May, 1965. Copyright 1965 by the American Institute of Architects.

85. Joseph Conrad, *Victory,* J. M. Dent & Sons, Ltd., Publishers, London, 1915. Courtesy Trustees of the Joseph Conrad Estate.

86. William Nickerson, *How I turned $1,000 into a Million in Real Estate,* Simon and Schuster, Inc., New York, 1959.

87. See Sylvia Wright, "The Drip Spoon Plate Society," *Harper's Magazine,* New York, February, 1963.

88. Daniel Friedenberg, "The Coming Bust in the Real Estate Boom," *Harper's Magazine,* New York, June, 1961.

89. See Arthur Gallion and Simon Eisner, *The Urban Pattern,* D. Van Nostrand Company, Inc., Princeton, N.J., 1950. See also William R. Ewald, Jr. (ed), *Environment for Man,* Indiana University Press, Bloomington, Ind., 1967.

90. Joint Committee AIA and AIP, *Planning and Community Appearance,* Regional Plan Association, New York, 1958. See also Michael Wornum, "A Case for Aesthetic Control," *Landmark '65,* University of California, Department of Landscape Architecture, Berkeley, Calif., 1965.

91. See *Nations Business,* September, 1966. See also John Dustin Kemper, *The Engineer and His Profession,* Holt, Rinehart and Winston, Inc., New York, 1967; and Beakley and Leach, *Engineering: An Introduction to a Creative Profession,* The Macmillan Company, New York, 1967.

92. Lewis Mumford, "UNESCO," *New Yorker,* New York, Nov. 12, 1960.

93. Garrett Eckbo, remarks at Urban Design Conference, Harvard Graduate School of Design, 1959.

94. Robert L. Zion, "New Parks for our Cities," AIA *Journal,* Washington, D.C., December, 1963.

95. Lawrence Halprin, *Cities,* Reinhold Book Corporation, New York, 1963.

96. Stamo Papadaki, *Oscar Niemeyer: Works in Progress,* Reinhold Book Corporation, New York, 1956.

97. See Bernard Rudofsky, *Architecture without Architects,* The Museum of Modern Art, New York, 1964; and Sibyl Moholy-Nagy, *Native Genius in Anonymous Architecture,* Horizon Press, New York, 1957.

98. Garrett Eckbo, "Architecture and the Landscape," *Arts & Architecture,* Los Angeles, October, 1964. See also Steen Eiler Rasmussen, *Experiencing Architecture,* M.I.T. Press, Cambridge, Mass., 1964.

99. Wayne Williams, *Recreation Places,* Reinhold Book Corporation, New York, 1958. Alfred Lederman and A. Trachsel, *Creative Playgrounds and Recreation Centers,* Frederick A. Praeger, Inc., New York, 1959.

100. Garrett Eckbo, "Creative Design of the Landscape," *Landscape Architecture,* Louisville, Ky., January, 1965.

101. Introduction by Shuzo Takigu et al., *Noguchi,* Bijutsu Shuppan-Sha, Tokyo, American distributor Wittenborn, New York, 1953.

102. Garrett Eckbo, "Urban Design: A Definition," AIA *Journal,* Washington, D.C., September, 1963. Copyright 1963, by the American Institute of Architects. See also Edmund N. Bacon, *Design of Cities,* The Viking Press, Inc., New York, 1967; Margaret van Barneveld Cole, *The Urban Aesthetic,* Cordes Printing Company, St. Louis, Mo., 1960; Robert Venturi, *Complexity and Contradiction in Architecture,* The Museum of Modern Art, New York, 1966; and Jeffrey Cook, *Architecture Anthology,* College of Architecture, Arizona State University, Tempe, Ariz., 1966.

103. Ruth Brecher and Edward Brecher, "Getting to Work and Back," *Consumer Reports,* Mount Vernon, N.Y., February, 1965.

104. Eugene Ionesco, *Rhinoceros and Other Plays,* translated by Derek Prouse, Grove Press, Inc., New York, 1960.

105. Includes material from Southern Regions: Very Preliminary Report, Urban-Metropolitan Open Space Plan, April 1, 1965 (which led to the final Urban-Metropolitan Open Space Study of Nov. 1, 1965) by Eckbo, Dean, Austin & Williams, an input for the California State Development Plan being finalized by the State Office of Planning, Sacramento, Calif., as of January, 1967.

106. Samuel Zisman, speech at American Society of Landscape Architects annual meeting, Dallas, Tex., 1964.

107. Sir William Holford, in Daniel R. Mandelker, *Green Belts and Urban Growth,* The University of Wisconsin Press, Madison, Wis., 1962.

108. Le Corbusier, *New World of Space,* Harcourt, Brace & World, Inc., New York, 1948.

109. First definition from unpublished notes by Eckbo, Dean, Austin & Williams. Second definition from open-space provisions of the Housing Act of 1961 (75 Stat. 149), Title VII, sec. 706.

110. *Architectural Review,* London, September, 1948.

111. Samuel Parsons, *The Art of Landscape Architecture,* Putnam's and Coward-McCann, New York, 1915.

112. Erling D. Solberg, *Open Space Control,* U.S. Department of Agriculture, Agricultural Research Service, Farm Economics Research Division; Santa Barbara County Planning Department, *Methods of Acquiring and Improving Open Space,* Santa Barbara, Calif., Sept. 30, 1959; Housing nd Home Finance Agency, Urban Renewal Administration, *Preserving Urban Open Space;* S. B. Zisman, "Open Spaces in Urban Growth," unpublished lecture delivered to American Society of Landscape Architects annual meeting, Dallas, Tex.; Planning Department, City of San Diego, *Urban Open Space: Synopsis 1960,* San Diego.

113. Garrett Eckbo, "The Quality of Urbanization," *Centennial Review,* Michigan State University, East Lansing, Mich., 1966.

114. Bruce Catton, *The War Lords of Washington,* Harcourt, Brace & World, Inc., New York, 1948.

115. Norman Bel Geddes, *Magic Motorways.* Copyright 1940 by Norman Bel Geddes. Reprinted by permission of Random House, Inc., New York.

116. Bill Dredge in a news story about the Society of Automotive Engineers, Los Angeles *Times,* Jan. 16, 1961.

117. George Getze in Los Angeles *Times,* July 22, 1965.

118. George Getze in Los Angeles *Times,* Aug. 8, 1965.

119. Los Angeles *Times,* Smog Supplement, Jan. 8, 1951.

120. Victor Gruen, *The Heart of Our Cities,* Simon and Schuster, Inc., New York, 1964, chaps., 16, 17. See also Wolf von Eckardt, *A Place to Live,* Delacorte Press, New York, 1967.

121. Donald E. Carr, "The Poison Air around Us," *Saturday Review,* New York, Feb. 27, 1965.

122. *Architectural Review,* London, August, 1948.

123. L. H. Bailey, *Standard Cyclopedia of Horticulture,* The Macmillan Company, New York, 1914.

124. Stephen F. Hamblin, *Lists of Plant Types,* Harvard University Press, Cambridge, Mass., 1929.

125. Roland S. Hoyt, *Ornamental Plants for Sub-tropical Regions,* Livingston Press, Los Angeles, 1938; *Planting Lists for Southern California,* Livingston Press, Los Angeles, 1933.

126. Albert D. Taylor, *The Complete Garden,* Doubleday, Page & Company, New York, 1921.

127. James C. Rose, in *Pencil Points,* New York, April, 1939.

128. Donald Wyman, *Trees for American Gardens,* and *Shrubs & Vines for American Gardens,* The Macmillan Company, New York, 1949 and 1951.

See also Gary Robinette, *Off the Board, into the Ground,* William C. Brown, Dubuque, Iowa, 1968.

129. From *An Epidemic of Genius.* Copyright © 1960 by Ira Wolfert. By permission of Simon and Schuster, Inc.

130. Reprinted by permission of Dodd, Mead & Company from *Chinese Gardens* by Dorothy Graham. Copyright 1938 by Dodd, Mead & Company, New York.

131. Norman Corwin, "Services for Lag B'Omer," unpublished discourse delivered at annual tree planting services at Brandeis Institute, Brandeis, Calif.

132. Dorothy Dixon, "These Are the Champs," *American Forests,* Washington, D.C., January, 1961.

133. Sanford Farness, in *Resources, the Metropolis, and the Land-grant University,* University of Massachusetts Co-operative Extension, Amherst, Mass., 1964.

134. Garrett Eckbo, letter to *Arts & Architecture,* Los Angeles, September, 1964.

135. Vernon De Mars, in *Progressive Architecture,* New York, December, 1958.

136. From *The Architectural Forum,* New York, January, 1959.

137. Seymour Melman, professor of industrial engineering, Columbia University, addressing Town Hall, Los Angeles, Calif., Jan. 19, 1965; reprinted in *Saturday Review,* July 31, 1965.

See also Melman's *Our Depleted Society,* Holt, Rinehart and Winston, Inc., New York, 1965.

138. Dr. George A. Kelly, in Los Angeles *Times,* Jan. 18, 1959.

139. Andrew T. Weil, "Harvard's Bruner and His Yeasty Ideas," *Harper's Magazine,* New York, December, 1964. See also Edward T. Hall, *The Hidden Dimension,* Doubleday & Company, Inc., Garden City, N.Y., 1966; David Lowenthal (ed.), *Environmental Perception and Behavior,* The University of Chicago, Department of Geography, Chicago, 1967; and Robert E. Stipe (ed.), *Perception and Environment: Foundations of Urban Design,* Institute of Government, University of North Carolina, Chapel Hill, N.C., 1966.

140. John Knox Shear, in *The Architectural Record,* New York, July, 1956.

141. Erno Goldfinger, "The Sensation of Space," *Architectural Review,* London, November, 1941.

142. John R. Bracken, *Planting Design,* The Pennsylvania State University Press, University Park, Pa., 1957.

143. William H. Whyte, Jr., in Editors of *Fortune, The Exploding Metropolis,* Doubleday & Company, Inc., Garden City, N.Y., 1958.

144. John Burchard, in *The Architectural Record,* New York, July, 1956.

145. Discussion of Jacques Maritain in Granville Hicks, "The Autonomy of Art Affirmed," *Saturday Review,* New York, Feb. 13, 1960.

146. Jerry Bauer, interview with Alberto Moravia, *Saturday Review,* New York, Oct. 28, 1961.

147. Excerpt from Thomas Wolfe, *You Can't Go Home Again,* Harper & Brothers, New York, 1940.

148. Maxine Greene, review of George Boas, The Limits of Reason, *Saturday Review,* New York, Apr. 8, 1961.

ILLUSTRATION CREDITS

INDEX